ANALISA Ι
O'RUL.

11th HOUR MIRACLES!

SURVIVING A BONE MARROW TRANSPLANT

2007

11th Hour Miracles!

To my husband, Brian, the love of my life and my reason for giving it my all.

To my brother, Alfred, for his kind selflessness in giving me his marrow that saved my life. And to my brother, Jim, for giving me the courage to hang in there at my lowest point.

To my parents, Victor and Estela Marquez, for handling life's challenges with humor and dignity. And to my in-laws, William and Rosemary, for being pillars of strength and integrity.

To our beautiful boys, Brian and Blake, for making our dreams of having a family a reality.

To my dear comrades, both living and fallen, and their families who have valiantly fought their own transplant battles.

To all our friends and family who buoyed me up with their love and prayers.

And finally, to Dr. Richard Champlin, Dr. Winston Ho, Dr. Stephen Nimer and the host of nurses and staff at UCLA Medical Center, for their expertise and dedication to making me whole again.

TABLE OF CONTENTS

FOREWORD

WHY I WROTE THIS BOOK

Many of us have traumatic experiences in our lives, which like clay mold us individually. If I was to learn from my diagnosis of leukemia, then I wanted others to learn with me. *11th Hour Miracles!* is an incredible success story of my bone marrow transplant, from the beginning of my diagnosis to the healthy life I now lead.

When my sister, Stella, died of lung cancer at age eighteen, I was fourteen years old. There were truths learned about faith, dying, and living life to the fullest. Then, when my own diagnosis came at age twenty-seven, just when we were about to start a family, it was a reminder of lessons that needed to be relearned—a reminder of how precious life is and how easily our dreams can be crushed.

In 1989, as I began my transplant, I wished I had attained a better insight into the process. When I learned that no book had been written from a patient's point of view, I made a personal commitment to God and myself that if He saw me through my transplant, I would share my experiences, both physical and spiritual, with others. The need and the responsibility to document each phase of the transplant gave me purpose, and a determination to "get the best of my illness, rather than let it get the best of me!"

Writing *11th Hour Miracles!* has been a major part of the healing. For as I began writing, and the tip of my pencil began scribbling the words, the eraser on the other end began to erase the pain. Writing has done what no psychologist could have ever done for me. When I have been entrenched in writing, it's as if the videotape has been rewound and I'm playing my life all over again. I see the events unfolding, like a movie, as though they happened yesterday.

I also wrote this book to remind others that amid the torturous process, when medicine is in complete control of your life and you have *no* say in the matter, that yes, the patient *is* cognizant and very much in tune with what's happening. And one person *can* make a *huge* difference by a touch of the hand, a word, or a listening ear.

As I told my friend Mieke years ago, when she asked how my book was coming, "It's like putting up wallpaper on a large surface. I've got all this great sticky material ready to go up, step by step. When I'm done, I'll iron out the wrinkles, and with God's help, it will be of great value."

At times I've wanted to put *11ᵗʰ Hour Miracles!* in a drawer, forget about it, and get on with my life, since this is all so personal. To an extent I have done so for many years. However, whenever I've shared my story with others or have spoken in front of groups, the story remains just as important, just as vivid, as if it happened yesterday—and this story must be told. I learned that in order to get *11ᵗʰ Hour Miracles!* published, I needed to have the *same* determination and faith that was required to survive my transplant—to take the bull by the horns and just do it! I want to send this book out blazing with conviction of its meaning and hope. Therefore, as the saying goes, "This is my story and I'm sticking to it!"

(For copyright purposes some of the names herein have been changed.)

DOCTORS' COMMENTARIES

Bone marrow transplantation is a highly effective treatment for leukemia and other cancers. It involves administration of high doses of chemotherapy drugs and radiation to kill the malignant cells. The treatment also kills the normal blood forming cells, so it must be followed by infusion of bone marrow stem cells from a normal donor to restore blood production and immunity. It also can damage the normal tissues of the body, and life-threatening complications frequently occur. Recovery is a slow, tedious process over many months. It is a harrowing experience for any patient, who must deal with the physical and emotional stress of their cancer, the side effects of treatment, as well as the uncertainty whether the disease will ultimately come back. Analisa recounts her personal experience from learning her diagnosis, its initial treatment, and finally considerations for the bone marrow transplant. She describes what it is like to cope with the stress and side effects of therapy, and adjust to the ups and downs experienced during her treatment. Ultimately, it is a success story, with her overcoming all obstacles and regaining her life and family. It's truly an inspiring story.

—**Richard Champlin, M.D., MD Anderson, Houston, TX**

This is a personal story of courage and faith of one young woman's battle for survival. She placed her life under the care of physicians to undergo a treatment for leukemia that at that time was relatively new and fraught with unknowns. Apart from the excellent state-of-the-art medical care that she received, she also relied heavily on her religious beliefs to draw spiritual and emotional strength to carry her through the arduous treatment.

She was courageous in participating in an investigational study with the drug DHPG (now named Ganciclovir) and helped define the role of this medication in the prevention and treatment of a serious viral infection that occurs in patients undergoing bone marrow and stem cell transplantation.

The accumulation of information and knowledge obtained from the efforts of patients such as Analisa has led to marked improvement in the success of this form of treatment for leukemia and other serious blood diseases. Eleventh hour miracles have become a true realistic treatment!
—Winston G. Ho, M.D., St. Joseph's Hospital, Orange, CA

Doctors can always learn by listening to their patients. In her book, Analisa shows the totality of the bone marrow transplant experience from her perspective as a patient, wife, mother and child. It is a moving experience that will help others understand what we transplant doctors see every day, namely the extraordinary strength of the human spirit.
—Stephen D. Nimer, M.D., Head, Division of Hematologic Oncology, Memorial Sloan-Kettering Cancer Center, New York, NY

PREFACE

There's something happening on 10 West today. This day has been coming for six months and now it's here. What is it going to be like? I've heard so much about it. Am I scared? Actually, I'm not. In fact, I'm as calm as a bird on a summer's day, and am rather energized about the events that will happen here over the next several weeks. Like many others, I'm here to see miracles. I'm here for my own miracle.

The building is big. The halls are plush, with a teal blue carpet that climbs the walls, giving a warm and inviting feeling. I'm aware of the people and the surroundings as I anticipate meeting those who will take part in changing my life. My first contact is Nickie, a nurse. She has a warm smile that could set anyone at ease. I inform her that I'm here.

"Oh, you must be Analisa. We've been waiting for you," she says. "Let me show you to your room."

Well, I'm here, I think to myself, as I look around and ponder. I'm here to have a bone marrow transplant.

INTRODUCTION

The summer of 1988 was a very busy time for us. My husband, Brian, was doing well in his career with AT&T. I, too, was working for AT&T, temporarily. We worked in the same building, so we often traveled to work together. Having lived in Belle Mead, New Jersey for one and a half years now, we were thoroughly enjoying the beauty of the East Coast.

I remember riding to work along the lush green two-lane roads, driving over rolling hills, never quite knowing what was on the other side of those hills—probably as much traffic as was on my road, I'd think. Stuck in traffic, one of us would lament, "Where do all these people come from?" If they took all the trees away, we'd be astonished to see how many people really *do* live in New Jersey!

It seemed we were always running late. Nevertheless, I managed to admire the beautiful trees and changing seasons. On the way to work, not a day went by without seeing deer, raccoons, or possums running in the fields or dead on the road. Having been born and raised in a Los Angeles suburb, we never thought of New Jersey as being so verdant; thus being called the Garden State.

Having been married for seven and a half years, the topic of children often crept into our conversations as we rode to work. After being told on that "black" Tuesday in December 1984 that we would never be able to have children, we often wondered what would become of us. It was a big blow. For a childless couple, the longing for a family can be all-consuming; something you just never quite get over. However, we were handling it well and trying to stay busy.

Here in New Jersey, we contemplated our next move. Brian was thirty-three and I was twenty-six. We wondered if we should adopt or try other options. Having just learned about a new GIFT (Gastro-Invitro Fertilization Technique) procedure, we had ourselves evaluated. We proved to be perfect candidates. A doctor in South Jersey accepted us. We were thrilled...and nervous. Could this be our chance to finally have our own baby? Little did we know that it was just the beginning of our problems.

That summer, we were entrenched in church responsibilities. As members of the Church of Jesus Christ of Latter-day Saints (also known as Mormons), Brian was involved in missionary work and I was a counselor in the Young Women's organization, teaching the teenage girls. It was rewarding. The girls kept me feeling young.

My best friend, Mieke Nielsen, and I were visiting teaching partners. We were assigned to visit a few women each month to see how they were doing and to leave a spiritual message. We were also taking a summer real estate course at the local college, in preparation for our real estate licenses. Before and after class we eagerly compared ideas, planning someday to be big, successful real estate tycoons. We loved talking about it over onion rings and ice cream sundaes. Mieke had a dual degree in real estate and accounting. She was intelligent, a risk taker, and had a knack for starting her own businesses. She was down-to-earth, and yet sometimes flighty. I think that's why I liked her so much. We'd rendezvous at the nearest fast-food locations (which, in New Jersey, were scarce) and plot our course.

July was a very busy month. I was working full-time and under a lot of pressure with school, church, and the idea of getting pregnant. We were on an emotional roller coaster. Because the prospects of getting pregnant were very important to us, I ignored my feelings of fatigue and felt I could shake it off with a restful vacation. We had been nervous and prayerful about our decision to undergo the GIFT procedure, since it would be costly and time-consuming. The chances of a successful pregnancy were low. Nevertheless, we purchased the expensive medication needed to induce my fertility.

Toward the end of July, we called the doctor to let him know we were ready to begin the process. The receptionist put me on hold. A moment later she returned, saying, "I'm sorry, the doctor is no longer doing the procedure."

"What?" I shrieked. "We just purchased the prescriptions!"

"He's run into some technical difficulties and is no longer doing the Invitro."

I was outraged. We had invested all our time and emotions into this one chance, making several trips to South Jersey for painstaking examinations. We were ready. They knew it, and now we were told no.

The doctor didn't even have the courtesy to speak to us. Later, we figured he was probably being sued. The pain and discouragement of unfulfilled hopes quickly surfaced. Our prospects for a family would be put on hold again.

By the end of the month, everything came to a head. It was the week of my real estate final exam. I was responsible for two youth activities, a dinner party, and a Sunday School lesson. I turned to Brian and said, "I'm so tired. I honestly don't have ten minutes to myself this entire week. If I can just make it through this week, I think I'll be okay."

Exhausted, I began to think again that a vacation would do us both a lot of good. We were emotionally drained. Somehow there had to be a reason for our trials. Only time would tell.

Well, I made it to the end of the week and then I crashed! On August 1, I ended up in the hospital for ten days with severe stomach pains. It was my first hospital stay, and the most horrifying experience of my life. I underwent a multitude of tests to determine the cause of the high fever, excruciating abdominal pain, and severe diarrhea. I lost ten pounds and thought I was going to die. In addition, the hospital conditions were poor. The air conditioning broke down during a record-breaking heat wave. The humidity was unbearable, and there was no running water for two days. You couldn't even flush the toilet! To make matters worse, I was in an orthopedic ward, so the nurses were not familiar with my type of illness.

It took four days for doctors to finally diagnose me. They were concerned because my white blood cell count was abnormally high. White cells fight infection, and for women, the normal range is from 6,000-10,000. When one gets an infection, the white cells increase slightly. I was admitted with a count of 25,000, which to the doctors, constituted immediate surgery (like an appendectomy). They were ready to open me up, but decided to run more tests instead. Two days later my white count climbed to 66,000. The doctors really began to worry. They treated me with steroids, and within a day the pain subsided and my white count decreased.

After I underwent a colonoscopy, Dr. Stephen Shapiro came in to see me. "Well, it definitely looks like inflammatory bowel disease—colitis. It's a chronic disease, but it's treatable."

Oh, I have a disease, I thought. Although they suspected my

elevated white count was caused by the severe colitis infection, the doctors remained cautious.

About the fifth day, as I began to improve, another doctor came in to say that I was growing a fungus in my blood. I underwent several more tests and was given antibiotics. Three days later, we were told that the "fungus infection" was a complete mistake; that one of the doctors had misread the lab results.

Despite all the problems, I was released on August 12. The entire experience was a nightmare. Brian was glad to take me home. I questioned my confidence in hospitals and doctors, and decided that if I ever got sick again, I'd take a much more assertive stand in terms of my health care.

For the next four months, I recovered slowly and returned for monthly check-ups. My white count continued to fluctuate, so Dr. Shapiro referred me to a hematologist/oncologist, Dr. Kathleen Toomey.

Dr. Toomey suggested that I undergo a bone marrow test to rule out leukemia. It was December, and as the holidays approached, it was a sad time for us. We felt jinxed. December had often brought bad news to me—to us. I recalled December of 1975, when Stella, my sister, died of lung cancer. She was only eighteen years old. I remembered that year and how lonely Christmas was without her. Then, in December of 1984, Brian's urologist told us we would never be able to have children. How devastating that was. Now I had what Dr. Shapiro termed Crohn's Disease (a more serious form of colitis), and we were on the brink of receiving even more disastrous news. Indeed, we felt jinxed. I related my fears to my doctor, asking if I could wait to have the bone marrow test in January. She suggested that I not delay. While family and friends rejoiced in the holidays, Brian and I prepared for an uncertain future. We were worried.

PART I
PREPARING FOR A BONE MARROW TRANSPLANT

CHAPTER 1
RECEIVING THE DIAGNOSIS

It was a quiet Christmas season in New Jersey. We canceled our trip to California. Over the years, we had learned to make Christmas by ourselves enjoyable. As usual, it always took an effort to keep from feeling blue about not having a toddler or two around the house, and this year was no different. The prospects of my having leukemia overshadowed the festivities, yet I managed to stay busy. I was doing well until I bumped into a friend at church.

"Analisa, aren't you and Brian going to Los Angeles for Christmas?"

"No, we've decided to spend it here in New Jersey," I answered cheerfully.

"Oh, it must be just terrible for you…without kids. Christmas is for kids. I bet it's hard for you guys, and actually boring!"

Stunned by his remark, I was furious, but calmly replied, "Yeah, we just don't fit in, do we? But we have wonderful Christmases—we *make* them enjoyable."

I didn't let him know just how much pain he had inflicted on me. It wasn't the first time someone had made an innocent, yet ignorant remark about our situation. Later, in tears, I related it to Brian, still not believing what our friend had said. Although we had more important problems to worry about, it made us sad and tainted the holidays all the more.

On December 27, 1988, I went in for the bone marrow test. We were nervous. I had heard all kinds of rumors about bone marrow tests and how painful they could be.

Dr. Toomey set our minds at ease. "Occasionally, colitis can mimic leukemia, and according to your history chart, I don't think you have it," she said. Grabbing me by my knees as I sat on the examining table, she gently said, "Don't you worry; today we're going to prove that you are healthy."

The nurse held my hand as a six-inch steel gauge needle was inserted into my lower back pelvic bone. With several sharp tugs she retrieved several small amounts of blood and marrow. The procedure took about ten to fifteen minutes. Yes, it was very painful; however, the pain lasted for only seconds. The fear of having the bone marrow test was more frightening than the test itself.

We asked several questions about the disease, but she preferred not to discuss it.

"We'll talk about it if it arises," she assured. "There is no need to worry yet. Just enjoy the holidays. We'll have the first results in a week, and the chromosome tests back in three weeks."

I was treated as an outpatient, and although I was sore, we went Christmas shopping the rest of the day.

It's amazing how much we depend on doctors. The one or two words they say can make or break us. In the coming months, I was to realize that a touch of the hand or a smile could convey a thousand words of caring. Dr. Toomey made me feel important. We left her office worried, yet hopeful that all would go well. We still did not understand the serious nature of what the outcome might mean. I guess we were just too afraid to discuss it.

THE WAITING

Waiting for test results, especially around the holidays, was nerve-wracking. However, we still tried to enjoy the festivities. There's always nostalgia around New Year's. You look back with regret, wishing you had accomplished more; and to the future, with new resolutions you probably won't keep. On New Year's Eve, we attended a party at a friend's home, the Bartholomews. As midnight approached, everyone cheered and chanted as we watched the "ball" drop in Times Square on TV. I nudged Brian. "Well, another year has gone by and it's still just us, sweetie…and who knows what 1989 will bring?"

"Yeah…1988 has been a busy and difficult year. Maybe `89 will be better," he remarked.

Sherlene had us write down our New Year's resolutions with the intent to send them to us at the end of 1989. My list was short and to the point. You can bet what was at the top! My mind quickly darted into the future, wondering what and where we would be when we received these resolutions again. We left the party feeling good, not letting others in on our concerns.

BLACK MONDAY

During the first week of January, Dr. Toomey called to give us the good news. I did not have leukemia!

"The chromosome tests are still pending and those results will be the most conclusive. Given the reports already, the chromosome tests should check out okay," she said.

We were so happy. She had relieved our worst fears. Without giving it a second thought, we quickly got on with our lives. But the happiness was short-lived.

On January 23, 1989, we received the dreadful news. As with any disaster or calamity in one's life, one always remembers the moment clearly. I was at work. I had given Ed, my boss, my termination notice, and was scheduled to quit the following Friday. I hadn't quite fully recovered from my colitis problem. I tired easily and was looking forward to taking time off. In addition, I still needed to take the real estate exam, since my colitis episode had forced me to postpone it.

It was a busy Monday morning when the receptionist called.

"The results are in and Dr. Toomey would like you and your husband to come in."

"Great, I'll be in tomorrow."

She paused, and then said, "You may want to bring your husband."

"Okay," I hesitantly said.

I hung up and promptly called Brian. Suspecting trouble, he wondered why she hadn't given me the results over the phone.

"Call her back and see if we can come in today," he told me.

The thought that something was wrong hadn't even occurred to me. It was almost noon. Dr. Toomey's office was only five minutes away. So, I called back, and the receptionist said it would be fine to come in now. "Will Brian be with you?" she asked.

"Uh, yes."

"Good."

My heart started pounding. All I could do was take a deep breath and say a silent prayer. I told my boss I had to leave and would probably be late returning after lunch. He assured me it would be okay.

Brian's department had recently moved to another building down the street. I dashed over to pick him up. While I waited, I searched my feelings. Surprisingly, I didn't feel too worried. Surely I couldn't have leukemia. Maybe they had found something else that wasn't as serious. Not wanting to look for trouble, I just wanted to know. I needed to see Brian. I knew that as soon as I saw him, he'd calm my fears. As he came out of the building, I eagerly read his face. He looked calm. All we could do was embrace. Not too much was said. As he drove, we held hands.

I turned on the radio for diversion. To my surprise, the station began playing "Without You" ("I can't live, if living is without you…") by Harry Nilsson. Instantly, it brought back memories of Stella and her death. I sighed, fearing it was a bad omen; our worst fears were about to be confirmed. Before we went into the office, Brian offered a short prayer.

As we walked in, the awful chemical odor that permeated the office hit us like a brick. Because it was the lunch hour, the office was empty. The receptionist assured us that Dr. Toomey would be with us shortly.

As we sat in the lounge, I glanced around the office and noticed all the cancer pamphlets on the wall. I wondered how this office would impact my future. In a few minutes my fate would be revealed. Suddenly, I didn't want to know. I wanted to freeze this moment in time and savor our innocence. What I didn't know couldn't hurt me. I wished I wasn't here. Why did it have to be us again? The receptionist called our name and in we went.

Dr. Toomey chatted with us to sort of break the ice. We told her our workplace was so close-by that we could have run across the field to see her. She grinned, not really paying attention; she had other, more important things to discuss. Then, with my chart in hand, she looked at both of us and said, "The results of your chromosome studies came back positive for CML: Chronic Myelogenous Leukemia."

My mouth fell open in disbelief. We were speechless. We had no idea what leukemia was—only that it was a cancer often found in children and occasionally in adults. It just couldn't be true, I thought.

"It appears you have tested positive for the Philadelphia Chromosome. Apparently, chromosomes nine and twenty-two are passing wrong information to each other, which make it clinically diagnostic for CML." She went on. "You're very lucky, Analisa. I believe we have found this in its early stages."

My mind raced around. All I could think of was Stella and how she had suffered. Cancer ate a person alive.

"I know what I'm in for," I said sorrowfully. "I've gone through this before with my sister…and now it's my turn."

She was quick to reassure me. "Times have changed, Analisa. That was 1975, and your sister's illness is totally unrelated to yours. You shouldn't compare them. CML *is* treatable, and in some cases curable."

There were so many thoughts and questions. Suddenly, life was crashing in on me. I've already been through this, I thought. I've suffered watching a loved one die. Why now me? I looked at Brian and started crying. He looked worried and helpless.

She continued to tell us how CML is basically a chronic blood disorder, which affects the white blood cells. The white cells multiply excessively and abnormally, anywhere from five to twenty times the normal amount, and become useless in combating infections. Eventually, these leukemic cells begin attacking the body.

"There are many different kinds of leukemias. Out of all of them to have, CML is probably the best one," she said. "It can be treatable and even curable," she repeated.

We listened as she counseled us about our options.

"You could let it take its course and be treated with drugs and therapy to control it as long as possible. Or, you could be treated with Alfa-Interferon, a very costly procedure requiring self-induced IV injections three times a week. This would cause the leukemic cells to go dormant, but it is not considered a cure. Finally, you could try for a cure by having the risky procedure of a bone marrow transplant."

She went on, "Bone marrow transplants have been successful in curing leukemia, but it's a highly dangerous procedure. You'll want to do this only as a last resort. Right now you are in no danger. The chances for your survival are higher by treating it with other means than to have a bone marrow transplant. Research on bone marrow transplants is advancing rapidly. Maybe six months from now the procedure may not be as severe. Perhaps you wouldn't have to suffer as much. Nevertheless, at some point—three to five years down the line—you will have to have one in order to be completely cured."

Then Brian asked, "How much time does she have, Doctor? Can she live twenty years without having the transplant?"

"No."

"How about fifteen?"

"No."

"Ten years?"

"It would be very unlikely. She has about three to five years. But I think we caught this early. You're lucky. Most people don't realize they have it until it's too late. Be grateful you came down with colitis."

We looked at each other, trying to absorb it all.

"You have a lot to consider. It's basically a numbers game, to bargain for more time. Any decision you make will have pros and cons to it. CML is common in adults ages twenty to forty. The time to do a transplant is when you're still relatively young and in good health. It's a gamble. You'll just have to weigh the options."

She went on to say that having a BMT (Bone Marrow Transplant) would require a bone marrow donor, preferably from a sibling with a perfect HLA (Human Leukocyte Antigen) blood match. (Human leukocyte antigens are proteins that help the body's defense system tell the difference between its own cells and other cells.)

"I have three brothers," I said.

"Good. This should be your first priority: to have your brothers tested. If no relatives match, you'll have to go through the National Registry to get an unrelated donor."

She suggested we research the transplant centers out West, either in California or Seattle, where statistics are high and where there is state-of-the-art equipment and ongoing research.

Although Dr. Toomey was knowledgeable and informative, it was too much to swallow at once. What were we in for? A bone marrow transplant was hard to fathom. I sensed she felt sorry for us. Here we were, a young couple in the prime of our lives, now faced with a critical dilemma. She tried to give us hope, and encouraged us to read and become informed about CML so we could make the best decisions.

"It doesn't have to be the end of the world, Analisa. We'll just take it one step at a time. The idea will be to buy as much time as possible."

When Brian and I came out of her office, the receptionist said, "That will be seventy-five dollars."

I wanted to scream! I turned to Brian and said, "Gee, we still have to pay, even for the bad news!"

He wrote out the check and we left.

Before returning to work, we sat in the car and stared at the bleak field of trees in front of us. It was a cold, ugly winter day. The gray clouds reflected our feelings. Suddenly, I hated New Jersey! Everything around me looked dead, and now I'm dying too, I thought. We held each other and cried.

As we contemplated future events, it just couldn't be real. Life had been great. We had good jobs, owned our townhouse, had just purchased another one with our neighbor, and were in the process of buying a new car. Now it all seemed so unimportant. All we wanted was to preserve our precious love. We were everything to each other. The thought of losing each other was unbearable. Nevertheless, Brian assured me that we'd get through this. "We'll just take it one day at a time," he said.

Feeling numb and speechless, Brian prayed that somehow we would be taken care of. As we discussed our future, we realized that we would need to pray for a miracle—many miracles! We wiped our tears away, determined that God would have to see us through this. Although depressed and worried, we returned to work.

Ed asked how my appointment had gone. "Not too good," I told him. "They're still checking on a few things." I passed it off as no big deal, knowing that if he inquired further I'd break down in tears. It took every ounce of concentration I could muster to work that final week and train new people. When my department gave me a farewell party, it was a supreme effort for me to put on a happy face. Inside I was miserable, knowing that suffering was imminent.

The hardest part was telling our parents. Surprisingly, they took it well—at least they seemed to. Perhaps they were merely in shock. Telling them relieved a tremendous amount of stress. They gave us plenty of encouragement and support.

The only family nearby was Brian's sister and brother-in-law, Robin and Craig Nelson. Since they and their two daughters lived in Newtown, Pennsylvania, only forty minutes away, they were a great comfort to us. Robin and Craig were married a month after us. And since then, Robin and I had become like sisters and especially closer in the past two years. We enjoyed exploring the East Coast together; taking trips to Boston, New York, and Washington, D.C.

A LIGHT OF WARNING

Within days of receiving my diagnosis, I recalled a dream I had had earlier that week. I thoroughly believe we are sometimes warned when certain events in our lives are about to take place. Surprisingly, I realized I *had* been warned! It was a most unusual experience.

I remember it vividly. It was Saturday night, January 21, 1989, two days before learning about my leukemia. That night, I retired to bed at 10:00 p.m. because the next day we were to drive to Baltimore, Maryland, to pick up Brian's brother, Bill. Bill was scheduled to take a class in Emmetsburg, Maryland. The day was going to be long, so I wanted to get a good night's sleep.

Brian and I had been watching TV. After getting ready for bed, I called out to Brian to join me. He had the habit of falling asleep with the TV on, while I usually tossed and turned for at least a half-hour before dozing off. But this night was different. I lay in bed feeling calm and relaxed.

Brian heeded my request, and came up and went into the bathroom. The room was dark, except for a thin ray of light coming through the door, which he left slightly open. I peered at the light, and then closed my eyes. The next thing I knew, I was leaving my body and soaring through darkness. I felt a marvelous feeling of peace and joy. I *knew* I was leaving this earth! The joy in my soul was so wonderful; I didn't question my departure. I knew I'd miss Brian and my family, but I wanted to go and had no doubts. Fully aware of what was happening, I said to myself, "This is it; it's all over; I'm done. Here I go!" Traveling further into the darkness, I continued to feel indescribable joy—complete and exquisite. I thought, any second now I'm going to see the "light."

Suddenly, as though coming around a corner, I saw a tremendously bright light. It was so brilliant that the moment I beheld it, I instantly felt electricity strike my body, entering from the top of my head and exiting through the tips of my toes.

I awoke in shock! My heart was pounding and I was trembling, as though I had been thrust back into my body. I was almost there, I thought; I *was* there! My gosh, this really happened! I closed my eyes and tried to get back, but there was no way. I felt rejected and short-changed. Desperately searching for understanding, I began crying and praying quietly to myself. A feeling of warmth and peace came over me, and I felt I had been given a great gift. I did not know why, nor did I fully understand it, but I *knew* that its meaning held great significance.

As I lay there, pondering in the darkness, I beheld the ray of light still shining from the bathroom. The experience, which seemed to last a long time, probably lasted only a few minutes, or seconds. I didn't want to tell Brian immediately. I needed to ponder it on my own first.

Three things came to mind. First, if this is what death is like, it is the most peaceful and wonderful experience imaginable. Second, I felt rejected and that perhaps I wasn't ready to "come into the light." Maybe I needed to get my life in order. Finally, perhaps I would be involved in a near-death experience, and/or die. The experience was so real that it left a profound impression on my whole being. It had occurred for a reason, and I would be looking for that reason.

While driving to Baltimore the following day in the early morning hours, the bright headlights of the oncoming cars reminded me of my dream. So, I shared the experience with Brian. We discussed death and dying, never considering a catastrophic illness. After listening to my conclusions, he agreed that maybe it was a warning of a life and death situation. The only question I had was whether I would die.

Now, after learning of my diagnosis, I reflected on this dream over and over again. It gave me great comfort. Although I wasn't sure what my fate would be, I *knew* God was aware of me. With faith, He would help us make the right decisions.

CHAPTER 2
PREPARING FOR THE CRISIS

The shock of my diagnosis took days, even months to fully sink in. While driving to work or talking to friends, I often pinched myself. This couldn't be true; this couldn't be happening to me, I'd think. It's all a bad dream and soon I'll wake up. But I never did.

Ironically, less than a week later, the Leukemia Society called, asking for a contribution.

Dismayed, I asked, "Am I on some kind of a list? I can't believe it. A family member has just been diagnosed!"

She apologized and said there was no such list. It was hard to believe it was a terrible coincidence.

The first thing plaguing my thoughts was how I was going to handle this crisis. What attitude was I going to adopt? I definitely had a choice. At first I felt in control. I couldn't break down if I didn't know what I was breaking down about. I needed more facts.

So, I frequented the nearby library to get the latest information on CML. It was awkward reading about "my" cancer. The more I read, the more I felt numbness come over me—a very somber feeling. My world was becoming smaller. After three trips to the library, I decided I had read enough.

In public I observed others, often wondering, why me? Why am I being picked on? Life is just not fair! A part of me wanted to be very bitter. But I knew if I couldn't be strong now, I'd never make it through the months ahead.

I shared my findings with Brian. Often we just sat and cradled each other. Our love seemed to flourish more than we could both imagine. I feared for his strength and worried that he wouldn't be able to handle it. I was glad this was happening to me and not him.

"I'm going to take care of you, baby. I'm going to be with you all the way," he'd say with a tender tone.

I loved him like crazy. I likened our relationship to the song "Evergreen" by Barbra Streisand. He was gentle and kind, tall and handsome with dark brown hair and brown eyes. His looks were a cross between those of Harrison Ford and Charles Bronson, and he had the personality of John Ritter. His strength and determination became my anchor.

DEALING WITH FRIENDS

After revealing my condition to the rest of our family, we decided to tell nobody else, except Mieke. It was crucial that no one know until we first understood the facts and weighed our options. Since I felt relatively good and basically happy, the last thing I needed was everyone's sympathy. I didn't feel sorry for myself, nor did I want anyone else to. Having to constantly update others on my condition would wear me down and shatter my strength. If I paced myself and stayed in control, I'd be fine.

I recalled the wise counsel given to us by Los Angeles Temple President, Allen C. Rosza, on our wedding day in 1982: "When problems and struggles arise in your life, try to solve them on your own first. Don't run and tell the whole world. Because long after the problem is solved, others will still be trying to solve it for you." His advice rang clear. I swore Mieke to secrecy, but before the day was over, she told her husband, Paul. I wasn't surprised, but I knew our secret would be safe with them.

Mieke had suffered many adversities herself. She too was a survivor—a couple of failed marriages, financial success to financial disaster, and now she was starting all over again. She didn't treat me differently. She knew I just needed friendship. We needed each other. Countless times during the ensuing months, at a moment's notice we'd gravitate toward each other for strength. We'd dive into deep discussions about life, happiness, money and spiritual things. We'd rendezvous at the nearby McDonalds and lick away our fears over ice cream sundaes with lots of nuts. We plotted how we were going to get out of "this mess." We laughed and cried, and often discussed the principle of "justice and mercy," and how there is justice and mercy in all things. We were both in need of mercy, and agreed there was no other choice but to feel happy about our circumstances.

Finally, one day Mieke inquisitively asked, "How come you're holding up so well, Analisa?" She seemed bothered by my joking, nonchalant attitude.

Feeling provoked, I defensively replied, "It's the only way I can deal with it. It's all I can do to keep from shaking in my boots! If I'm not strong now, I'm never going to make it." I was feeling well and that's all that mattered.

However, a couple of weeks after receiving my diagnosis, the first feelings of real fear surfaced. One day, while contemplating my situation, the painful memories of Stella's death hit me like a brick. I felt horribly doomed. A terrible depression came over me and I couldn't do the simplest tasks. Crippled with fear, I saw myself heading down the same path to eventual destruction.

This harrowing feeling lasted two days. On the second day I received a call from Fran Price, the Relief Society President, in charge of all the women in our ward (congregation). Her responsibilities were to oversee the women and to extend love and support where needed. She had been trying for weeks to come visit me, but I was either busy or unavailable. Truthfully, I didn't want her to come, for fear I'd have to unload my problems. But this day she insisted, and feeling so upset, I consented.

Fran was a sweet, soft-spoken woman with white hair, and old enough to be my mother. As she sat in my living room, I wondered why she had come.

"I'm not quite sure why I'm here. I've just felt prompted lately to come and see how you're doing," she said.

She knew about my colitis problems last summer and about our "childless" situation. She began explaining how her daughter had just adopted a baby, and wanted to share her experience with me. "I want you to know, Analisa, that if that's what you're worried about, don't worry. Everything will work out."

At first, I was amazed that she was able to detect any kind of problem. I had done a good job of disguising my feelings, and was sure no one knew about my illness. As she spoke, I wondered for the hundredth time how many people had tried to solve our "childlessness." Everyone always had a friend or relative he or she was eager to tell us about.

I expressed my appreciation. Then, with a smile and a need to vent my feelings, I blurted out, "Fran, not having children is the least of our worries right now." In tears, I divulged everything.

Her visit ended up being a wonderful experience and an answer to prayer. Needless to say, she was shocked to learn of my illness and never would have guessed it. Nevertheless, she admitted she was glad. "Now I know why I had to come and see you. I couldn't figure it out."

We were both grateful. Her presence and sincere listening completely lifted my burden. I never again felt that horrendous, crippling feeling of depression. I knew in my heart that God was watching over me, was aware of my needs, and had sent a little angel my way.

I looked to the future as though it were a movie with many scenes yet to be played out. Brian assured me that with a prayerful attitude, things would fall into place and we would be led each step of the way. We began to nurture that belief.

I acted and truly felt as though nothing was wrong. At times I felt extremely happy. It wasn't really a denial; I just had to continue on with life.

In early February we went ahead and purchased our new car. Jokingly, I told Brian, "Maybe we should wait. There's no sense in buying me a car if I'm not going to be around to enjoy it!"

"No!" he insisted. "I want to buy you the best little car, and I want you to have fun driving it."

Well, who could resist? We purchased a cute, red and gray Pontiac Grand Am. They were popular in the East, and sporty-looking. Ironically, my new license plates read, "CBC 95K"—the acronym in medical terms meaning, "complete blood count 95K." It was an eerie description of my health problems! I felt labeled and hated that license plate. My disease was following me everywhere. Nevertheless, we enjoyed our new car.

With the news of my illness, instantly there arose a strong need to cherish every day with Brian. On Valentine's Day, I wrote him a simple poem:

> Roses are red, violets are blue,
> I'm so glad I'm married to you.
> May 9, 1980 was the night we met,
> A wonderful day I'll never forget.
> You were handsome, gorgeous and sweet,
> I knew in an instant, we were meant to meet!
>
> We fell in love right from the start,
> Although it took awhile to capture your heart.

Two years of dating; we had a blast,
Nurturing a relationship we knew would last.

And when we got married, boy what a treat,
The presents, Hawaii; it was all so neat!
You've made my life so colorful and real,
I cherish every moment this love that we feel.

We've shared so much in these last seven years,
Buying houses and cars amidst all the fears.
Three years in Idaho and two in New Jersey,
So many blessings almost leave us feeling unworthy.

Although we sometimes wonder what will become of us,
As long as I have you, I won't make a fuss.
It's the love we share that will help us get through,
The days to come when we might feel blue.

We're a rare couple you and me,
Perhaps a model couple for others to see?
And although sometimes we question, "Why?"
The Lord has plans for us, we cannot deny.

Until then, it'll just be Brian and Ana,
But someday I know we'll have our Briana.
We'll have good health and that little family,
Perhaps a white picket fence, where we'll live happily.

So each day of our lives, let us always be strong,
With a love like ours, we just cannot go wrong!
Brian, you're wonderful; Brian, you're "me",
And I'm so thankful I have *you* for eternity!
Thanks for marrying me.

For Valentine's, we took the train into New York City and enjoyed a romantic dinner at the top of the World Trade Center. Our bill was high, yet we were still hungry. So, afterward we went to eat Chinese food. It was a great evening.

Going in for a blood test once a month was miserable. The reality of my illness would hit me as soon as I walked into Dr. Toomey's office. It was like getting on a roller coaster. Sometimes my white count was up, other times it was down.

"My whole life revolves around this two-second poke in the finger," I'd tell the nurse. Each time I waited, hoping and praying she'd look up and say, "Your counts are normal; there's nothing wrong with you," but she never did.

I'd have a list of questions for Dr. Toomey, and would absorb all bits of hope or encouragement she would offer.

Driving home I'd feel so lonely. The songs on the radio took on so much meaning. Instead of sulking over sad songs, I began collecting good songs, and spiritual ones, too. Brian and I began listening to them until we were blue in the face.

As the weeks and months followed, there was a growing need to stay extremely busy—distracted. We continued to be active in church. We tried to follow the admonition found in Matthew 16:25. Basically it says, "When you lose yourself in the service of others, you find yourself."

One day I took a woman to the doctor. I listened to her lament for hours about her back problems. I thought to myself, "If only you knew what I was up against...it wouldn't compare." Nonetheless, I found great joy in serving.

My mom, dad, and brother Jim flew out for two weeks to extend their support. Although the weather was cold, we gave them a tour of the East, including Washington, D.C. It was good to see them and they encouraged us to hang in there and be strong.

GETTING A SECOND OPINION

In March, my illness began accelerating sooner than expected. My white count started hovering around 45,000. Dr. Toomey decided to put me on a low dose of Hydroxyurea, an oral form of chemotherapy. She assured me I was still in no serious danger yet.

"All your other blood counts are normal and could remain so for a very long time."

We were shocked, thinking we still had years to decide what steps to pursue. At first, I responded well to the one-a-day pill. But a month later, it had to be increased to three pills a day. The thought of being on medication so soon made me sick.

"I can't live like this, Brian. My world is closing in on me. Little by little, I'm going to be eaten alive. We've got to do something. Somebody else needs to know about my condition."

Determined to get the best care possible, we asked Brian's mom, Rosemary, to check out UCLA for us. She promptly obtained the name of Dr. Richard Champlin, Director of the Bone Marrow Transplant Unit at UCLA Medical Center.

Having seen his name in a few leukemia pamphlets from Dr. Toomey's office, I knew he was world-renowned and one of the doctors who went to Chernobyl, Russia, after their nuclear accident. I held onto his telephone number for a couple of days, wondering what this Dr. Champlin would do for me, and what role he might play in my life.

He was probably such a busy man it would take days to reach him. However, when I called, amazingly he himself answered the phone. At this point, my feelings were so sensitive that just the sound of his voice would have turned me away, if I had felt uneasy about him. As we spoke, I readily gained trust in his gentle voice, and he seemed interested in my case. I explained my current condition, and he agreed that I would eventually need a bone marrow transplant.

He said, "I don't want to scare you, but we suggest having the transplant within one year of diagnosis to ensure curability. Do you have any brothers or sisters?"

"Three brothers; two in Los Angeles and one serving a Mormon mission in Peru."

"Good. There's a twenty-five percent chance for each brother that one of them may match. So, you have a seventy-five percent chance."

"Gosh, I didn't think I'd be having the transplant so soon."

"We'll take one step at a time. Getting a match is the most important step before we can do anything else."

He also restated that CML could stay chronic for years, but it was common to last only three years before going into "blast crisis," the stage where cancer cells multiply erratically and death is certain.

I was astonished at his urgency. We had just purchased tickets for a trip to Mexico City and Acapulco for the first week in April. However, he suggested that I not take the risk, but come to California and see him instead. After we hung up with him, Brian and I just looked at each other. Suddenly the pressure was on, with a definite urgency to take care of my problem now.

As we pondered over the books and pamphlets again, I wondered what price I would have to pay to get my health back. Our lives seemed like one big question mark. What was to be learned from all of this? And who was to be affected? Remembering how Stella's illness had touched many lives, I knew my present acts were setting the stage for my own "unfortunate performance." Each decision would have to be made carefully and prayerfully. However, time was running out and decisions would have to be made soon.

Like a seesaw supporting each other, we did our best to laugh a lot—trying to do what the current popular song said, "Don't worry, be happy!"

As the weeks passed, we mulled over the seriousness mounting and the decision to go ahead with the transplant if one of my brothers matched. I looked at it this way: I was twenty-seven years old; we had a terrific marriage; and we wanted a family. If we waited it out, the harder it would be on my body and the further it would delay a chance for a family. Perhaps we could take care of this CML now, allow a few years for recovery, and then adopt a baby while we were still in our thirties.

As we discussed my future, I burst into tears. "Brian, I love you. I can't bear the thought of losing you and leaving you behind."

"I don't want to talk about it. You're going to be fine," he insisted. He reassured me, "If you do die, I will never marry again."

But I knew in my heart that if I died, women would be knocking at his door before he could even make it to my funeral! I was sure of it. Brian was *my* jewel, and the thought of him with someone else truly motivated me to commence fighting with all my heart, mind and soul. The thought of us being ripped apart provoked in me so much anger. I *could not* and *would not* allow it to happen. We were perfect together—we were one.

At times he admitted, "It would be nice if we could die together in a car accident or something—just to get this life over with. Life is so hard!"

These fatalistic conversations caused numbness to come over me again and again. Sometimes I'd catch him staring at me, deep in thought. Immediately, I'd ask him, "What are you thinking?"

"Nothing...I just love you so much."

"I need your strength to survive, Brian. You are going to be my greatest ally."

"I know we can do this," he'd insist.

Although life was becoming increasingly difficult, I was determined to keep a sense of humor, no matter what. I had to hang tough. It was too early in the game to fall apart. Crying would have to come later. Although at times, I'd almost start trembling with fear.

Other times I felt extremely happy. I took joy in the simplest of pleasures, like ice cream with Mieke, or a delicious meal at Robin and Craig's home. These small moments were precious, for however long they would last.

The task that lay ahead seemed to invigorate me. I was gearing up for the biggest marathon of my life. I could feel myself changing day by day, becoming more daring, more aggressive. What do I have to lose? I thought. I often pondered over the medical books, wondering again what price I was going to pay to get well, and would it be worth it?

In time we would divulge my illness to the rest of our friends and petition their faith. Until then, our only concern was getting a perfect match.

Foregoing our trip to Mexico in April, we met with Dr. Champlin. My brothers, Victor and Jim, came along to have their blood tested. Alfred, my brother in Peru, still knew nothing about my illness. We were hopeful and confident that Victor's or Jim's blood would match, so that Alfred could continue serving his mission. We were confident that the Lord would not disturb the work he was doing; that perhaps through his service our family would receive greater blessings. I also didn't want him to know until we had all the facts.

On April 4, 1989, we walked into the UCLA Bowyer Clinic. It didn't feel normal to be in a doctor's office, especially an oncology one. I'm not supposed to be here, I thought. I scanned the room inconspicuously, wondering what everyone else was there for and automatically comparing myself. It was sobering.

We first met with Dr. Alexander Black. He was very nice and thorough. After having my blood drawn, he gave me a routine checkup, reviewed my records, then left to get Dr. Champlin. We waited a long time—the saga of being in a doctor's office. I tried to envision what Dr. Champlin would look like. Would he be the Marcus Welby type, or the Dr. Seuss? Establishing a good relationship was crucial, so I worried about our making a first impression. It could either turn us on or off.

When Dr. Champlin walked in, we were quickly put at ease. He was much more the Dr. Welby type—a nice-looking, gray-haired man in his mid-forties. He came across as serious and knowledgeable, and I sensed in him a genuine concern for my welfare.

Although he wasn't very talkative or enthusiastic, I felt I could work with him and put my trust in his expertise. He examined me, reviewed my records, and confirmed my diagnosis of CML. Then he explained the necessary steps for a bone marrow transplant.

Victor's first question was, "How is the procedure for the donor, and will it hurt?"

Dr. Champlin replied, "The donor's marrow will be removed from the lower back hip bone, requiring the donor to be hospitalized for about three days. There will be some pain and discomfort, but after a long weekend, you should be able to return to work."

He stressed the importance of a perfect sibling match; six out of six elements of the blood must match. "A transplant could be done with a five out of six match, but the odds would lower your chance of survival."

I flooded him with a list of questions I had written. He seemed to answer all of them quite thoroughly. He explained, "The common protocol is to have lethal dosages of radiation and chemotherapy given in intervals over a one-week period to eradicate your own marrow. The new marrow is then injected intravenously. It instinctively migrates to the bones and we wait to see if it grows. It takes three weeks for it to be diagnostically visible, and one year for the new marrow to grow to full maturity."

"Will I be able to have children?" I asked.

"Given your age of twenty-seven, it's difficult to tell. The transplant could likely put you into early menopause."

"How long will the recovery be? And how much will the transplant cost?"

"Plan on giving yourself at least a whole year. The critical part will be the first six months. You will be susceptible to any kind of infection. The cost may vary; $80,000-$150,000 or higher, depending on complications."

When he finished, I needed to let him know I wasn't just another number on a medical report. Wanting his full attention, I looked him straight in the eye, but he had a tendency to look down when he spoke.

He seemed shy, but sincere. I said, "Dr. Champlin, if I was your wife, would you encourage me to have the transplant this year?"

"Yes, I would not wait," he said as he looked up. "I want to see you old and gray...and your chances right now are good."

In a sense I was a walking time bomb. My white cells could accelerate out of control at any time. If my cells reached "blast crisis" stage it would mean almost certain death, even with a transplant.

I asked him if we could talk to anyone who had already been through a transplant. He left, and then returned with a thirty-six-year-old woman who was dressed in shorts and actually looked quite healthy. She too had CML, and had undergone her transplant nine months earlier. Her name was Sally; she was a chiropractor by profession. She was in for a routine checkup. We appreciated her willingness to share any advice.

"It will be the very hardest thing you'll ever do. It will take every bit of strength. If you have any unfinished business with family, friends or wills to make, take care of them now so that you can put all your energy into getting through this."

In awe, I studied her. Her hair was short, with salt and pepper strands, and she was very tanned. I took comfort in looking at her. No one would have guessed she had been through a transplant.

But as she spoke, it was as if I was listening to someone who had just climbed a huge mountain and now was briefing me on the obstacles.

She said, "I don't want to scare you, but I think that it's very important you be informed on what to expect."

"I want to be prepared as much as possible," I said anxiously.

"Just think of the worst experience you could ever imagine and it will be just that, and probably worse. Many don't survive." She nodded her head as though not wanting to divulge the whole truth. "You'll be sicker than you can ever imagine, and you'll need every bit of support you can get from family and friends."

"How do you feel now, and how long did it take for you to start feeling better again?" I asked.

"It's been a very slow process, but I was lucky. I entered the hospital last July. By November I was able to go roller skating at Venice beach, and in January I returned to work part-time."

She said the staff at UCLA was excellent. Her sister was her donor, and she stressed the importance of a sibling match.

Finally, I asked if there were any other suggestions or advice she could give me.

"Just try to stay active and walk around as much as you can, in your room or in the halls. Do your mouth swabs daily so you won't get mouth sores, and bring baby wipes for the bathroom. They will be a lifesaver!"

Then she paused and looked at me solemnly, "I'll keep you in my prayers. You'll probably come through it okay, but it'll be hard."

She had survived, and it *was* possible to lead a normal life again! I took mental pictures and notes so I would remember her. If she could do it, perhaps I could too. Meeting her gave me courage. Later on, I often recounted the memory of Sally.

We left the hospital that day and went to eat at a restaurant in Santa Monica. We were laughing with Victor and Jim and having fun, trying to guess who my donor would be. Life seemed so normal, and I wanted to keep it that way. But inside I felt the pressure weighing on my heart, gnawing at me. A faraway voice was calling me in another direction. I could ignore it for a while, but I couldn't let it go. The knowledge of my illness was ever-present—like a pack of wolves preying on me. However, I couldn't and wouldn't give in! Like a helium balloon, I was rising to each step, hoping and praying no one would pop me. I felt strong, yet so very fragile.

That afternoon at my parent's house, we told them about our visit. "Dad, I feel like I have a huge ocean in front of me to cross, and Sally has made it to the other side. I can't make it all the way by myself. No matter how much I try I'll only be able to go a certain length. Only with faith will the Lord have to step in and guide me the rest of the way."

Solemnly he agreed that much would be happening in the coming months. As usual he gave me great advice, encouraging me to stay positive. My parents were strong and could handle a crisis well, but I worried how this one would affect them.

After Victor and Jim were tested, all we could do was wait. God willing, one of them would match. Things were happening fast, and I began to wonder about Alfred, and how we would tell him, just in case he might have to come home. He was so happy and having much success in Peru. His letters were inspiring, and it was evident that he had matured greatly in only six months. Mission rules dictated that except for emergencies, families were only allowed to communicate through letters.

Unbelievably, the very next day the phone rang, and I was shocked to hear Alfred's voice! He was so excited, saying he felt a strong need to call home. He had just been transferred to the jungle and wouldn't be writing to us for a few weeks. He took a chance, and wanted to let everyone know he was doing fine.

I was able to tell him everything and, most importantly, let him know what was going on without frightening him. He took it all so well.

"No problem, whatever you need. I'll come home for you, Ana," he said calmly.

"We'll do everything we can to keep you on your mission; it's not an emergency yet. We'll let you know as soon as we find out."

Dad, on the extension, asked, "Alfred, do you think you have Ana's blood type?"

Alfred paused. "Yeah, Dad, I'm probably the one," he said humbly.

We bid our farewells and all promised to pray for a perfect match. It was such a relief to know that Alfred knew! It was more than a coincidence that he had called. It was a miracle.

While in Los Angeles, we took a side trip to San Luis Obispo with Brian's parents. While I tried to enjoy myself, Brian remained solemn. One evening while we were eating in a Chinese restaurant, I was eager to read my fortune cookie.

"Okay, everyone, this is it. This fortune's for me; this will tell me how everything will go," I declared. I opened it and read, "By Fall all your troubles will be far away."

Tears came to my eyes as I clutched that wonderful fortune. "Thank you, God, I pray it will be true," I whispered.

Brian kept the fortune in his wallet, so he could remind me of it when things got rough. Although my life felt like one big question mark, these little miracles were, like drops of water, one by one adding to my reservoir of faith. We left Los Angeles feeling a little more hopeful.

BACK IN NEW JERSEY

Absorbing the concept of the transplant all at once was overwhelming. So I began pacing myself, setting goals, and embracing each step—

creating the foundation to be physically, emotionally and spiritually prepared. I soon learned it would require continual adjustment and readjustment.

PHYSICALLY

I borrowed Robin and Craig's stationary bicycle and began riding regularly. Dr. Toomey suggested I eat as much as possible, since I would most likely lose weight during the transplant. Finally, a free ticket to indulge in food without guilt! I savored my meals, imagining what it would be like not to eat for a while. Some days I felt good; other days I felt worn out.

EMOTIONALLY

I continually reassured myself that this leukemia wasn't going to get the best of me. Rather, I was going to get the best of it; whatever that would be—hopefully good health. I collected positive, uplifting music and literature, and surrounded myself with positive people. I couldn't tolerate anyone with a negative attitude. For now, I was in control and wasn't about to let anyone pull me down. Like the story of the little engine going up the hill, I kept repeating to myself that I think I can make it.

SPIRITUALLY

Spiritual preparation was the most important factor before, during and after the transplant. Victor and I had joined The Church of Jesus Christ of Latter-day Saints in 1975, through the influence of Stella. Stella had joined when she became ill, and thereafter displayed incredible faith during her battle with lung cancer. In her weakened state, she cried tears of joy the day Victor and I were baptized. Three months later she passed away. Even on her deathbed she bore an unshakable testimony of the Gospel and of Jesus Christ—an impression that was unforgettably etched on my mind. I was determined that if I ever got sick, I would follow her example. Later, in 1981, Alfred and Jim were baptized. Although our parents were supportive, they remained Catholic.

Now faced with my own battle, we felt grateful to embrace all the church's teachings and prepare ourselves spiritually. There would be no time for "catch-up" later. As Brian and I discussed the transplant frequently, we realized it would surely become "an exercise" in faith.

Day by day, through prayer, pondering, and serving others, we listened more intently—yearning for answers to the questions of "why." Thereafter, I found greater relief in attending all my meetings. One of our former church presidents, Spencer W. Kimball, once said, "God does notice us, and He watches over us. But it is usually through another person that He meets our needs."

If I was to suffer, I wanted to learn every truth possible. I chose to focus on searching for answers instead of wallowing on the questions. Could I truly put my trust in God, and would He put His trust in me? My sincere feelings were that I would not let Him down if He would give me a chance to survive. We wanted to bind the Lord with faith. It was such an important aspect of my illness that I almost titled this book *An Exercise in Faith*.

In my collection of inspirational poems and stories, I found one that was especially soothing:

<u>Trials</u>
By Lynell Waterman
Reprinted by permission. ©John Mark Ministries.com

You perhaps recall the story of the blacksmith who gave his heart to God. Though conscientious in his living, still he was not prospering materially. In fact, it seems that from the time of his conversion more trouble, affliction and loss were sustained than ever before. Everything seemed to be going wrong.

One day a friend who was not a Christian stopped at the little gorge to talk to him. Sympathizing with him in some of his trials, the friend said, "It seems strange to me that so much affliction should pass over you just at the time when you have become an earnest Christian. Of course, I don't want to weaken your faith in God or anything like that. But here you are, God's help and guidance, and yet things seem to be getting steadily worse. I can't help wondering why it is."

The blacksmith did not answer immediately, and it was evident that he had thought the same question before. But finally he said, "You see here the raw iron which I have to make into horse's shoes? You know what I do with it? I take a piece and heat it in the fire until it is red, almost white with the heat. Then I hammer it unmercifully to shape it as I know it should be shaped. Then I plunge it into a pail of cold water to temper it. Then I heat it again and hammer it some more. And this I do until it is finished."

"But sometimes I find a piece of iron that won't stand up under this treatment. The heat and the hammering and the cold water are too much for it. I don't know why it fails in the process, but I know it will never make a good horse's shoe."

He pointed to a heap of scrap iron that was near the door of his shop. "When I get a piece that cannot take the shape and temper, I throw it out on the scrap heap. It will never be good for anything."

He went on, "I know that God has been holding me in the fires of affliction and I have felt His hammer upon me. But, I don't mind, if only He can bring me to what I should be. And so, in all these hard things, my prayer is simply this: Try me in any way you wish, Lord, only don't throw me on the scrap heap."

As days passed, a sense of humor and a desire to remain light-hearted became extremely important. I took on a sort of slaphappy attitude. If I couldn't laugh about myself, I'd never make it.

Still, my heart was ever-serious, and I felt a need to write. It was during these months that I became determined to write a book. It gave me focus and a purpose to survive. It made me happy to know that someday this story would indeed be told. Oddly, my vision was strong. At times I felt excited to look ahead and see how the future events would unfold. Still, doubt and uncertainty crept in continually. It was a daily exercise to push them away and maintain faith. God had always been there for me. And I was now hopeful that even Stella would somehow be working on my behalf.

CHAPTER 3
GETTING A MATCH

We remained in a holding pattern, keeping our fingers crossed and hoping that Victor's or Jim's blood results would prove successful.

"I still don't want anyone to know, Brian."

"I'll have to tell my work. Maybe I can take time off or put in for a transfer back to California."

"That would be a dream come true," I said. It would likely be our only way back to California. Jobs with AT&T in Los Angeles were scarce. We would settle for San Francisco, or even Arizona.

Brian's organization agreed to investigate a transfer. We were grateful that AT&T was understanding and willing to help.

The possibility of having the transplant that summer was becoming real. So, in mid-April, I took the New Jersey Real Estate Exam. I was determined to get my license, even if I only worked for a couple of weeks. At times it was hard to study, for I would tire easily. However, it kept me occupied.

A few days after we returned to New Jersey we received a call from Dr. Champlin. "Analisa, how are you feeling?"

"Okay," I said nervously.

"We have the results in from Victor's and Jim's blood tests." He paused. "I'm sorry, neither of them match your HLA blood type."

It was like a dagger to the heart. I was shocked. We were so confident that one of them would match. A thousand questions ran through my mind.

"They only matched three elements out of six," he said.

"Could it work with three?"

"No, it would put you at an inordinate risk. You probably wouldn't survive. But look, we have one more chance. You have one more brother, and he just may be the one. There is still a twenty-five percent chance he'll match you."

"Really?" I asked apprehensively.

"Yes. I've seen patients with five or six siblings and none of them match, and others with only one and they match perfectly. So, let's keep our fingers crossed."

"What if Alfred doesn't match?"

"Let's do one thing at a time." He suggested we bring Alfred home as soon as possible.

"Gosh, I hate to bring him home. I know he wouldn't mind; I just didn't plan on doing this so soon."

"I don't think you have a choice, Analisa. Just bring him home to be tested. This is a matter of life and death," he said with concern.

"I guess you're right, Doctor," I sighed. "We'll get back to you as soon as we get more information on him."

The mounting pressure made me nauseous. Suddenly, my whole life depended on Alfred, who was out proselytizing in the jungles of Peru! It just couldn't be true. How could God allow this? I searched for answers. We were so proud of him, and I often cried over his letters and his humble desire to serve. We felt sacredness toward his work as a missionary.

Brian came home early from work that day so we could contemplate our plans.

As I searched my heart, I began to feel that perhaps Alfred *was* meant to come home. Suddenly it all made sense, and I very much wanted his "perfect missionary marrow"! A very special feeling came over me, and soon Brian and I began focusing all of our faith on dear Alfred. He would be the one, God willing. He would be the one to SAVE MY LIFE.

We wondered how he was holding up. He had been suffering from dysentery. In some letters he said he was eating liver and beans for breakfast and dinner.

We called our families and told them the news. We talked at length about Alfred and his precious marrow. Because he was on a mission, everything had to be approved by his Mission President. He, in turn, would get approval from church headquarters in Salt Lake City, Utah.

Nervous, and rusty in my Spanish, we called the Mission President. Brian commented later that I didn't even so much as stutter. Our first desire was for Alfred to continue serving as long as possible.

The following day, Alfred called. "No problem, Ana, I'll come home for you. Just tell me when."

"It's not urgent yet. It's just urgent that you get a blood test. We're going to try every option before we bring you home.

Our telephone connection was lousy and it was difficult explaining to Alfred how to tell the doctors, in Spanish, what we needed. Nevertheless, he was willing to try.

Over the next few weeks, we ran up the phone bill calling Peru, Salt Lake City, and UCLA to explore all possibilities. We learned that once a missionary returns home from a foreign country, for whatever reason, he/she cannot go back to the same country, due to visa regulations. Therefore, Alfred would have to complete his remaining eighteen months in the States.

I felt tremendous guilt. Bringing him back for a simple blood test and not having a match would put him back on his mission in less than a week. The travel costs would be enormous, and knowing he couldn't return to Peru would be disheartening. Naturally, if he matched, it would be great! He would become my donor, stay in Los Angeles for a couple of months, and then go on to finish his mission elsewhere.

One evening while discussing our options with Paul and Mieke, we received a call from the Mission President in Trujillo. He could have Alfred on a plane to Los Angeles the very next morning. He was calling to get our approval. At that time, flights to L.A. were occurring only once a week due to political problems in the country. Therefore, he needed to make the arrangements quickly. We told him we would call him back in two hours with our decision.

Peru was currently unstable and Americans were somewhat in danger. Every day that Alfred was there, I worried for his health and safety—especially now that I coveted his marrow. To know he could be home and safe within twenty-four hours was incredibly tempting. But somehow I felt uneasy about it. It seemed too easy. Paul and Mieke decided to leave so we could think it over more carefully.

Brian and I talked and then prayed about it. It was one of the hardest decisions we've ever made. We decided to put our faith on the line and leave him there. I desperately wanted Alfred's blood to match mine, but it had to be done under the right circumstances. Somehow we needed to demonstrate faith, and in time maybe the Lord would bless us.

We felt good about our decision to put everything on hold. We would explore all possibilities first, such as Alfred's blood being sent to the States via overnight express mail, but the next day we learned it could not be done.

BARBARA WINDER

On May 4, 1989, I attended a special church "Women's Conference" where Barbara Winder was going to speak. She was General President of the church's Relief Society, the oldest and possibly the largest women's organization in the world. It was formed in 1842 to provide relief, strength, and sisterhood among women and their families. I was anxious to hear her message.

The theme for the conference was "A Season and a Time." Sister Winder spoke of trials and strength. As I listened with a heavy heart, I wondered how she could possibly help me. Suddenly, I felt a desperate need to let her know of my situation. If I could just ask for her faith and prayers, it would be good enough for me.

So before the meeting was over, I ducked out of the chapel and made my way to a bathroom stall. With my heart pounding like a drum and my hand trembling like a leaf, I began scribbling a quick note on the back of the program. I could hardly write, yet I poured out my heart, beseeching her to pray that Alfred's blood would match mine.

My only request was for her to ask the General Authorities—the Prophet and the Twelve Apostles, in Salt Lake City, to please pray for us. It was so crucial to request their faith that my heart was full of emotion. I wiped away the tears and hurried back to the chapel, just as a crowd was lining up to meet her. When my turn came, I handed her the note and said, "It's very important that you read this note at your earliest convenience." I thanked her for coming and then left.

In the parking lot, I ran into Mieke and told her about my daring request. I felt so very happy to know that the leaders of the church might pray for my well-being. The note included my address; I hoped that she would write back. It was times like this that the smallest events brought such comfort and peace.

Two days later, Saturday, Alfred called. "There's a missionary named Elder Dave Christensen who is completing his mission and returning to California on Tuesday. He can bring my vials of blood. My companion and I are preparing to take a bus to Lima, to have my blood drawn late Monday night. Elder Christensen and his parents are leaving on the red-eye, which will arrive in Los Angeles at 8:00 a.m. Tuesday morning, May 9."

We were ecstatic! From New Jersey, we busily made the arrangements, calling UCLA to get information on the correct vials to use. The nurse instructed us to have the Peruvian nurse use the supposedly universal, purple-top vials. As long as we could get the blood to UCLA within twenty-four hours, the blood could still be fresh enough for testing. I informed the UCLA nurse that my parents would pick up the vials around 8:30 a.m. Allowing time to get through customs and the morning rush hour, my parents should arrive at UCLA at about 10:00 a.m. The nurse said she would be standing by to receive it.

So on Sunday morning, May 7, Alfred and his companion took a seven-hour bus ride through the mountains of Peru to a Lima hospital, to have his blood drawn the following night at 8:00 p.m. Time was of the essence. The sooner the blood could be tested, the more reliable it would be. We could only hope that all the coordinated efforts would prove successful, and that the Peruvian nurse would use the correct vials. Again, we felt our faith put to the test, hoping and praying all would go well.

On May 8, our seventh wedding anniversary, Brian and I awoke extremely nervous. All we could do was wait. I worried about Mom and Dad, and wondered how they were coping. I was grateful they could be there to help us. The following day, Dad called to let us know how it went.

"It was just like something out of the movies. The traffic on the 405 freeway was horrible. The drive from the San Fernando Valley to LAX, which normally takes forty-five minutes, took us two hours! We were rushing and almost got into an accident. Just as we arrived at the airport, we were pulled over by a policeman for stopping over the crosswalk. I explained our urgency to him, and luckily he was understanding and let us proceed without giving us a ticket. By the time we arrived at the gate, the plane had just arrived."

Brian and I nodded our heads as we listened to Dad.

"We eagerly waited as passengers came through customs. We had a sign with Elder Christensen's name on it, but it didn't take long to spot each other. This missionary stood out like a beacon in the night. We all shed tears as he carefully handed over the vials with "green-top" caps!

His mother said he proudly carried the precious vials in his coat pocket near his heart, and never took off his coat during the entire nine-hour flight! A big football player, he wasn't about to let anyone get in his way of delivering this blood."

Elder Christensen also had a letter from the hospital, in case he was stopped by customs. He said they chatted about Peru; meeting Alfred and the Mission President the night before; and how the missionaries would be fasting and praying for positive results.

My parents were impressed with this family, whom they had never met before, and the love and concern they expressed in just a few minutes. Dad said, "It's as if we had known them for years. Then, we quickly said good-bye and we were off. At 10:10 a.m. we arrived at UCLA, where a nurse was standing by, waiting to receive it. When we walked in she said, 'Are you Victor Marquez?' 'Yes,' I said, 'are you Cindy?' 'Yes,' she said."

Dad carefully handed her the two vials. She looked at them for a moment, puzzled at the green tops. She shook them and said, "They look just fine to me," and off she went to the lab.

Weeks later, Alfred told us about the treacherous bus ride to Lima, and how it was one of the scariest rides of his life. The conditions were terrible, with no seating on many parts of the trip. He told us about the visit with Elder Christensen, his parents, and the Mission President. After Alfred handed over the vials of blood to Elder Christensen, a prayer was offered. Alfred said, "It was a humbling moment for all of us, filled with tears, joy and faith."

Mission completed! We were so excited to know everything had gone just as planned. It was the best wedding anniversary gift we could have received. We were now over one big mountain.

There were so many people praying for us. All we could do now was hope for a big miracle...a perfect match!

WAITING FOR A MATCH

With Alfred's blood arriving safely, we savored every happy moment. But the next few days passed with moments of hope, then fear, as we anticipated the results—which would be in by Friday, or Monday at the latest.

Staying busy was my best tool against worry. So I planned a big Chinese dinner party for the following Sunday, Mother's Day. We invited Robin, Craig, Paul, Mieke, her daughter, and other friends.

I tried not to worry, but by Friday I was a nervous wreck. Every bad thought began plaguing me as I waited for Dr. Champlin's call. It was like playing the Lotto—six out of six elements of his blood had to match perfectly with mine. The odds were a seventy-five percent chance against me! What would I do if Alfred didn't match? I couldn't bear the thought, nor had I even entertained the thought until that very moment. The truth about my future was a phone call away. I was nauseous and truly scared.

Brian called from work. "How are you holding up?"

"I can't handle this, Brian. I can't wait another minute without knowing if Alfred's my match," I confessed.

"Have you tried calling Dr. Champlin?"

"I've left a message for him, but they're three hours behind so we may have to wait until evening to hear anything."

"Don't worry. I'll come home early," he said tenderly.

Like a tumbleweed blowing in the desert, I slowly began to fall apart. I felt lost, alone and terrified of the outcome. I could hardly wait for Brian. When he arrived, I fell into his arms. He held me close and tried to console me.

"Maybe we ought to say a prayer," he suggested.

"Okay."

Never in our lives did we pray for something so hard than we did at that time. I could see the pain and worry in his eyes. He had lost weight from worrying. When I was strong, he was weak; when I was weak, he was strong. We were a great team together. We held each other for what seemed like hours.

"I can't do this dinner party on Sunday without knowing the results. I feel sick," I said.

"I know. Just relax, we can cancel it."

Solemnly, I stared out our back window at the lush green grass, which led to a beautiful grove of trees. I thought about Mother's Day; it had always been a bummer. Now I dreaded it more than ever.

"Gosh, Brian, my greatest desire is to have a perfect match, so that Mother's Day can be a day of celebration—a hope that maybe I can still be a mother someday."

Around 9:00 p.m. I called UCLA again, but still no Champlin. Impatiently, I paced the floor, nervously wringing my hands. The minutes dragged by like hours. I called again. This time, they paged him. They said it was very likely we'd have to wait until Monday for the results. I was miserable and desperate, with the uncertainty of my future eating me alive.

"Can't they see how important this is to me? Can't they see this is a matter of life and death?" I complained.

By 10:00 p.m. Brian suggested a game of Scrabble to kill time. It was our favorite game.

Then at 11:00 p.m., the phone rang. My heart was pounding so hard it could've awakened the neighbors. Calmly, I eyed Brian as he dashed to the phone. Lying on the couch, I stared at him like a hawk in complete concentration of its prey. He shrugged a nod to me as he said, "Hi, Dad."

Carefully I listened, all the while thinking how wonderful it would be if Brian just looked up at me and said, "It matched." But how could he? My dad wouldn't know.

Brian responded to Dad's questions. "No, we haven't heard anything. Ana's not doing well; she's really down and we're both very nervous. It's been a bad day."

Suddenly, Brian paused as though my dad was telling him something. Brian was listening intently and saying, "Uh huh...uh huh... uh...really...are you sure? Are you absolutely sure?"

As I studied Brian, trying to read his face, he slowly got a big smile. In amazement, his eyes met mine, and with a big grin he exclaimed, "Ana! IT MATCHED PERFECTLY!"

"Oh, my God! Oh, my God! Thank you! Thank you!" I cried out as I ran to the phone. "Oh, Dad, are you sure? How did you find out? Oh, this is the happiest moment of my life! I can't believe it! I'm so thankful. God has answered our prayers!" So overcome with joy, all I could do was cry as Dad recounted the events of the day.

"Earlier today I called the nurse to whom we had delivered the blood. She remembered me, and understanding the importance of the results and the fact that you were in New Jersey, waiting, she said, 'I'm not supposed to do this. I could get in big trouble, but I do have the results and I'm happy to say that your son Alfred matched Analisa's blood perfectly—a six out of six match!'"

My dad was overjoyed, but said he cautiously asked her to double check. He said she left the phone, then returned and said, 'Yes, it says right here in black and white, Alfred's HLA matches Analisa's.' "She made me promise not to tell you, since Dr. Champlin should be the one."

So, Dad waited all day to hear from us first. By 11:00 p.m., he figured we hadn't heard anything; otherwise, we would have called him. When Brian mentioned we were having a bad day, he couldn't hold back the news any longer.

"Your mom and I cried when we heard the news. We even went to a Catholic church to give thanks."

We said our good-byes, for I suddenly felt the need to fall on my knees and give thanks. Brian and I hugged each other, crying aloud, "It matched! It matched! Thank God, it matched!" I have never before felt such a gratitude and indebtedness to God than I did at that time. It was the most humbling and wonderful experience of my life.

Heavenly Father had indeed answered our prayers. What started as a dreary, dreadful and bitter day turned into the sweetest and happiest day ever. My life had hope.

It became clear that oftentimes the Lord makes you wait until the "eleventh hour" before coming through with the answers. It was wonderful to know that Sunday *would* be a day of celebration, a day of hope, and a day to rejoice in our most important miracle—Alfred's perfect match!

That night we lay in bed and recounted the events of the day. Somewhere in Peru was my dear Alfred. He was going to be the one. The blood flowing through this young missionary's veins was going to save my life. I was so excited; I couldn't wait to report the news to him. That night we fell asleep glowing.

MOTHER'S DAY

On Mother's Day, we went to church grinning from ear to ear. I could hardly contain my excitement. As usual, a woman came up to me in the hall and expressed concern about how difficult Mother's Day must be for me. Beaming, I quickly responded, "Oh no, it's just great!" She looked puzzled. I smiled and continued walking.

After church, in the foyer, we visited with our good friend, Larry Fraze. We quietly mentioned to him that the results were tentatively positive and that the doctor would call on Monday to confirm. Brian noticed a few heads turning and curious looks coming from others standing nearby.

On the way home Brian and I chuckled.

"They probably think I'm pregnant and am waiting for the doctor to let us know." (A few people knew of our intentions to do the GIFT procedure.)

Brian laughed. "Hah! If they only knew what was really happening, they'd never believe it!"

Although we were pleased to have kept our secret from the ward thus far, we knew the news was bound to seep out soon. The thought of others expressing words of sympathy terrified me. Like a gymnast walking the beam, sympathy would throw me off balance. It was easier to spare everyone the pain. For now, I was happy knowing Alfred matched, and I wanted to hold on to that happiness for as long as possible.

The next day, Dr. Champlin called and cheerfully gave me the news. I acted surprised.

"I suggest you go ahead with the transplant soon, like in June," he said.

"That's next month! I need a little more time. How about July?"

"Fine. I just don't want you to wait too long. The sooner the better."

We agreed that on July 1, I would enter UCLA Medical Center, giving Alfred a month and a half to tie up loose ends, and allowing Brian to make plans with AT&T.

That night I called Alfred's Mission President, so he could notify Alfred of his perfect match. A few weeks later I received this inspiring letter from Alfred:

May 1989

Dear Ana and Brian,

How are you doing? Thanks for the peanut butter. Boy, it was good. Pres. Aguayo called and told me I had the same blood! I was so happy! I prayed so much that I would match. You know, when I was in Lima and they were retrieving the blood, the spirit indicated to me that I had the same blood. I just knew I was coming back home! I even fasted and prayed to see whether the Lord wanted me to go or to stay. The spirit said, "Go help your sister."

So, I'll be home on June 30th. Please don't feel bad for interrupting my mission. These things happen. They're challenges. I'm very happy that I can help you. And I know everything is going to be all right, because the Lord will prepare the way. I'll come back, help you (and you will recover fully), baptize Mom and Dad, and finish my mission in Texas or wherever. Our zone here did a special fast for you. Everyone is involved. I love you all very much and I thank the Lord for all these experiences, for without them I wouldn't grow.

I'll see you soon!

Love,
Elder Marquez

The month of May was spent preparing for the transplant. Basically, I felt good. My only symptom was fatigue. I wrote letters, thanking everyone.

I soon got word that I passed my real estate exam. On May 15, I began working as a rental agent. It was important to do what I had always yearned to do, and to keep everything normal for as long as possible. The work was hard and challenging. Nonetheless, in the first few weeks I executed my first lease. A rare achievement, my manager remarked. I received my one and only check with a great sense of accomplishment and satisfaction. A month later, I quit.

Mieke and I still met frequently. She had taken a job in Jersey City, and one day I rode to work with her.

"I've been thinking about cutting my hair, in preparation for losing it all."

"That's a good idea. I know a hairstylist in Somerville," she said.

Later, I mentioned it to Brian, and he agreed. That night as a joke, I put a stocking over my head to see what it was like to be bald. We laughed.

Brian assured me, saying, "I'll always love you, no matter what you look like."

That weekend, Brian and Mieke went with me for my final cut. We skimmed through the books and picked out a style that the hairdresser suggested would look good.

Then he started cutting away. I wasn't too scared. This was only the beginning. I had to get accustomed to changes. As locks of hair fell to the floor, I pondered where, if ever, I'd be the next time I got a haircut. After he finished, we were all pleased with my new look.

Each day was still a struggle. I often dreamt that it was all a mistake and that I really wasn't sick. But I'd always wake up to the truth, with a huge pit in my stomach. Nonetheless, we pressed forward feeling that the Lord was helping us each step of the way.

I often listened to inspirational music to strengthen my determination and hope to survive. I recalled many instances in life when God really did answer my prayers—not always in the way I wanted, but they were always answered.

For instance, when Stella was gravely ill, after two years of struggle and during her final hospitalization, our family continued praying for a miracle that she would get well. On her final night, having lost the energy to speak, she calmly stared at each one of us. Her hair had just started to grow back. She looked peaceful and beautiful, and as though she was staring right into eternity. Later, as Dad drove home, he tearfully said it was time to pray for the Lord to take her.

That night, with a heavy heart I asked the Lord to do His will and not mine. Then I cried myself to sleep. It was the most difficult task I had ever done in all of my fourteen years.

Early the next morning, Stella passed away. Our prayers *were* answered, even though it wasn't what we wanted. From then on, I resolved to stay in tune with what the Lord wanted, rather than what I desired. This determination helped me search for understanding, even when we were about to undergo the GIFT procedure. When a "no" answer came back like a slamming door, and a cancer diagnosis to boot, we could only have faith that there was a reason for this. Now, facing my cancer, I was very hopeful that this time the answer to our prayers would be "yes."

Although everything was going well, we still felt a tremendous need for peace. We needed something to anchor our faith. So we called our Bishop, Bob Smith. He was a caring man who often got emotional at the pulpit when he spoke. Although we had become quite close to him and his family, we swore him to absolute secrecy as we tearfully related our sorrows, triumphs, and pending misfortune.

Shocked, he exclaimed, "I had no idea you've been going through this these last several months."

"We'll be leaving the end of June," Brian said.

"I strongly suggest you share your trial with the rest of the ward members," the Bishop said pensively. "They need to hear this, Analisa."

"I know. I was planning to request their faith just before we leave, but I can't bear their sympathy," I said.

As he sat in our living room, it occurred to us that he was related to President Howard W. Hunter, one of the General Authorities of the church—an Apostle, no less—in Salt Lake City. Later that night, Brian and I discussed the idea of requesting his wife's help in arranging a meeting with President Hunter for us. It would be an opportunity equivalent to a Catholic meeting with an Archbishop, or the Pope!

Events were happening daily. I was excited to receive a letter from General Relief Society President Barbara Winder. She had read my note and put my name in the Temple to be prayed over. She wanted an update. I wrote back and told her of Alfred's match. Thereafter, we continued to correspond.

Brian and I then approached our Bishop and his wife, Karen. Through them, we were able to arrange a special meeting with President Hunter to receive a priesthood blessing. We were elated. Our meeting was scheduled one week prior to entering UCLA Medical Center. It would be the crowning point in preparing us for the transplant.

Everything was falling into place. Blessings were coming quickly and at times when we least expected them. Perhaps there was a reason for all the suffering I would pass through. Our days in New Jersey were coming to an end, and I decided that the Sunday before Father's Day, June 11, would be a good day to disclose my situation to the ward members. It would be Fast and Testimony Meeting, where anyone from the congregation is invited to share their testimony or a special experience.

On Saturday, June 3, Mieke called. "The news about you is getting out Ana. It was bound to happen sooner or later."

"I'm surprised we've been able to keep it a secret this long."

"You'll never guess what happened. Andrea Velucci found out. It wasn't my fault, honest! I'm just warning you, in case people come up to you tomorrow."

Andrea was a good friend, but I wanted to announce it myself, and not through others. And though we had told Andrea's husband, Gary, a few months prior, we were sure our secret was safe.

"How did it happen?" I asked.

Mieke began, "It's so ironic. The other night they and another couple were over for dinner. After we ate, Andrea helped me clear the table. In the kitchen, she began asking how you guys were doing. She said, 'Hey, are they still planning on doing that surgery? I know they're concerned about Ana's health and the expense.' Surprised that she knew, I said, 'Oh, I guess she told you about it? Yeah, they're going to do it next month.' Then Andrea said, 'Oh, that's great. They've been planning it for a long time.' Then I said, 'Yeah, they didn't want anybody to know.' I figured she was talking about the *transplant*. Then she said, 'I guess they'll find out within a few weeks whether it worked.' Then I said, 'Well, actually it'll be at least three to six months before they know for sure.' Andrea said, 'Really? Well, when are they going to do it?' And I said, 'Well, she's scheduled to enter the hospital July first, and they'll start her on the radiation and chemotherapy the same week.' Immediately after that, Andrea didn't say a thing, and she went into the bathroom. I walked back into the dining room to finish serving dessert, and didn't think anything of it. Soon after, they left."

Mieke went on, "That night, she called me up to tell me why they left so suddenly. She wanted to find out from Gary what was going on. She figured Gary knew, since a few months ago he had come home from your house acting very strange. Then she declared, 'I thought the whole conversation in the kitchen was about Brian and Ana getting *pregnant* with invitro-fertilization! I had no idea about the transplant or that she was even sick!'"

I couldn't believe Mieke's story. It was almost hilarious.

"Andrea promised not to tell anyone. But, don't be surprised if she comes up to you tomorrow, Analisa."

"Well, I'm just afraid of everyone's reaction. I want to announce it once, request their prayers, and then quietly leave for California."

Sure enough, the next day at church, Andrea marched right up to me, gave me a big hug, and said, "Oh, Ana, I'm so worried for you!" We chatted for a bit, all the while fearful about being overheard.

Knowing that I would divulge my whole life the following week saddened me. I would be cancer labeled. I dreaded the awkward position others would be put in to express their feelings.

The following Sunday, Fast and Testimony Meeting came and went. Before I knew it, the meeting was over and I didn't get up. I was miserable. I had made a commitment to the Lord, and to Bishop Smith, and I failed to come through.

That afternoon Bishop Smith called. "Analisa, I was hoping you were going to get up today."

"I know Bishop. I'm sorry. It just didn't feel right."

"Well, next week is Father's Day, and I'd like you to be one of the main speakers."

Surprised, and with heartfelt humility, I responded, "Oh, uh, of course, Bishop. That would be fine."

"We want to hear your recent experiences, but also remember that it's Father's Day."

The responsibility of delivering my "talk" properly made me nervous. Yet, I was grateful.

"Sure," I said.

That evening, as I thought about it, it seemed to make sense. Mother's Day had been a terrific day, and now I could only hope that Father's Day would be the same.

That week I pondered and prayed long and hard about how to deliver my talk. Finally, one morning I awoke, and the words flowed like a fountain out of my hand onto paper. The next morning it happened again, and before I knew it my talk was completed. There was no doubt I had help writing it.

I was so nervous; I rehearsed my talk in front of Brian. We both cried, realizing the true crisis we were facing.

"I'll stand right next to you, Ana."

"I may need you to hold me up," I said sheepishly.

Our love was stronger than ever, and we struggled to preserve our faith by not discussing our fears so much. Each step was bringing more challenges and triumphs, as our lives were fast becoming an open book.

CHAPTER 4
FATHER'S DAY

On Father's Day we both nervously arrived at church. Brian sat in the front row as I took a seat on the stand. Attendance was high. As I looked over the congregation, I felt a rush of shivers come over me. Everyone looked beautiful and I dared not look at their faces for fear I would burst into tears. Instead, I thought of funny jokes to maintain my composure. Whatever happens I thought, just keep reading!

The moment came. I stood up and poured out my heart to our friends. A portion of my talk went like this:

Brothers and Sisters,

I'm grateful to speak to you on this Father's Day. My heart is full. I've prayed the spirit might be with me as I share with you recent events that have occurred which leave me *very* grateful on this day.

On this day *all* men ought to be honored, whether they be a father, brother, uncle, friend or missionary. Each of us has been influenced by "some man," in one way or another. It is befitting to honor them, including our Heavenly Father.

As for me, I'd first like to mention Brian. He's wonderful and has been great to me. Lately, I have looked to him much like I would a Father—seeking compassion, understanding, and strength. And he has been there for me.

Many of you know of his cleaning habits, and I just have to mention the latest. The other night I came home from the movies with the ladies to find every piece of furniture moved and the carpet vacuumed! I'm glad I wasn't there! *Does he deserve to be honored, or what?* I won't say any more, because I know it makes you all sick! I just want to say thank you, Brian. I love you!

We're grateful to serve in this ward. Our callings have given us the opportunity to be father and mother figures to your children. Whatever our circumstances may be, *we all* have the responsibility to get to know the youth and children of the ward.

At times, it's been difficult understanding why we have been denied the blessings of children. And at other times, *we know why*. We feel the Lord is very much aware of our situation and has other things in store for us. Actually, at this time, children are the least of our worries. Nonetheless, whatever the circumstances, whether Primary teacher, visiting teacher, or home teacher, we ALL need fatherly strength from one another, and someone who honors his priesthood.

Next, I'd like to acknowledge my own father. My parents aren't members of the church. But, after fourteen years, they are the closest they can be to becoming members. I spoke to them this week and my heart is soaring because they will be getting baptized on July 2nd! It's one of the many miracles happening lately, as our family will finally be united in the Gospel of Jesus Christ.

As kids, my dad spent much time with us. I recall many words of encouragement. He always made us laugh. When we decided to join the church, he sat us down and told us to join the church *only if* we were going to be faithful the rest of our lives. His advice left a strong impression, and now I am able to give him the same counsel.

In my youth and dating years, he was always there to give a much needed "pep" talk. I recall many nights sitting on the dresser, with my feet on their bed, telling them about the day's events. I thrived on his advice. Afterwards, I'd go to bed feeling good, like I could make it.

He taught me to be positive and appreciative, and to have a sense of humor—*no matter what the circumstances*. To be sincere in everything I did. My mother never worked, so they raised five children on one salary. My father worked for an airline company in Burbank, California. Therefore, we traveled much. I can honestly say we never had *one* babysitter! I don't know how they did it, and they don't know either! He often stressed the importance of making great memories with his family, saying we were his greatest joy.

Because of the airline discounts, we stayed in beautiful hotels, rented nice cars, and enjoyed terrific vacations. He said he didn't make a lot of money and we weren't rich by any means, but that we should always be grateful for these blessings that allowed us to live like kings! As kids, we'd laugh and tell him, he was our king.

As I've grown older, I've realized the financial struggle and sacrifices he went through to raise us. We have had to aid them and it has been difficult. And yes, we tell him, he still is our king.

Two other people I want to honor today are my Heavenly Father, and my brother, Alfred, who is serving a mission in Peru. Alfred is coming home in two weeks to literally save my life! As some of you know, Brian and I will be going home to Los Angeles next week for about two months, so I can undergo a bone marrow transplant.

These last four months have been very challenging. Yet, we have seen many miracles happen and we keep wondering what is going to happen next. I've been able to share many of our experiences with some of you, but to make a long story short, I will tell you of the most important miracle that has happened.

I then shared with them our eleventh hour miracle, Alfred's perfect match, and I read his letter. I said he was coming home to save me physically, and in a sense to save my parents spiritually. I ended my talk on a happy note, sharing a cute Father's Day card I found in a store.

It was difficult to get through. When I sat down, I was greatly relieved that it was over. A comforting feeling came over me. I looked at Brian and he was in tears. Almost everyone was crying. Bishop Smith stood up and expressed his support.

Afterward, Brian and I experienced an overwhelming outpouring of love. One man, a father of eight children, offered to pay our mortgage while we were gone. Another man exclaimed, as he shook Brian's hand, that the spirit testified to him that I would be fine. Then a missionary came up and testified the same. The day had been a success. Now everyone knew.

Many showered us with words of encouragement. Some who had fought their own battles with cancer shared their triumphs with me. One lady admitted she was going through a rough time and had decided to give up church altogether, until today. She said, "I can't believe you didn't tell me! Here you were taking me to the doctor, when you've been so sick!"

After we left, I felt an urgency to run home or somewhere and tell God, "Thank you! Thank you! We did it!" It was all His doing, not mine. Indeed, all these months I felt like an instrument being fine-tuned in His care, and today my recital went flawless.

With another Father's Day celebration planned, we gathered with family and friends for a repeat of Mother's Day. At home, we continued to receive calls from friends pledging their support.

AN UNUSUAL VISIT

That afternoon, just as we were about to sit down to eat, the doorbell rang. It was a woman from church whom I had met briefly. She was a beautiful, talented woman in her forties. I knew that, for unknown reasons, for months she had been secluding herself. It was obvious she was very upset. "Come in," I said.

As we sat in the living room, I tried to perceive the intent of her visit. Her distressed look was puzzling. Was she going to shower me with sympathy (my most dreaded fear)? I was unsure. Her first sentence indicated that was not the case.

"How could you do what you did today? I wasn't there, but I heard about it, and cannot understand why you did what you did."

Caught off guard, I was puzzled by what she was trying to tell me. She went on, "I too have the same kind of illness, but yours is worse." Then she paused and without hesitation said, "Analisa, your illness is much more serious than mine. Aren't you afraid you are going to die?"

This being the happiest day of my life (since my diagnosis)—other than the day I learned of Alfred's match—I felt my strength being terribly challenged. I don't recall all that I said to her, only that I spoke in self-defense. What had been a perfect day was being threatened by what appeared to be the adversary.

"My struggles and fears with this disease are constant. All I can control is my attitude. This disease is not going to take away my attitude and my hope," I insisted. "I will not let it get the best of me!"

I tried to give her some positive advice. And, although her visit lasted only twenty minutes, when she left I was emotionally drained and disturbed by her pain and sorrow. It was as though she had come specifically to find out for herself just how strong I really was, and perhaps wanting to break me down.

Brian and the others encouraged me to enjoy my meal and not to worry about it, but I couldn't stop thinking about her. That visit was evidence to me that the adversary was, and would be, working diligently to tear down everything I had worked *so hard* to achieve. It made me fearful of the emotional and spiritual challenges I'd have to face going forward.

(A few months later, I was sorry to learn of her sudden passing away from heart failure.)

FINAL WEEK IN NEW JERSEY

The last week in New Jersey was spent packing, visiting with friends, writing letters, and gathering important memorabilia. I also wrote a pep list. This list would be helpful to refer to in moments of despair.

On Monday, I called Dr. Champlin to inquire about the UCLA bone marrow transplant information packet he promised to send me.

"You never got one?" he asked. "I'll Federal Express it out to you today."

The next day it arrived. I was eager, yet almost nauseous to read it. It was several pages long, describing the 10 West wing, what to expect, and what to bring. At first it was easy reading; encouraging patients to bring their own music, books, and VCR. I could wear sweatpants, my own pajamas, and bring my pillows and blankets. I could even bring a stationary bicycle. I would be encouraged to make my room as homey and comfortable as possible for the six to eight-week stay. Spouses were even encouraged to sleep in the same room, so patients could receive as much support as possible.

I thought, okay, I can handle this; it doesn't seem that bad. But the more I read, the worse it got. The seriousness of the procedure quickly became clear. The lethal dosages of radiation and chemotherapy I would receive, and the problems arising during and afterward, were sickening. By the time I was through, I wondered how in the world anyone could survive this transplant.

A somber mood came over me, a glazed-over feeling. I couldn't believe what I would have to go through. How would my little four feet, eleven and a half inch frame withstand such a beating? I felt like a candle in the wind bracing for a hurricane. I tried to dismiss my worst fears. It was a continual struggle to psyche myself up and think positively.

"It's gonna take a big miracle to survive this, Brian."

"We can and will get through this, Ana. I'll be with you every step of the way; you won't be alone."

He put his big arms around me. I felt great security, and wondered how he would hold up. "I just have to survive this, Brian. I'm doing it for you and you only," I insisted.

On Tuesday night I hesitantly attended my last church meeting. It was there that I came across one of the most beautiful quotes I had ever read. It was a poor, worn copy of a colored picture that caught my eye on the bulletin board, a picture of Christ. To one side of His face it read, "I Never Said It Would Be Easy." On the other side of His face it read, "I Only Said It Would Be Worth It." Its message was so powerful that, without a second thought, I snatched it off the wall and tucked it in my purse. It would prove to be an invaluable reminder while I was in the hospital. I was grateful I went to church that night.

DENTIST VISIT

Since I was likely to get mouth sores during the transplant, I made an appointment with our dentist. Dr. Fraze was also our past Bishop and a dear friend. That week I learned that he was having problems and facing a divorce. It seemed like everyone was going through hard times.

I frowned at being there. The dental hygienist had no mercy on me, even though I begged her to go easy. Dr. Fraze filled a cavity, and then asked me to come into his office.

My heart was full as I kept thinking of his situation. He had no idea that I knew, and I struggled to hold back the tears, as this would be our good-bye. I wanted him to know we loved him and would keep him in our prayers, too.

As we sat in his tiny office he said, "Analisa, you are teaching all of us how to deal with difficult situations and trials. We are all learning from you."

My heart was breaking for him, and likewise his for me. I appreciated his kind words. He then asked if we could say a prayer together. I felt touched by this sweet man as he poured out his heart for me. Little did he know he was teaching me. I wanted to assure him all would be well with *both* of us, but doing so would have initiated a sob scene. Instead, I thanked him and gave him a hug. As we struggled to hold back tears, we quietly said good-bye.

I left his office thinking what a wonderful, rare blessing it was to see a dentist for a cleaning, and then to pray with him afterward. I got into the car, my gums still raw and hurting. I chuckled to myself. Perhaps it should have been the other way around—to pray first, and then have my teeth cleaned! Nevertheless, I was glad I had it done.

SAYING GOOD-BYE

As our departure day of June 22 neared, it was difficult saying good-bye to everyone. I was sad, but there was an urgency to get the transplant over with and get on with our lives. I couldn't wait to get on the plane destined for the West.

We were scheduled to spend a day in Salt Lake City and two in Idaho, visiting friends, and then continue on to California. Alfred would arrive on June 30, and my parents were to be baptized on July 2—just two days prior to my entering UCLA.

I visited with Dr. Toomey one last time. My blood counts were still in check. She wished me well, and I *promised* her I would be back to visit her again.

On our last day Brian worked a half-day. AT&T approved a leave of absence and a thirty-day personal leave. It was comforting to know he would be at my side for the next two months. His management would continue searching for a position for him out West. There were no guarantees. However, we were extremely grateful for the company's support.

As for the insurance company, there were no hassles. Except for the customary deductibles, they agreed to pay for everything. What a blessing not having to worry about money and insurance!

Our last day was an emotional one, as I gazed over the furnishings of our little townhouse. Would I ever return, I wondered? Faith was propelling me, reminding me that too many miracles had occurred for it to be otherwise.

That afternoon, I made a call to a lady named Donna. She had come up to me after church and said she was once a nurse stationed at the Bone Marrow Transplant Unit in Hawaii. I was eager to get her opinion and advice on the transplant process.

Her words confirmed Dr. Champlin's. "This will be the hardest thing you will ever go through, and it is very possible that you could die."

"Well, have you seen people survive?" I asked cautiously.

"A few, but there were many who didn't. With your brother matching, and your early diagnosis, it will help a lot." She paused, "Did the doctors tell you *everything* you are going to go through?"

"Well, yes. I received a packet a couple of days ago and I've read it."

"All I can say is just be prepared for the most horrible thing that can happen to you, because it will be just that and worse. I'm telling you this because it's important that you know that you can always say no."

I began crying, thinking of the huge mountain before me; a mountain which I would have to climb alone. Like Sally, Donna emphasized taking care of unfinished business. She wished me well and said she would keep me in her prayers.

"You'll probably be all right," she finally said. "But remember, it takes at least one to two years to completely get over it. Your hardest challenge will be isolation. Stay active and keep up the mouth washes."

When we hung up, I cried even more. I somewhat expected to hear those remarks. It was just hard to hear them over again. This was the beginning and there was no turning back. God willing, I would survive this transplant.

I sat in the living room and again looked at our nice belongings. I thought of the wonderful life Brian and I had made together, and realized I must write him a letter and hide it away somewhere in his drawer—just in case something happened to me. Donna said I owed it to him; that it would be a great source of strength to him if I did not survive.

As I thought about it, I recalled the time I felt great joy in receiving a letter from Stella, three years after she died. It was in December of 1978, and more than a rare coincidence. Stella passed away in December of 1975. Several months prior, her home economics teacher made the students write a letter to themselves with a list of goals they hoped to achieve. Mrs. Cox planned to mail the letters back to the students three years later.

It just so happened that three years later I was in the same home economics class. While sewing at my machine, I overheard a conversation between Mrs. Cox and another student, about a girl who had died of cancer, and how unsure she felt about mailing the letter for fear it would upset the family. I listened as she told how this "beautiful young girl" had written a ten-page letter.

Increasingly curious, I spoke up and asked, "Excuse me, what kind of cancer did this girl have?"

"I think leukemia," she answered.

"Oh," I said disappointedly, "my sister died of lung cancer three years ago."

Puzzled, she stared at me and asked, "What was her name?"

"Stella. Stella Marquez."

"That's her! That's her!" she exclaimed. We both gasped. It was unbelievable! She went on to say that she put the letter in a safe place and would have to spend time looking for it.

Several days went by. Finally, the last day before Christmas vacation, she handed me the letter. The stamped, self-addressed envelope was addressed "Stella Marquez c/o Analisa Marquez"! While other students worked on class projects, I quietly began reading Stella's letter. She wrote in Spanish, English and French. I cried as I read how she knew she might not be around when this letter would be sent. Nonetheless, she was going to make the best of each day. She wrote of the peace and happiness she had found in the church, and how she was unafraid of the outcome of her life.

During the three years since her passing I had struggled with loneliness and depression. Stella and I were so close that our neighbor nicknamed me "her shadow." I was overwhelmed with emotion to read her ending words, "With Love, Your Shadow."

Her letter filled a void and gave me joy and peace. A little miracle had occurred that Christmas in 1978, like she had taken time out to visit me.

Now, as I wrote Brian's letter, I wondered what I could say. Writing a letter seemed to show a lack of faith. However, I awkwardly began writing to my beloved. It didn't seem fair, since my heart and soul were telling me that physically I was okay. I struggled to make it simple; giving whatever advice I could, no matter what the end result would be. My last sentence simply said, "God willing, we will read this letter together soon and maybe we'll smile about it."

I then recorded a short message on tape to my family. When I finished, I added another cassette to the machine to record some music. I turned the radio on and began writing another letter to Mieke.

Ironically and to my astonishment, the station began playing an old song, "Who Loves You" sung by the Four Seasons. (A disc jockey that Stella dated had once dedicated this song to her on the air.) I hit the "record" button, and listened with excitement to the words of one of my favorite songs. Here are some of the words:

"Who Loves You"
Words and Music by Robert Gaudio and Judy Parker. © 1975 (Renewed 2003) JOBETE MUSIC CO., INC. and SEASONS MUSIC COMPANY. All Rights Reserved. International Copyright Secured. Used by Permission.

"When tears are in your eyes and you can't find the way,
It's hard to make believe you're happy when you're gray.
Baby, when you're feeling like you'll never see the mornin'
light.
Come to me...Baby you'll see.

Who loves you pretty baby?
Who's going to help you through the night?
Who loves you pretty mama?
Who's always there to make it right?

And when you think the whole wide world has passed you by,
You keep on trying but you really don't know why.
Baby, when you need a smile to help those shadows drift away,
Come to me. Baby, you'll see.

Who loves you pretty baby?
Who's going to help you through the night?
Who loves you pretty mama?
Who's always there to make it right?

For years I had wanted a copy of it. How appropriate it was to record it at this very moment, as though Stella was watching over me. It was a small miracle. The rest of the day I reflected on her and her courageous example. My attitude toward my illness was mainly based on the example she had set.

When Brian got home, I told him about my day. And, as we made the final preparations, I teased him, "Oh, there's going to be nobody here to vacuum these rugs for the next two months!"

At last I hid Brian's letter in his dresser drawer. I would tell him about it on the plane. I debated leaving other notes in places he wouldn't expect, like "I love you" rolled up in the toilet paper. Humor would help if I didn't survive. But the more I thought about it, I couldn't bring myself to do it. One letter was enough.

Mieke and her daughter drove us to the airport. Paul had totaled their car the week before, so we agreed to leave our new car with them for the next few months.

As we left the house, Brian softly said, "I wish we could snap our fingers, fast forward two months, and I could be bringing you home instead."

We had shared some happy and difficult times here on Bree Court. If we ever had a daughter, we were going to name her Briana (Brian + Ana). When we first moved to Bree Court, I teased him, saying this would probably be the closest we'd ever get to "Briana." It made me sad to think it could possibly be true.

At the airport, I handed Mieke her letter. "I love you guys."

"We love you, too."

"I'll be back, I promise! Let's plan on going out for a Sundae with nuts—lots of nuts!"

It felt great to finally get on that plane and not look back.

UTAH AND IDAHO

Indeed, we felt happy as much as expected. There was no time for brooding. On the plane, I told Brian of his letter.

"I don't want to hear about it. It isn't going to be necessary," he firmly replied. He put his arm around me and insisted, "It's all going to go well."

Brian was my pillar of strength. I worried about his reaction to my hair loss; how he would respond seeing me so sick. He had become totally involved in my well-being—constantly asking how I was doing, how I felt, and if I was okay—almost to the point of smothering me. I often begged him, "Please be strong for me. I need that more than anything else."

On several occasions we often found ourselves thinking the same things at the very same time. I was crazily in love with him and was prepared to fight tooth and nail for him. We belonged together and I couldn't see it any other way, and dared not. He was suffering right along with me.

On the plane, we counted our blessings. Anxiously, we anticipated our scheduled appointment for the following day with President Hunter. This was going to be the most important interview of our lives.

Due to delays and stopovers, we arrived in Salt Lake City at 2:00 a.m. To our bodies, it was 5:00 a.m. Exhausted and weak, I was clearly coming down with a bad cold. In the morning I wrote in my journal:

We must continue to press forward in faith and not waver. The daily process hasn't been easy. I have to be positive and prayerful continually.

I realize we're not "special," *all* of us are special. Anyone can have miracles in their lives if they submit themselves to God, allowing Him to work through them. It's the enduring to the end that's difficult!

We've had our sad days. We've suffered much already and have yet to suffer a great deal more. It may be God's will that I die. But, I believe it isn't. It boils down to two things: He'll either heal me or He won't. I *must* believe He will...and I do! It's been a tough, tiresome learning process and our faith has been growing by leaps and bounds. I expect to have spiritual experiences. I hope today will be one with President Hunter. I look forward to his counsel.

We intended to fast, but we were so famished that we decided a hearty lunch would do us good.

"Brian, I feel like Dorothy and the Scarecrow presenting our plea to the Wizard of Oz," I said as I devoured my meal.

"I do too," he said, nodding his head.

We chuckled over scenes from the classic movie. In the end, each got their wish and Dorothy was able to go home.

"You'll come home, Analisa. You'll come home," he repeated.

Excited and nervous, we walked into the Church Office Building located just southeast of the Temple. As we waited in the foyer, we recognized other church leaders who often spoke at the worldwide conferences. They warmly greeted us as they passed. Then we were escorted to President Hunter's office.

Our hearts pounding like drums, we walked up to the man sitting behind a large executive desk. President Hunter was in his eighties and used a walker to get around. He, too, had suffered his own physical trials—a deteriorating back problem that left him crippled. Just a few years prior he had lost his wife. He was a man who had given decades of selfless service to the church, spoken to millions of people around the world, and who—by virtue of his calling as President of the Quorum of the Twelve Apostles—is an extremely busy man.

His first soft-spoken words were, "Please forgive me for not getting up. I'm crippled."

A feeling of great humility came over me. I questioned our worthiness for being there with our selfish requests. Quietly, Brian and I sat down at arms-length in two high-backed chairs. I felt like a tiny mouse in mine and wanted to scoot closer to Brian.

We intended to let him do most of the talking so we could receive as much counsel as possible, but it didn't turn out that way. Instead, he invited us to talk about ourselves, our heritage and our membership in the church.

He asked me first. I nervously began imparting to him all the miracles leading up to this moment. He listened intently and asked questions. I could see the sincerity in his soft yet piercing look. It was as though he could see right through me. It was humbling. Brian and I could not hold back our emotions as we explained our situation.

I looked over at Brian as he took his turn speaking. He looked handsome, dressed in a beautiful dark suit. I loved him more than ever as I listened to him tearfully pouring out his heart, expressing his love for me, and his earnest desire to have me alive and with him for the rest of his life.

It's hard to describe the feeling of being with an Apostle of Jesus Christ, a Prophet. After Brian finished, President Hunter looked up at both of us and softly said, "So, you're here to have a blessing." He then turned to me and gently asked, "Analisa, do you have the faith to be healed?"

A million thoughts ran through my mind: Do I have the faith? How much does it take? How does the Lord measure it? Is it enough? Then, remembering all the blessings we received up to this point, with some certainty I replied, "Yes, I believe I do."

He then smiled, looked over at Brian, and said, "Well then, let's heal her."

We were overcome with joy! He asked me to come and sit next to him. He and Brian placed their hands upon my head and he proceeded to give me a beautiful and sacred blessing of health. It was a long prayer and he mentioned Job a lot. He blessed Alfred, that through him I would receive the help I needed. He pleaded and beseeched the Lord for His mercy on me. He blessed the doctors and nurses—that they would know how to analyze and care for me. He also blessed us with children. All this and more was promised to us, according to our faith.

Afterward, I hugged him and told him I loved him. He looked at me with his piercing eyes for what seemed an eternity, then softly said, "Don't worry. You'll be okay, Analisa."

I took full comfort in his words, believing and knowing they were true. After leaving President Hunter's office, Brian and I rushed to the nearest tree, to sit and jot down as much as we could remember. Our visit with him was a humbling, powerful and unforgettable experience. We had been given this most precious gift of all—to be healed! From now on, we could funnel all our faith to this end—that the Lord *would* see me through, according to our faith, and His will. We walked around the Temple taking pictures and feeling great.

We were scheduled to drive to Idaho Falls, three and a half hours away, to visit our friends, the Scotts and the Packs. But we were so exhausted with jetlag that we decided to stay one more night in Salt Lake City. We left them messages, hoping they would understand the circumstances.

We topped off the day by going through the Salt Lake Temple. Certainly it is one of the most beautiful temples. While there, a kind worker took an interest in us and gave us a personal tour. He shared bits of history and pointed out the ornate design that beautified every room. The pioneers sacrificed forty years to complete this incredible edifice. We told him of our earlier visit with President Hunter and he was happy for us. It was a wonderful way to end a perfect day.

IDAHO FALLS

We arrived in Idaho Falls the next day at noon, missing our scheduled 10:00 a.m. tee-off with our friends. By this time, my cold was really coming on strong and we were still exhausted. All we wanted to do was relax, visit, share good memories, and fill our friends in on what was happening. Surely, they would understand. Apparently, they had planned a big surprise dinner for us, and our missed golfing appointment only made matters worse.

When we arrived in Idaho Falls we went boating with Clark and Julene Scott. The Scotts owned a smoked turkey and wild game processing business. It was interesting to tour their facility and see wild game stacked high in their walk-in freezers waiting to be processed. Through them we had our first experience of tasting elk steaks.

That evening we went out to dinner with Lynn and Cindy Pack. The Packs owned a dairy farm. We have fond memories of the times we spent on their farm—learning to milk cows, having corn feasts, sharing meals together, and riding horses and snowmobiles in the back country of Idaho.

The following morning all six of us went out to breakfast like old times.

By the time we arrived in Los Angeles on June 24, my cold had reached its peak. Dr. Champlin decided to postpone my admission to UCLA until July 10. This gave me an extra week to recover, spend time with family, and purchase my wigs.

Meanwhile, I met with the gastroenterology staff. They reviewed my New Jersey records and concluded that I did *not* have Crohn's disease. They had no explanation for my 1988 colitis attack—only that it might have been the leukemia's way of surfacing. They were of the opinion that the bone marrow transplant might actually help my colitis, since the process would kill my immune system, thereby destroying the colitis. Like Dr. Champlin, they didn't know anyone with colitis who had undergone a transplant. That was real encouraging! I tried not to worry.

I was impressed with the kindness of the staff. The nurse tried to put my worries at ease and offered to visit me on 10 West.

ALFRED ARRIVES

On June 30, the long-awaited moment arrived. Family and friends gathered at LAX to cheer Alfred's return. Running late, we met him in the baggage claim area. Who would have believed, when he left in November, that he would be coming home early to fulfill an extraordinary new mission!

Alfred, a five foot and eleven inch, handsome, reserved young man with boyish features, who often spoke with a smile on his face, displayed his usual cool disposition. I was thrilled that this twenty-two-year-old "little brother" would give me his life-saving marrow. We chuckled that perhaps his marrow would make me feel four years younger!

All the way home he talked enthusiastically about his mission. He recounted the moment he heard the news of his match. He related how several Peruvian families had walked five miles to see him off at the airport, and how they pledged their faith and prayers on our behalf. I marveled at his maturity. In only six months he had changed from a boy to a man.

On the way home, I surprised him with the news that Mom and Dad were getting baptized on Sunday.

He was so excited—he could hardly believe it. Finally, after fourteen years they were going to keep the promise they had made to Stella just before she died. All these events were allowing me to enter the hospital with a most unshakable faith.

The next day at church I was "all ears" as I listened for final words of wisdom. It was Fast and Testimony Meeting again, when people stand up to share their thoughts and testimonies.

Alfred immediately darted to the podium. This usually shy young man poured out his heart, relating his experience upon learning of the detour of his mission, and then the joy of learning of his perfect match.

He said that he knew he must come home, yet he wanted to receive a special confirmation. Humbly he expressed how the Sunday before his return, the entire mission gathered for a special conference. Leaders from Salt Lake City were in attendance, and he was asked to say a few words. As he thought of what he might say, and wondered why our family must go through these challenges, he turned to the scriptures. He found his answer in scripture known as Doctrine and Covenants 105:18-19:

> "But inasmuch as there are those who have hearkened unto my words, I have prepared a blessing and an endowment for them, if they continue faithful.

> "I have heard their prayers, and will accept their offering; and it is expedient in me that they should be brought thus far for a trial of their faith."

His words were piercing. Indeed, God was hearing our prayers.

That evening, Mom and Dad were baptized. It was a festive day. I soaked up whatever joy I could, even though life felt imperfect and unpredictable.

FOURTH OF JULY

We spent a hot, but fun, Fourth of July day at the house of my brother Victor and his wife, Cindy, in the high desert of Palmdale, California. I valued the time with my niece and nephews. Also invited were their friends, John and Sandy, and their three beautiful children.

On the way home, Brian and I couldn't help but talk about Victor and Cindy, and John and Sandy, and compare our lives to theirs. John, a computer whiz, was thriving financially. They had just moved into a new home, purchased a new van, and today announced the arrival of a new five-thousand-dollar bedroom set. Victor and Cindy were also doing well, and Cindy was expecting their third baby in October.

We handled ourselves well under the circumstances, but we couldn't help but feel envious. It made me sad and threatened to put a damper on our thriving faith.

"Isn't life unfair?" I expressed. "Everyone our age is into their families and careers. And then there's us—we're just trying to stay alive."

"I know. No matter what we do, we can't change the fact that our lives are different from everyone else's."

I gazed out the window and sighed. "Gosh, we are in for the biggest challenge ever. I'd give a million dollars to be in John's and Sandy's shoes."

"I know, Ana. Me too," he sighed.

There was no turning back now—too much was at stake. We could only keep looking forward.

PART II
THE HOSPITAL—UCLA MEDICAL CENTER
JULY 10 TO AUGUST 15, 1989

CHAPTER 5
ENTERING 10 WEST

U nable to ignore the urge to write, I found expressing my thoughts on paper very soothing. And though I was unsure how to write a book, I was determined to do so. When Stella died, I had wanted very much to share her story with others, but had never followed through with it. So this time I kept notes, and Brian made some entries too.

July 10, 1989—journal entry

Well, here I am sitting in the lobby, waiting to move into "Hotel UCLA," and I am as calm as a bird on a summer's day. Everything has been going smoothly. With so many people praying for us, I honestly couldn't feel sad or worried even if I wanted to. It's a strange blessing, difficult to express, but every time I begin to worry it immediately washes away. My fears vanish as if there is no room in my heart for worry.

The first day was Orientation. Nickie, my nurse, greeted me with a warm smile. "We've been waiting for you," she said, showing me to my room.

As I looked around, I thought to myself, I'm here; I'm finally here to have my bone marrow transplant. She interviewed me thoroughly, and then gave me a rundown of 10 West, the Bone Marrow Transplant Unit. Her sweet disposition convinced me that I would be in good hands.

Throughout the day, several doctors and nurses dropped in to introduce themselves and to brief me on what to expect. I was amazed by how many people would be involved on a daily basis: the intern, Dr. Hart; the resident, Dr. Fazio; the fellow, Dr. Michaels; and the attending physician, Dr. Champlin. Also in attendance would be Dr. Ho, the hematologist; Dr. Winston, the infectious disease specialist; a dentist; about a dozen nurses; a psychologist; a social worker; a dietician; and the chaplain. Later on, when complications arose, it almost became a problem to keep track of everyone.

Each asked, "Do you really know what you're going to go through?" Each clearly reiterated all the problems that could arise. By the end of the day I was worn out and distressed, unable to take one more gory detail. I insisted that I had done all my "homework," read about the transplant, and had prepared myself as much as possible. Still, they seemed to question my emotional status. Perhaps my jovial attitude was puzzling to them. Finally, that evening I declared to Dr. Champlin, "I know this is going to be extremely hard, and I could die during the transplant, but I am here to be cured. I will do my best from my side of the bed, and you do your best on yours, and together we'll work to get me well."

Dr. Champlin seemed satisfied and nothing more was said.

My room was nicely decorated with blue wallpaper, and even had a small refrigerator. I put some pictures up to make it homey. I delayed changing into a pair of pajamas and getting into bed right away, because it didn't feel right and I didn't feel sick. Later on, as I folded my day clothes, I could only imagine the day when I would put them on again. It seemed like a world away. I put on my pajamas that looked like sweats. If I was going to be deathly ill, at least I'd look cool!

Brian's mom, Rosemary, beautifully penned some daily quotes and displayed them on a small easel, to give me something to focus on each day. Out my window, I had a clear view of Westwood. To the right I could see Santa Monica, the Pacific Ocean, and in the distance, the planes landing at LAX. Just to the left, between several buildings, I was thrilled to see yet another small miracle—the Los Angeles Temple where Brian and I were married seven years earlier. It represented everything in which we believe. I took comfort knowing it was only a glance away. For months I would find myself staring at it and the world outside.

We soon learned that 10 West was the "penthouse" of the hospital. Here, patients received royal treatment. The halls and rooms were carpeted, and meals were of the highest quality—lobster, filet mignon, etc. The servers even dressed in white shirts, black vests and bowties. I enjoyed my first meal, a lobster tail the size of my hand! Unfortunately, it turned out to be one of the only meals I was able to eat. Thereafter, Brian ate most of them.

I don't remember where my family was the first evening, only that I was alone. So I asked the nurse if I could roam the halls. To keep from feeling claustrophobic, I decided to make the halls an extension of my room, instead of confining myself to within my four walls. I put on my Sony Walkman and roamed the hospital as I listened to some old Carpenters songs. I ended up on a bench just outside the busy building and watched people come and go. As I listened to the soothing words, I silently reassured myself that I was going to be okay.

For a brief moment I plotted an escape. I wanted to get up and just start walking and not come back. No one would notice, would they? But I couldn't run from this problem—this disease that was supposedly killing me. I'd have to take the bull by the horns, roll with the punches, and fight with all my heart and soul.

There were so many doctors, each with a different personality and bedside manner. I would have to win their hearts in order to get the best treatment. Building good relationships was crucial. I wanted to be important to them, not just another statistic. Besides, I was sure I would get through this, and I wanted them to know it.

I wondered about the people who would come into my life—how each would play a role in getting me well. I began to imagine that 10 West had just employed me for the next six weeks. It would be the shortest, yet hardest job I would ever have, but with team effort I would survive. Working *with* and *not against* my nurses and doctors would promote a better environment for survival.

In ten days I would receive my new marrow. It seemed an eternity away. The doctors counted the days backwards, starting with "day minus ten." Each day, as radiation and chemotherapy were given, my blood counts would decrease, resulting in a depleted immune system by day zero. At that point, my blood counts would be near zero and I would be ready for Alfred's marrow. I would then be kept alive with blood transfusions and medications until the marrow would, hopefully, engraft. Family members were scheduled to donate blood platelets to me as needed. The process seemed incomprehensible.

I finally made my way back to my room. With Brian near, I would be okay, I thought. Again I worried just how well he'd hold up. Could he handle it? I looked forward to him sleeping next to me in the small rollaway bed.

VISITING THE RADIOLOGIST

The next morning, a volunteer showed up with a wheelchair to escort me to the radiologist. I asked my nurse if I could walk instead. I wasn't about to use a wheelchair if I didn't have to.

The visit with the radiologist was brutal. There were three doctors. The first one examined me. He was so young I couldn't help but ask his age—twenty-seven. The second measured me from head to toe, including individual limbs, to determine how much radiation could be tolerated. I asked several questions. As we talked, he brought up the subject of faith. He was Episcopalian. I told him I was LDS (Latter-day Saint) and expressed some of my views. He seemed pleased, saying it would help me a lot.

Each one made his evaluation, then left. I wondered what they thought. Perhaps I came across too vivacious, but that's how I am. Inside, I felt like a lamb going to the slaughterhouse. It was important that they see me as a real person. I even had on makeup, though I was dressed in pajamas. Perhaps they felt sorry for me. I felt sorry for myself, as I glanced up and caught my reflection in the mirror. I didn't want to be there. The room was cold and the waiting seemed eternal.

Finally, a third doctor came in, followed by his two colleagues. As they stood around me, this doctor, with dark brown hair and glasses, began giving me a forty-five-minute, unmerciful dissertation on the amount of radiation I would receive. He graphically described the gross effects it would have on my body immediately after, and the complications that could arise in the months and years to come. He spared no details. On his lapel was a button that read, "Us Rad Animals <u>Do</u> Save Lives!"

As he spoke of the horrific effects, he smiled with every remark, as though trying to minimize its magnitude. He was honest and forthright.

"Let me tell you how much radiation you will receive. A routine chest x-ray is one-fiftieth of a rad. The amount you'll receive will be one thousand one hundred and twenty-five rads, given in five doses of two hundred and twenty-five rads each. Each dose takes a half-hour and will be given every twelve hours. Virtually, you'll be susceptible to any kind of infection during the first few months. Therefore, you are going to be very sick very quickly. You might develop heart problems, liver and kidney problems. You will likely develop mouth sores. You will develop several rashes and your skin will become dry and peel. The most serious infection is CMV (Cytomegalovirus). If it occurs in the lungs or liver, it is often fatal. If it occurs in the eyes, you may loose your eyesight. In rare cases it has affected the nervous system. Over time you may develop cirrhosis of the liver, and you will likely develop cataracts within ten years. You won't be able to have children, and of course you'll lose your hair."

As he continued on and on, I began feeling sick and helpless. Surely these words weren't meant for me! How in the world could anyone survive this treatment? It seemed impossible! I asked several questions. When he was through, he said, "Many don't survive, but some do, and we are hoping that you will."

By the time he finished, I was numb and on the verge of tears. However, an unknown strength was holding me together, and I was actually surprised that I didn't break down. Any normal person hearing such horrible details would have lost control. Why bother with the transplant? It's going to kill me anyway. But I must not think this way, I told myself. People did survive! I saw a woman who did, and she looked good.

"How do you feel about all this?" he asked.

"I have no other choice. I have to do this to get rid of my leukemia. I want to live," I said, teary-eyed. "I guess I have to believe in what your button says."

I thought he had delivered his speech heartlessly. It was cruel and inhumane. However, what he did was standard procedure. I had to know. They had to inform me of all possible outcomes. Losing my hair would be nothing compared to everything else.

Finally, they released me to my room. Slowly, I walked back to 10 West. Like a stranger dropped onto an unknown planet, I wondered why and how I had ended up in this kamikaze situation. There was no way out now! I truly felt alone. Each day was going to get harder and harder. "God, help me!" I whispered. I hope to prove everyone wrong, and be one who survives.

Strangely, I was unafraid and resolved not to dwell on the radiologist; rather, to think of President Hunter's blessing and to concentrate on getting through each day, each step, and each process. Later, Brian handed me a letter he wrote to me that day, and it helped lift my spirits.

My Dearest Ana,

I promised you I would write you a letter each day you are in the hospital and I intend to keep that promise. So, here is my first letter to my wife.

Ana, there isn't a half-hour that goes by that I don't think of you. I know what is meant when a husband and a wife become "one." I feel and have always felt you are a part of me. I yearn for you each minute. Sometimes we don't realize how much one means to the other until something like this comes into our lives. But heck, we've been through some tough times already. Even though this trial sometimes seems overwhelming, I *know* it's just another that we, both of us, will tackle together and get *behind* us.

I am *so very thankful* for President Hunter's blessing to you. Ana, never forget that this came from the lips of a humble, yet powerful servant of God. If he said those things, isn't that good enough? You bet it is!

ALWAYS remember this in moments when you feel like tearing. Ana, I am going to try and write an inspirational message in each letter. So, here goes a poem. I'm going to describe the day we had.

Today we went to UCLA,
The Medical Center, a visit to pay.
This was the day that Ana went in,
To prepare to receive marrow from her next of kin.

Yes, Alfred was the one who miraculously matched,
This wonderful news throughout Jersey was definitely "catched."
Everyone has been praying for my sweet wife,
To bless and plead for a long, long life.

I know this will happen as sure as I write,
As sure as we get our mosquito bites.
So, I'll gather up the things that I will bring to you,
The comb, the VCR, and the blue slipper shoes.

I'm sorry this was short and rather dumb,
But what do you expect from your big, big...?

I love you honey,
Brian

This was the only letter he wrote to me.

The first part of the week involved several tests, including a bone marrow biopsy, pulmonary function, electrocardiogram (EKG), dental x-rays, the implanting of my Hickman Catheter (central venous catheter), and the radiation and chemotherapy treatments.

I was quite nervous about having another bone marrow test. The muscle relaxant helped. Angie, my nurse, held my hand and caressed my face as Dr. Michaels, the fellow, aspirated the marrow from my back hip. Afterward, Angie kissed my forehead and said, "You did good." She made me feel safe. I looked forward to any positive feedback I could get from the nurses.

HICKMAN CATHETER

During the first week, they implanted my Hickman Catheter, an IV line that hooked directly into one of the main veins of my heart. For the next four months, this spaghetti-like tube protruding from my chest, with two yellow caps at the end, would basically be my "lifeline." I wouldn't have to worry about eating for several weeks. From my catheter, blood products would be drawn and most medications and nutrients given.

I remember the procedure, when the doctors made two small incisions in my chest. They blocked my face with what seemed like a cardboard box and surgical tissue. The surgeon was an unpleasant-looking, older man. Although I was drugged up, I could hear what they were saying. During the procedure, I heard one doctor swearing because he couldn't get the catheter in. I could feel the pulling and tugging, and it seemed to take forever. Impatiently, I groaned and managed to utter, "Gosh, what's taking so long? Hurry!"

Quite surprised, they responded, "Can you feel that?"

"Yes!"

"Uh, we're just having a little trouble here, but it's okay."

He told the assistant to give me more anesthesia. I don't remember anything after that. Perhaps they didn't think I could hear them or would remember, but I do.

I was wheeled back to my room. With patches on my chest and patches on my lower back from the BMT test, I ached in both areas and felt nauseous.

Every day the nurses cleaned my catheter. Alcohol and bedadine solution became my new perfume. I was given special soap and shampoo for bathing, and no showers were allowed. We were told that the steam could cause Legionnaires Disease. After bathing I'd have to powder up with Nystatin, to prevent me from catching fungi infections.

Each day I submitted myself to the orders of the day. My body became keenly aware of what was happening. I began categorizing everything by moguls and mountains. My first mountain was just getting here; second was having another bone marrow test; and third was getting through radiation treatments.

GETTING TO KNOW MY COMRADES

Like entering the woods, it was strange to be in a hospital. What a different world, to be among the sick. Brian and I got to know several families. At first, we stared at each other cautiously. But as we came to know them, we weren't quite so afraid; quickly realizing they were people just like us who had come down with some awful disease. It became important to know them. There were about ten others on 10 West going through a similar transplant. Many had diseases other than leukemia.

One man who became dear to us was Rick. He was a forty-two-year-old construction worker who came in a week after me. He looked just like Kenny Rogers—handsome, with a clean white beard, and a cheerful attitude. He too had CML. I briefed him on what to expect his first week. We talked about how we were going to lick this thing!

Another man was David, a twenty-two-year-old Yale student with Hodgkin's disease. Down the hall was a man named Harold, who was also Mormon. Next door was a man named Glen, who was engaged to be married as soon as he got out of the hospital. Next to him was Peter, a forty-two-year-old man who had already been there for more than two months and was still in isolation. Anthony was a twenty-one-year-old man from Northern California, who entered the same day I did. And finally, there was Ragen, who came in about two weeks after me. I was the only woman. There were others, but we never saw them. Only the name on the door indicated there was another poor soul suffering.

As we got to know these patients, we passed notes back and forth to each other for support. It became important to ask my nurses each day how my comrades were doing.

Brian spent a lot of time with their families. They got to know each other better than the patients did.

CHAPTER 6
RADIATION AND CHEMOTHERAPY

<u>July 12, 1989</u>—journal entry

This morning, I'm getting my first radiation treatment. Nurse Mitchell says the hardest part will be the elevator ride. He gave me some Valium and "gut sterilizers." They started making me feel queasy. I take seven "horse pills," four times a day (a total of twenty-eight!), to protect my stomach, lungs and mouth from all the treatments. Right now I feel very calm, yet realize it's going to get harder. The nurses keep telling me I have a great attitude. They have been terrific. I know the Lord is with me. I've been able to share our story with others. So far, it hasn't been that bad.

The radiologist had me lie still on a table in front of a big laser machine. She asked a few questions; it seems everyone wants to know my age. Her eyes imparted that perhaps she thought I was quite young and was sorry to subject me to this awful treatment.

For thirty minutes I could not move a muscle while I received my first treatment. After it was over, she handed me a bucket. "Here's this in case you need it."

Surprised, I put it on my lap. I didn't expect the radiation to affect me so quickly, but shortly after I got back to my room I threw up. The rest of the day I was nauseous and restless. Brian kept a journal and tallied how many times I threw up. After the sixteenth time, he stopped counting. Later in the evening I went down again for treatment number two. I was given three types of anti-nausea medication. The nurse assigned Brian to check all "hats" (meaning my output containers and emesis buckets). All intake and output had to be measured, including water.

On Thursday, I had radiation treatments three and four. The day passed by in a fog. I only remember that I was very sick. Only one more left, on Friday. All throughout, I could feel my body spitting out emergency signals to my brain: "Caution, warning, danger, help!" My "physical computer" was going on the "blink." Brian recorded some of my remarks:

"I'm being backed up into a corner and there's no escaping; it's like quicksand! I'm getting sicker each day—my next mogul, chemotherapy. After that my hair will fall out, and then the transplant a week from today. They keep me busy; I'm always going downstairs for tests. People are always coming in. I've thrown up a lot so far, but nothing overburdening yet. I just feel grateful I'm in a good hospital. My faith is growing. Last night I met a woman named Liz. Enthusiastically she said, "You and I have something in common." She paused and then said, "Our faith!"

"Are you LDS?" I asked.

"No, but my initials are LDS."

I told her about Alfred's match, and her eyes welled up with tears. She said she got goose bumps. It's these small moments that brought the most peace and comfort. I was determined to share a positive attitude whenever possible—the rewards were double.

That day I also began mouth swabs four times a day with water and baking soda to prevent mouth sores. Due to low platelets, using a regular toothbrush could actually cause me to bleed to death! I was extremely lucky. During the transplant I never got one major mouth sore, but the ones I did get were extremely painful.

After radiation, I began chemotherapy (Cytoxan). My world was becoming smaller and daily tasks were increasingly difficult. I wrote out my feelings, thereby gaining some of my greatest strength. It was within the first week that I again resolved to write a book. Unsure of how to go about it, I knew it was important to keep good notes. The trauma I was receiving on a daily basis was so incredible; it seemed natural to write and let others know the hell I was going through.

One day I asked Nickie, "Has anyone written a book about a bone marrow transplant?"

"No, not from a patient's standpoint," she said.

That night I told Dr. Michaels and Dr. Fazio that I was going to write one.

Dr. Michaels replied, "Oh, do you know how to write a book?"

"No, but I know I'm going to do it!"

The experiences were so vivid that to have this goal made good sense. I felt an obligation to share with the world the bone marrow transplant experience from a patient's point of view. Therefore, I made a promise with the Lord that I would, if I could just live to tell about it.

PHYSICAL DETERIORATION

The treatments were taking their toll on my little body. It was evident I was loosing total physical control. So I listened carefully to my body, following its lead and what it required of me. Mentally, I had to quickly decide to turn inward or outward. It was easier to turn outward and to share my feelings. Many patients turned inward.

Although it was a struggle to keep things in perspective, without letting the treatment consume me, instinctively I focused and refocused through each day of pain. I reflected much on the spiritual and emotional preparation I had done, and I felt strong.

Sometimes, I focused on happy times of my life, like lying on the beach in Acapulco without a care in the world; driving with the music on; or I visualized fields of flowers in full bloom—anything to keep my mind off reality.

The throw up sessions were like an aerobic workout. The chest pain caused by the radiation intensified with time, making my insides feel raw. By the end of the second week, the pain was so bad I started getting back spasms and was ready to give up, believing that my heart was going to give out. Surely I wouldn't last through the weekend.

By Friday night, nurse Kristen finally suggested some painkillers. Though I was scheduled to go on Methadone, she gave me Dilaudid, and within minutes the chest pain ceased. I couldn't thank her enough for saving my life! I was so relieved to know I could make it through the weekend. Kristen, very knowledgeable in the field of BMTs, visited with us for long periods of time, coaching me on what symptoms to expect from each medication.

Hour by hour, I fluctuated between tranquil moments and violent throw up sessions; clearly I was deteriorating. Brian continued to help me bathe and take short walks.

Part of the days I spent watching TV. Amazed at all the food advertisements, I began making a mental list of the meals I intended to eat when I got out. When I shared this with the doctor, he was pleased that I was still thinking about food. However, soon that idea changed!

Meanwhile, Brian enjoyed my lavish meals. Daily, I was given an elaborate menu from which to choose. Yet making any decisions, especially about food, became a torturous task. Just hearing the servers wheel the carts down the hall would cause me to throw up! To be on Total Parental Nutrition (TPN) through an IV, and not have to worry about eating anymore, was such a relief.

Brian was holding up well. I never knew I could love him more than I did at this time. We became closer than ever. He was there at every turn, handing me the emesis bucket, tissues or water. He cleaned my buckets, helped me bathe, and gathered up my laundry. I started calling him my "sunshine face," because amid the awful throw up sessions, he remained his cheerful self. Nothing seemed to faze him, except when I wasn't doing well emotionally.

Loss of coordination and concentration came quickly. At every turn my body took the blows of this "physical holocaust" (hell) created by the radiation and chemotherapy. My body fought violently to maintain control. However, it finally gave in, becoming *totally* dependent on external medicine for survival.

I was sweaty and oily and could feel my body purging itself of moisture. I developed several rashes, and each day the doctors examined them thoroughly and checked for new ones and allergies. I went from one IV machine to two, then three, then four.

One day, nurse Nickie asked, "How do you feel?"

"Like I'm running an obstacle course of moguls and mountains lined with hot coals. Gunfire is coming at me from all angles, and arrows from all directions. I'm being turned inside out and have to climb ten-foot walls. There's no doubt I'm getting hit hard!"

"Well, just so you know, you're still going to get much sicker before you get better."

"Brief me on what symptoms to look for, so it won't be so scary."

"Sure."

Nickie and the other nurses were like angels, helping me along. Experts in their field, they took care of us in twelve-hour shifts. I could tell them anything. They kept the doctors abreast of our conditions. My doctors were nice and equally excellent, but the nurses were extra special. Because UCLA is a teaching facility, the doctors alternated each month, and they only came in for a few minutes a day.

Indeed, the days got harder. Brian made sure that each day I got some exercise. I'd visit Rick and we'd compare notes. One day, the chaplain came and married patient Glen and his fiancé. A few days later Glen passed away.

Brian tried to keep it from me, but it didn't take long to figure it out. I never saw him, but I often saw his fiancé. It made me very sad; one day he was there, the next day gone. I tried to push away bad thoughts, reminding myself that I "worked" here on 10 West and wasn't "just a patient."

However, one minute I'd be fine, the next miserable. I was becoming hypersensitive to anything negative. My family came often, but I really couldn't have visitors; nor did I want them. Fresh flowers were prohibited because they could bring fungi infections. So our friends in New Jersey flooded me with cards and letters. I eagerly read them; each seemed remarkably tailored with just the right encouragement for the day. It was like a small daily miracle. Friends called, but they usually spoke to Brian.

In a hospital one has a lot of time to think, so I began to ponder more about my book, and what Dr. Michaels had said. I really didn't know how to write one. So much was happening and I needed guidance. Brian and I prayed daily for guidance and strength, and listened to inspirational music. That night, about 3:00 a.m., I woke up with incredible impressions to write. I wanted to ignore these promptings and get my much-needed rest, but the feelings were so strong I had to seize the moment.

Not wanting to disturb Brian, I gathered my strength, pushed my IV pole into the bathroom, sat on the side of the tub, and began writing.

A few minutes later, Nickie came in. "Analisa, are you okay?"

"Yeah, I'm just writing."

"You're what?" she asked, surprised.

Slightly embarrassed, I replied, "I'm just working on my book. I've got all these neat thoughts for an outline. If I don't write them down now, I'll lose them."

"I can't believe you, Analisa. Well, let me know if you need anything."

It was an extraordinary experience. I felt inspired! The words flowed onto my yellow pad. Before I knew it, I had a complete outline. To this day I have continued to follow it.

The outline was a terrific boost, and it was clear what direction to take. All I had to do now was fill in the blanks. I knew the Lord helped me, and it was comforting to know I wasn't alone in this. The next day, I eagerly told Brian. On several more occasions, I became familiar with these promptings to write and knew I must obediently heed them, lest I lose them.

Often I'd stare out the window at the Temple and think of my book. The ending would be Brian and I going to the Temple with a baby, to be "sealed" to us. (As Mormons, we believe that families can be together forever, never to be broken apart.) Half seriously, I even told Nickie one day that my book would be so good that they would make a movie out it. She just smiled, half-believing and said, "Just keep thinking that way."

Although each day my world was becoming smaller, spiritually I felt that I was growing by leaps and bounds. I thought of the Savior and what He went through, and I felt close to Him. As I searched for understanding, it seemed that answers to our prayers were always coming at the eleventh hour.

TRAINING THE NURSES

The nurses played a huge part in my survival. Each cared for about three patients at a time. Sometimes we'd have the same nurse for a couple of days. During their twelve-hour shifts, we got to know them very well.

Having to relinquish total care into their hands, I had a need to bond with them. Again, the better the relationship, the better the care. It was important to work diligently with them and not against them, when they checked my vital signs several times a day, cleaned the emesis buckets, helped me change or bathe, and gave me countless medications. Many spent hours advising and coaching me, each with their own style of nursing.

Many would often hold my hand, caress my face, and kiss my forehead during difficult moments, never knowing how very soothing their actions made me feel. Anyone entering the room had to wash their hands. So, between patients, Brian and I figured they easily washed their hands more than twenty-five times a day.

Each night around 10:00 p.m., a nurse came in to draw several vials of blood, clean my catheter, and change my IV lines—a procedure which took a good hour. By morning, the lab would have the results ready for the doctors' daily meeting. At the meetings, patients' records were reviewed and recommendations made. For quick reference, each doctor kept a three-by-five index card in his breast pocket detailing each patient's blood levels. The interns would make their rounds in the morning, and in the afternoon Dr. Champlin would make his.

In my condition, there wasn't much to do but observe the parade of people coming through. One day I was assigned a new nurse, Paul. The first day, he was very reserved and unapproachable. He'd enter, check my IV lines and vital signs, and not say a word. After a few times, I became annoyed, since I very much wanted a little tender care.

"I'm going to try something," I told Brian.

The next time Paul came in, I complimented him and asked him questions. We talked a bit, but he still wouldn't soften up. It made me agitated, but I was determined to not give up!

The following day, I was terribly sick and worn out. When Paul came to check my IV bags, I watched and waited for a "hello" as he carefully monitored my machines. Again, he said nothing.

"You're a nice guy, Paul. Thank you," I managed to whisper.

Startled, he looked at me and said, "So are you; you're pretty nice too."

I'm not sure what happened, but from then on his whole nursing demeanor changed. Before, he'd never say good-bye, but that night he came in and cheerfully announced, "My shift is over now, Analisa. I just came in to ask your permission to go home, or if there is anything you need."

So appreciative, I was speechless! From then on, he called me "cutie-pie," and our friendship grew. He was wonderful. It was a learning experience, and a little miracle, vital to my well-being.

The relationships with the doctors were equally vital. Though their visits were brief, they were crucial. Whatever they said set the mood for the day. I clung to their words and looked to them each day for relief, input and empathy. Brian was just as eager. They were excellent and always listened to my complaints, but I yearned for more compassion from them.

We accepted the fact that they were the experts, and needed to concentrate strictly on my physical needs. My success was their success.

Most of the compassion was left to the nurses. I often tried to break the ice with Dr. Champlin and his colleagues, but they always seemed to keep their distance. Very seldom would their real emotions surface, and when they did, it was so gratifying. It was then that I could measure my progress by what they were *really* feeling.

CHAPTER 7
TRANSPLANT DAY—JULY 20, 1989

Finally, the long-awaited day arrived. They called it "hump day." My blood counts were nearly zero; my body ready to receive Alfred's marrow. Alfred, who was admitted the night before, was scheduled to have his marrow aspirated by Dr. Winston Ho early in the morning.

Nickie came in to calm my fears. "Don't worry, Analisa. Most patients are usually nervous on transplant day."

I was to receive Alfred's marrow around 10:00 a.m. However, emergency room delays postponed it until 2:00 p.m. At 2:00 p.m., it was postponed again until 4:00 p.m. Anxiously, I waited. At 3:30 p.m., Nickie came in to say it would be yet another three hours! It was becoming a very long day.

By 7:00 p.m., Nickie was ending her shift and I still hadn't received my marrow. The anticipation was killing me. All I wanted was Alfred's marrow in me. Minutes passed like hours as I began to fear disaster would happen—like an earthquake, or a fire, before I could get the marrow!

I listened to music, but relief didn't come. I became restless and started to panic. What I had hoped to be a peaceful and serene event was turning into an emotional roller coaster. Brian tried to calm me, but all we could do was wait.

At 7:30 p.m., Nickie came in to say good-bye.

"How much longer, Nickie?"

"Your brother's in surgery now, so it will probably come later this evening. Don't worry; it will be here."

She and Brian leaned against the bed and held my hands as she began reminding me of our blessings. "Remember Analisa, you're so lucky! You have a wonderful husband to support you. He loves you so much. I hope I can find someone like that."

"Well, you might want to go to the Mormon Church—your chances might be a bit greater," I remarked softly.

She smiled as I began telling her how Brian and I met, the activities of the church, and how anxious I was to get the marrow.

"This was going to be a pivotal day—never to be forgotten. I've been physically and spiritually beaten up, and the pain and suffering is mounting. Not once have I felt as disturbed as I do today."

They listened to my lamentations, and I found no relief until I began sharing my feelings about our faith. As I did so, a rush of peace and tranquility came over me, turning all my sorrow into gratitude. I even recited our Young Women's theme to her.

"Nickie, I love God, and I know He lives and has blessed us tremendously—no matter how bad this is. I know the things I've learned all my life are true. I want this precious missionary marrow so badly. But, *if I died tonight—right now*—I would die happily…because I know I've shared my deepest testimony about our faith to you. That's all that's important."

"Oh, come on Ana," Brian said.

"No, I mean it! It's all that's important, and my love for you."

As I looked at Brian and Nickie, their tears were flowing and the spirit in the room was so strong. It would have been a perfect way to pass on.

"Thanks for being with me," I said.

Nickie left, but the serenity stayed and my burden was lifted. Finally, Alfred's marrow was brought in, and I was completely ready for it. Amazingly, it was exactly 11:00 p.m.—another eleventh hour miracle!

Brian and my parents were there when nurse Mitchell and another nurse formally verified who I was, what type of blood I was receiving, and from whom. The precious marrow, which resembled a bag of Kool-Aid, was carefully hooked into my IV line. It took exactly one half-hour to transfuse, instinctively making its way to my bones.

Meanwhile, my vitals were checked every few minutes for any adverse reactions. Then, all the nurses came in and sang, "Happy Birthday," complete with a cake and candle! This would be my new birthday, they exclaimed.

Again, we had to wait until the eleventh hour before receiving our most precious need! Even in the smallest details, I continued to learn something spiritual. It was as though my head was split open and a stream of knowledge was flowing in straight from heaven, easing my pain and carrying me forward. No matter how much I was suffering physically, I was usually riding a spiritual high.

The next day, we learned that Alfred had gone through some serious complications. While under anesthesia he began coughing, and water from the tube in his throat got into his lungs. Dr. Ho kept him in recovery much longer than expected. My parents were quite nervous, since his condition was unknown for some time.

Alfred stayed at UCLA for two nights. After he went home, he suffered severe chest pains, and Dad slept with him for the first few nights. Other than that, it went okay.

The following day I began thinking more about Nickie. "I'm going to match you up with someone," I told her.

She laughed, "Don't worry about me; think about yourself."

But I knew I'd do better if I kept my mind on everyone else. So I set her up with a new friend, Jason, from the Westwood Singles Ward who visited me on Sundays. (A few months later, they went out on a blind date. However, nothing ever came of it. At least I tried!)

CHAPTER 8
ISOLATION—MOGULS AND MOUNTAINS

Within a couple of days after the transplant, I was put in isolation. Coping was extremely difficult, taking my every effort to get through each hour. Making short-term goals became important.

I focused on growing white cells. This and other crucial goals kept my mind clear, so if setbacks occurred the disappointments would be minimal. Each goal achieved felt like a milestone. I took comfort, then concentrated on the next one.

In order to get out of isolation, I needed to have 1,000 white cells. They said it would take at least three weeks before I could take a walk outside my room. Any infection—either fungus, bacterial, or viral—could be fatal. Anyone entering the room had to wear a mask and wash their hands.

Each day I was examined for signs of engraftment, infection or fevers. If I "spiked" a fever it meant an infection was on the rise. The main concerns were infections or Graft vs. Host Disease (GVH), where the new marrow rejects the body. A little GVH was good, meaning the marrow was being stimulated. However, too much GVH could lead to complications—an attack of the liver, lungs, kidneys, colon or, in some cases, the brain. Many patients die because of GVH. A related donor greatly decreased the possibility of this disease.

TOTAL BODY TORTURE

Although relieved to have Alfred's marrow in me, the bigger problems were just beginning. In isolation, the nurses repeated that I'd still get worse before I got better. Indeed, they were right. Physically, I had no white blood cells to defend me against any infections. Nickie drew me a picture of a white cell so I could concentrate on growing cells. Anything helped to boost my morale, so I kept it under my pillow.

In isolation, the gross effects of chemotherapy and radiation boldly began manifesting themselves. My little frame fought back with a vengeance. I just hung on. There was no speeding up the process as my body took its own course. In addition, all the medications were affecting me. Each day was unpredictable. I got fevers, chills, rigors syndrome (where the body shakes violently), rashes, swelling of the hands, night sweats, diarrhea, constant nausea, severe heaving, dryness of the mouth, and excessively dry skin that eventually became scaly and peeled. In addition, I had racing heart palpitations, loss of hair, unsteadiness, joint pains and jaundice, along with the symptoms of fatigue, feeling cold, and hallucinations. In short, I was sick!

Just when I thought it couldn't get worse, it did. Many of these symptoms occurred simultaneously. I felt like I was being put through a shredder! This unbelievable trauma was putting me in touch with mortality. I called it "TBT"—Total Body Torture! Certainly, life had given me a raw deal.

SKIN AND PILLS

I turned five different colors, first, a pale white from the beginning effects of treatment. Then, a rosy color as my body purged its final moisture. Next, red as my skin became raw. Then, a black/bluish bruised color, revealing the internal havoc and destruction of my cells. Finally, I turned a charcoal color from losing my pigmentation. All this was due to a depleted immune system. At one point my hands became raw and swollen, the palms turned blood red and hot, and my skin peeled. I had to be given ice packs to relieve the swelling.

I was extremely nauseous, as if on a twenty-four-hour, wild coaster ride that only stopped intermittently. I wondered when it would ever stop. Good or bad days turned into good or bad hours.

Sometimes I'd think how inhumane this procedure was, and wonder what I had done to deserve it. However, I refused to curse God. I kept remembering the first and great commandment, which is to love God with all your heart, mind and soul.

With Brian's help I could still take baths, although with so many IV lines the task became increasingly difficult. I was now on four machines, each filling me with vital medications, painkillers and nourishment. I received blood transfusions too, and Mom, Victor, and Jim donated platelets on several occasions.

Time in isolation passed slowly. It took a supreme effort *not* to concentrate on time. In the bathroom, sometimes I spent time standing or marching along the sink, or writing. Oddly, the bathroom provided a welcome change from the cooped-up feeling of my room. It took a long time to bathe, so I would often "make a day" out of it.

On good days, I paced the floor or did breathing exercises. I was put on a low-bacterial diet, with no fresh vegetables, etc. I worried how I'd be able to eat again, and if my body would ever metabolize food properly. Since I was fed intravenously, I tried not to worry too much. Brian was happy to eat my meals.

Brian was there continually, like a mother hen, and did everything he could to make me comfortable. He monitored my medications and constantly asked questions. The moment I began to worry, he'd say, "Leave the worrying up to me; just hang in there."

One day, the nurse came in while I was sleeping. Seeing Brian hovering over me, she was concerned and asked, "Is everything okay?"

"Yes, I'm just checking to see if she's breathing," he answered.

Although our teamwork was incredibly good, there were days when the stress simply got to both of us. It was two weeks before we finally had a major blowup. Nickie said, "Not bad, considering you're spending twenty-four hours a day with each other. Under these circumstances, any healthy relationship is bound to have its moments."

Brian monitored everything as though his own life depended on it. For a period, it became a battle between us for me to continue swallowing twenty-eight pills a day. By the end of each day, the last set of seven pills was impossible to swallow, let alone stay down. The doctors said the more I took, the more protection I would have. So, it became Brian's mission that I take them all.

I became resentful, unappreciative, and outright rebellious. In my struggle to maintain personal control, I battled him over each round of pills before finally swallowing the last set of the day. It was such an ordeal that, at one point, I began to see him as a villain out to destroy me. I wanted to throw him out; he was too smothering. "Do this, do that, take your pills," he would say. Every time I turned around he was presenting me with a set of pills.

One night we got into such a quarrel that we almost could have hit each other, all due to the stupid Carafate (gut sterilizer) pills! The next evening, I got so upset I almost threw them, along with my emesis bucket against the wall. I couldn't take it anymore! All I wanted was relief.

It became important to take breaks from him; not out of a lack of love, but for survival—his and mine. These were traumatic times and our marriage was truly being tested.

One day I shared my distress with Nickie. "I just need to be alone. I'm so tired and nervous when anyone is around. I love Brian more than anything and would die if he weren't here with me. I just need a break. He's so involved in this. I'm afraid if I die, he'll die right along with me. He won't listen to me."

"I'll tell him, Analisa. Don't worry," she said.

She wrote him a "citation" note. Thereafter, he began spending more time with the other patients and their families, and taking walks. I, in turn, was able to get some rest and relax a little easier. Although I felt bad about it, it helped both of us.

In isolation, high fevers and chills persisted. One moment, I felt extremely cold, the next feverishly hot. "I hate the chills," I would declare to my nurses. They'd promptly furnish a heated blanket. When I spiked a fever, nurse Angie would place a washcloth on my head and say, "Let's put this on your little noodle." She'd check my vitals and kiss my forehead.

The days continued to be unpredictable. Sometimes I had only enough energy to last until noon, and then it would be downhill after that. On really bad days I would ask to be sedated, so I wouldn't have to deal with anything.

Other days weren't quite so bad. One evening Brian and I played an excellent game of Scrabble, scoring in the low 300s. I beat him by two points!

We also watched TV, although it was not my favorite pastime. One night we watched two tear-jerking movies. Ironically, one was *Windy City*, a story about a team of football players who grew up together, and one ended up dying of—what else? Leukemia! Although I could relate to the dying patient, I felt strangely removed from *his* situation. It honestly did not bother me. The following movie was the romantic comedy *Pillow Talk*, with Doris Day and Rock Hudson. It was totally enjoyable and epitomized our relationship. I appreciated these happy moments—the hard ones were always around the corner.

Brian's journal entries:

11TH HOUR MIRACLES!

July 31, 1989

Today was not one of Ana's best days. She threw up most of the gut sterilizers, and incidentally hasn't taken them for two days now. She's been spiking a fever as high as 102°. Analisa has been a bit cantankerous, like others in her situation. If I even mention the word pill, as in "have you taken your pills today?" she gets very angry with me. I know it's hard, but I wish she realized I'm *only* doing it for her good!

She's been edgy with me, but I know she's been in pain and discomfort. I just wish she would take those darn pills.

She's had so many visitors today I'm beginning to feel like it's Grand Central Station. She needs more quiet time.

Analisa wants *out* of isolation. I don't blame her. When she is down, we tend to argue. I asked if she wanted me to stick around. She said, "Yes, for today." I feel like she'll bite my head off every time I open my mouth. So, I have to be very delicate as to what I say to her.

August 3, 1989

Analisa has been suffering a lot for the last few days. I should say for the last three weeks—ever since she was admitted. I've been taking it pretty good. I have felt the Lord sustaining me through this. And I have remained quite positive as I explain Ana's condition to everyone.

But, tonight I feel some pain inside as I try to console her. No matter what I say or do, I cannot fully understand Ana's pain. Sure, I've been more or less in isolation for the past two weeks, but I get reprieves often. I can leave whenever I want.

I plead with God that the days ahead will bring more white cells, and minimal or no more nausea. Here are a few of the physical discomforts she has had to endure:
- Excessive, continual vomiting (day minus 9 to present).
- A rash over entire body after receiving Jim's platelets, and fevers the past three days.

- Raw hands. The Prednisone should help remove the rash. She's now on an "itching pill."

Yesterday she almost threw up in her bath water. Luckily there was a bucket nearby. Her little body contorts through all these functions. She told me, "Pain takes away the fear, but fear doesn't take away the pain." The chills are violent, especially today. Ana's been fighting fevers all week. The first sign is chills. Tylenol is given when fevers reach 101.5°; within a short period of time the fever breaks and Ana breaks out in a sweat. Later, it starts over again.

The doctors started Ana on Amphotericin, an anti-fungal drug. This was to combat the persisting fevers. Unfortunately, one of the side effects is chills. Ana had a violent rigors reaction today. Angie quickly brought in two heated blankets and had to lay against her to keep her from falling off the bed. She bundled her up like a mummy and instructed her not to move or take a bath until the fever broke.

She's been retaining fluids. With all the IV's, Ana's input is so much greater than her output. This accounts for her weight gain of 5 lbs, in one day. Dr. Champlin ordered a diuretic. Consequently, Ana's been going to the bathroom every 20 minutes. Her output was equivalent to 2-3 liters—equal to 3 lbs. On another occasion she gained up to 12 lbs. in a single day!

Marci, her nurse, came in and made a world of difference. We've been feeling so depressed this evening. Marci really boosted Ana's morale. I firmly see the Lord's promise to Ana unfold from the words of President Hunter, "that the doctors and nurses will be able to analyze you and help you with all your needs."

Marci said, "You're right where you need to be, your new marrow has already engrafted. The itching on the hands and feet, a rash starting to develop right now, means engraftment. Your body is adjusting to it." She kissed and hugged Ana, and then hugged me.

She said that Analisa could be out of isolation within a couple of days. They were words we desperately needed to hear.

Earlier this evening, Ana and I had a special experience. She has two pictures of Christ. One of them is in the bathroom, since she spends much time there. It's a picture of Christ teaching the people. Ana said, "If only I could touch these sandals." I hugged her. As she went back to bed, she cried out in grief over the pain she continues to suffer. She remembered President Hunter's blessing—how he mentioned the Prophet Job many times. She said she felt as if she was Job.

THIRST

Another day while in isolation I became excessively thirsty. I could not produce any saliva. My mucus membranes were bone dry. I felt like I was going to choke to death. The need for moisture in my throat was so great that I couldn't go without water to my lips for more than a few seconds. Yet I could barely swallow a few tablespoons of water and ice at a time. It was one of the most frightening and challenging days I recall. It wasn't a matter of quenching my thirst; it was a matter of survival. No amount of water was enough. Surely I would not live to the end of the day if this continued. Brian, tired of handing me ice chips and water, told the nurse, "I'm ready to throw a bucket of water over her head, and she still says she can't get enough."

All I could do was pray that this awful dryness would subside. I realized what it meant to really have thirst. At the end of the day the moisture slightly returned. (But for months, even a year after the transplant, I always needed a glass of water nearby.)

RIGORS

Several times a night I would need to use the bathroom. One night as I finished washing my hands, I began to shake violently. Just as the rigors attack began to intensify, Dorinda, my nurse, came in. "Analisa, are you okay?"

"Help!" I cried out.

Quickly, she grabbed me and assisted me to the bed. I was shaking so violently she had to lie on top of me to hold me down! As the shaking subsided, she bundled me up in a heated blanket.

These shakes were *extremely* painful. Every muscle would spasm, creating a bone-chilling reaction, and my nipples felt like they would fall off. These attacks would bring complete and total exhaustion to my already weakened frame.

Surprisingly, Brian slept through the whole incident. I thanked Dorinda repeatedly for saving my life. Had she not come in at that very moment, I would have fallen, hit my head, torn out my catheter, or maybe worse. She was heaven sent!

EMOTIONALLY

For the most part, I was positive and doing the best I could. However, the daily mood swings were rough and sometimes volatile. I often became depressed over the slightest incidents.

For example, I kept asking for a toothpick, but nobody would give me one. I was told that I couldn't have one because I could contract a bacterial infection, or poke my gums and bleed to death due to a low platelet level. I pressed Brian to get me one, but he refused. I couldn't believe it! I finally threw a fit. Dr. Fazio had to come in and reiterate why I couldn't have one.

"This is ridiculous! A toothpick is all I'm asking for!" I contended. "I'll be real careful. I just want to clean my teeth."

"No, Analisa, we won't give you one."

"Well, what makes you think I'm not going to tear off a piece of paper and fold it into a sharp edge?" I retorted.

"We don't know that, but you really shouldn't."

I battled him on this. The issue wasn't that I could die from using a toothpick; it was that I just wanted someone to appease me. I had been behaving extremely well up to this point—surrendering every part of my body to them. Requesting a measly toothpick, only to receive such a blunt refusal almost made me violent.

Later, as I rested, the nurse told Brian it was common for patients to go through periods of anger and hostility. Brian was always patient with my temper tantrums. And although I often gave him a hard time, he continued to be there, refusing to leave my side. Even when I didn't deserve it, he was good to me.

I was impressed with his stamina and determination to get me well. I thought for sure he would crumble, but the tougher things got the stronger he became. I had never witnessed more strength, patience and selflessness. His love was unconditional and his care was loyal. I promised him that if I got well, I would iron all his shirts for the rest of my life! I kept apologizing for not doing all the things I should have done in our marriage.

My emotions were like antennas on my head, fighting the trauma while searching for positive reinforcement. Certain commercials left poignant impressions on me, like the diet commercial where the actress from *LA Law* said, "Come on…you can do it." Her words spoke directly to me. Another was the C&R Clothiers commercial stating, "What a difference a day makes…"—where the male model looked sloppy one day, then gorgeous the next. I envisioned myself just the opposite—great one day, horrible the next! I knew I was really in a pitiful state when I could relate to the "I've fallen, and I can't get up!" commercial. At first it was humorous, but when it became reality, it became my greatest fear. We often watched *Star Trek* and "Beam me up, Scotty" made real sense.

Daily events were like watching my life on a movie screen, with everything in slow motion. As the main character, I was also the quiet observer, somehow detached from the situation. This detachment allowed me to write and visualize the outcome without hurting myself emotionally.

Also, becoming dependent, helpless, frustrated, and in some cases scared, caused me to reflect a lot on my childhood. During special moments as a child, I often remembered saying to myself, "I've got to remember this moment." I now found myself doing the same thing. Truthfully, it seemed to me that I could almost remember moments when I had felt safe in my parents' arms; my first baths; or perhaps even my birth; when I really didn't know what was happening. I'd share these feelings with Brian and the nurses. The transplant was, in a sense, a rebirth.

One day I said to Nickie, "This is awful. Am I going to have nightmares about all this when I go home?"

"No, don't worry about that right now," she said as she was making my bed.

I believed her, and for the moment I was content. Months later, I learned otherwise.

MAKING ANALOGIES

Often Brian asked, "What does it feel like?" He listened as I made analogies.

"Every event creates pictures that I would not have imagined otherwise. It's one thing to imagine what one might be going through, but it's another to live these things before even thinking them. It becomes your worst *living* nightmare! I feel victimized; my body violated and raped of integrity. I will never be innocent again. I'm too young to be going through these atrocities. I'll be "damaged goods"!

"I've been beaten up," I went on, "left to wallow and die in some ditch. I feel like I've stepped into a black hole—a physical holocaust with no way out. I'm running an obstacle course with arrows coming at me from all directions. I'm staring down the barrel of a loaded shotgun, waiting for it to go off. My body is literally dying; it's turned inside out. This burden is too hard to bear. I'm climbing Mount Everest with my fingernails. Out of millions of people in the world, why was my number picked to endure these trials?" I asked.

Deep pain again and again was becoming familiar. It brought with it a sort of nauseous dehumanizing feeling, reminding me of just how human I really was. *This is pure hell*—a living hell, I thought. I had the bull by the horns, but now I'm just hanging on.

My most vivid analogy was that of being tossed into an ocean with nothing but a scrawny little life jacket. Everyone around me was aboard huge lavish boats, cheering me on with, "Come on! Hang in there! You can make it!" The water was rough, and I felt like I was going under. It took all my effort to keep my chin up. I could see land in the distance, and knew the tide was slowly pushing me toward it. Sharks and piranhas surrounded me, waiting to eat me. At times, the sun was shining and the waters were calm—I could catch my breath, and almost paddle my way closer to shore. But suddenly the clouds would gather, and it was scary. The waves pulled me back, and under, and all hell would break loose! It could happen in an instant, with merely a word or a statement from someone, or during throw up sessions when my whole body was contorting. I felt doomed to drown in my illness. Nevertheless, everyone continued to cheer—begging me to hang on. How I wished someone would just pluck me out of this awful state! But they couldn't. They could only talk me through it and watch me struggle. Desperately I held on to my lifejacket—my faith, faith in God! God would keep me afloat until I got to the land of health and well being, I told myself.

Mentally, I was aware of everything around me. Brian and the nurses sometimes thought I was "out of it," but I was there—*very* much there. Although my body was in shambles, my spirit felt whole—more eternal, and at times stronger than ever. My spirit felt separated from my body, yet trapped in a bag of rotting bones. My spirit wanted to hide, but there was nowhere to go. I asked Brian, "Where can I turn in my body for a new one?

FAITH AND SPIRITUAL MOMENTS

Illness spares no one. Everything I had ever been taught boiled down to one thing—Faith. Everything else seemed insignificant in my present state. This was an exercise in faith—a hard workout—to believe that God and Jesus Christ do live, and that by having faith in them I could be healed.

I can't deny how many times a critical and helpless moment was overcome by a peaceful spiritual experience. I called them miracles, whether big or small.

Lying in the hospital, I came to many spiritual epiphanies. No matter how much Brian and my family tried to help, it was just me and the Lord, and *no one else*. The only thing I could do in my situation was *pray*; and because I could only pray, I began to think about God and Jesus Christ, realizing they were the only ones who truly understood what I was going through. Line upon line, prayer upon prayer, my suffering turned to understanding. Yet, it was still hard, because at times I felt all alone and deserted.

Life isn't fair. How can God allow this kind of human suffering? I wrestled with this until finally confessing that Jesus *is* the Christ. With this understanding came peace. For many, I suppose it never comes.

It has been said that God does leave us alone, for a while, but He never forgets us. My prayers were being answered, all of them. Still, it was very hard. I had to get through each day—learning to eat and drink, forcing myself to take walks, etc.

Each day I felt purged, both physically and spiritually. I was being stripped of all my pride, until nothing but pure humility seemed to be left. There were many instances where I felt God's mercy, as though He were softly saying, "I know thy pain…endure to the end and ye shall have everything!"

As the days got harder, my prayers became more intense and direct, with much serious petitioning. I had often prayed throughout my life, but now I hung on prayer. I found myself beseeching the Lord, even bargaining with Him, for mercy and strength. Through this process, a softening and a molding began to take place. I came to a clear understanding of truths I had never known, as if all truth was flowing through my veins. Sometimes it was euphoric and tiring. Still, I ventured to learn all I could, fearing God, and knowing that in a flash I could be gone. He was God, and I was a minuscule dot on this earth—nothing, compared to all He was and is! This learning came in bits and pieces.

Sometimes I'd close my eyes and see brightness all around me, and a feeling of hope would fill my heart. I felt close to the life beyond this life, as though separated from it by a thin veil.

One evening, there was a special moment when I *knew* the Lord understood my suffering the way no one else could. In a quiet moment of deep despair, I prayed. I felt a calm, sweet, clear voice enter my mind saying, "*I know your pain.*" In that instant, and in a small way, I knew His and He *knew* that I *knew*. And I also knew that someday He would look into my eyes and lovingly say, "Remember my child when I was with you? *I KNEW YOUR PAIN!*"

This spiritual experience carried me through much of my long period of suffering.

The days were unpredictable, and sometimes I feared sleeping. Surprisingly, many of the nights were calm and I was able to sleep fairly well, in spite of the frequent interruptions. One night, I dreamt there were two men standing on either side of my bed. As I looked up at them, I wondered who they were, what they were doing, and if they were related to me. They didn't do much; they just stood by, almost as if they were preoccupied. I tried to get their attention, but they ignored me. Yet I was comforted by their presence, as though they were assigned to watch over me. That morning I woke up unafraid to face the day, and the peaceful feeling lingered.

Later that day I was started on a new anti-fungal medication, Amphotericin. Angie warned me of its side effect—chills—and sure enough, I had a violent reaction. Angie said my nights might be difficult as well. But I wasn't afraid. I was confident that those two men would be there to watch over me again. That night, I didn't see them, but I felt their presence and knew they were there. I slept well. Those were the only two nights during the transplant when I had such an experience.

Another day while in isolation, I listened to a tape called, *I Walk By Faith,* by Janice Kapp Perry. I can't describe the joy I felt. Although I had listened to it countless times before, a particular song brought me greater peace than it ever had. I felt an urgency to share that peace with others. Here is a portion of the words:

"Learn of Me"

Lyrics by Joy Saunders Lundberg, Music by Janice Kapp Perry,
© 1985, Used by Permission.

I walk today along the path of life,
No more a child protected from the strife.
Now I must face whatever foes may come,
And fight with strength until the battle's won.

I tremble in fear the task is far too great,
On every side, the tempter lies in wait.
What can I do, I plead to him above?
Then hear him speak these gentle words of love:

"Learn of me and listen to my words,
Walk in the meekness of my light.
And I shall give you peace,
My love will never cease, for I am Jesus Christ."

When I was yet a child so clean and pure,
I doubted not, and knew God's love was sure.
I knew He lived for every bird and tree,
By breath and leaf were witnesses to me.

But now the world would fill my mind with doubt,
And so my soul, in search of truth cries out.
How may I know, I plead to Him above,
Then I recall these gentle words of love:

"Learn of me and listen to my words,
Walk in the meekness of my light.
And I shall give you peace,
My love will never cease, for I am Jesus Christ."

I was grateful for a perfect day!

SENSE OF HUMOR

The ability to laugh under these helpless conditions was terribly important and definitely minimized the stress. Morphine, Dilhauted and Ativan were an added bonus!

Occasionally I'd catch myself saying, "Oh God, give me strength"—which often invoked an automatic grin, reminding me of a co-worker in New Jersey named Lucinda. She, a typical East Coast Italian woman (if there's such a thing), often repeated those same words in her thick "New Joysee" accent. Although it was comical, it bothered me because it sounded disrespectful. Now, here I was on 10 West, saying it to myself ever so seriously. And, I was grateful for anything that could get me to smile at this time.

One stirring milestone occurred the day Brian shaved my head. By the second week, my hair, having become bristly, dry, itchy, and unmanageable—began falling out in clumps. One night I decided to have it shaved off. Good moods were short-lived, so I seized the moment. Impatient, I wanted it done right then. Nickie was too busy, so Brian reluctantly agreed to do it. Nickie brought in the clippers, and Brian began nervously shaving away.

"Are you sure you want to do this right now?" he asked.

"Yes! I want my head as smooth as a baby's bum, no nubs! So when it starts growing back I'll know it's for sure."

We chuckled as clumps of brown hair fell to the floor. There was no stopping now. About an hour and a half later, the dull electric shaver finished. Brian was a good sport about it, but I knew that he was tense the entire time.

Shaving my head took away all the nervous anticipation of losing my hair. It actually felt great, and gave me a whole new perspective and a good topic for conversation. My thought was that if it began growing back by September 1, maybe I wouldn't have to wear a wig to my ten-year high school reunion on November 10.

However, the next day my head broke out in an awful red, irritating rash, becoming extremely dry and itchy. I had to use cortisone cream on my scalp for several days. Brian would help rub it on, saying, "Time for your grease job."

I tried on different scarves and hats, and sometimes I wouldn't wear anything. Brian took a few pictures, but I only allowed one of my bald head. The family liked the bare look. They said I looked like Sinead O'Connor, the rock star. As soon as Victor saw me, he said, "Grasshopper, grasshopper, quickly snatch the pebbles from my hand"—-a reference to the old TV show *Kung Fu*.

Later, in a note to my comrade David, I described what was happening in isolation:

July 27, 1989

Dear David,

Sorry I haven't written. Isolation hasn't been too bad as far as boredom is concerned, there's always something going on. Sometimes it's nice to just rest and sleep.

Brian shaved my head on Sunday night. I must say it was <u>so</u> exciting. I put on a bunch of make-up and told Brian to go for it!

As with everything, there have been some really bad days and then some real good ones. My upper GI tract is so raw, every time I throw up I want to give up. The drugs have been miracle-savers. I'm on day +7.

Have they given you any indications when you're going to check out of this "Hotel"? Have you been able to eat again? I haven't. I attempted to nibble on some egg and potatoes, but my taste buds are "shot"; everything tastes like paste. So, I gave up eating.

Besides, my throat is so raw I can't imagine anything making it down to my stomach without getting stuck! Eating again is going to take quite some time. I've begun a mental list of all the foods I want when I'm out of here.

I'm wishing you the best, David. Your mother gave me a nice book. And yes, I do feel like a peach with my bald head and want to continue a "Peaches and Creme" attitude.

David, it's been a tough long road here; but I know a lot depends on attitude and faith. I have so much faith that the Lord will pull us through this. It's the only way! Have a great day—make it a great day! Your neighbor who understands…
Love,
Analisa

While on 10 West a new nursing student came on board. Her name was Hi. She was a young, quiet, petite Asian nurse. We often chuckled over her name, for I seemed to say it wrong whenever I greeted her. I didn't know whether to say "Hi" or "Hi Hi."

Brian and I often wondered what it would be like if she and Dr. Ho were married. Her name would be Hi Ho. "How would we greet them?" I asked.

He replied, "We'd say Hi Hi, Hi Ho."

"No, we'd actually say "Hi Hi. Hi Dr. Ho." It gave us the giggles. Sure enough, one day after isolation while walking on 10 West, we saw them coming our way together. I nudged Brian. "Look." Embarrassed and trying to say it correctly, I messed up and said, "Hi...Ho."!

FRIENDS

I didn't want many visitors. It wasn't necessary for friends to see me in such a crisis. If I died, I wanted people to remember me healthy, not sick.

The Westwood Ward members of the church were responsible for visiting the LDS patients at UCLA. I had never met any of these people before; however, we got to know each other well. The Relief Society President, Leona Matoni, Marney Buchanan, and several others graciously came to offer their support. Our church is fantastic that way. It's one of the church's greatest qualities. In times of trouble, no matter where in the world one might be, people are always ready to render service. I especially appreciated the men coming on Sundays to give me the Sacrament.

Through Leona, I learned of another Mormon girl going through a transplant—a teenager on the pediatric floor named Danielle. Her mother Ramona came to visit me a few times. Danielle, too, survived her transplant.

One day, while I remained in isolation, Brian went to the Temple. When he returned, he said, "Guess who I saw? President Rosza (the man who married us). I told him all about you, and he's going to come see you today."

I was thrilled! He came later that day. He still looked as handsome as I remembered, even with a mask on. I felt a little embarrassed for him to see me bald, ugly, and in such a helpless state. Still, I greatly appreciated his visit as we reminisced. He also said he would pray for me.

As he left, he told Brian it wasn't a coincidence they had run into each other that day. "Sometimes the Lord has a way of putting people right where they need to be, at the right time."

I considered his visit another miracle to help me get through another day.

COMRADES

I continued writing notes to my comrades. When I thought of them, I didn't feel alone. They could relate to this horrible experience. Sometimes, it was frightening because I could hear them heaving or moaning. My heart went out to them and to myself. What a sorry state we were in! Nevertheless, passing notes or messages helped. Here's one I wrote to Rick the day after he received his new marrow:

July 26, 1989

Dear Rick,

Happy birthday! Welcome to the other side of the fence! You can now count positive days (+1, +2...). The letter you received from your donor was beautiful. I'm sure you'll want to meet her someday.

I must say, there have been days so unbearable that the only reason I feel like I want to hang on any longer is because of Brian. I don't know how I could handle this without him. I'm sure there are still tough days ahead, but all in all, we'll make it!

They gave me a painkiller, Dilaudid. It's a miracle drug that almost makes throwing up a pleasure. Can you believe it? I've had better days now, but I haven't eaten anything yet.

All in all, I'm hanging on to this roller coaster and I think my ride is going to end soon, so I can go out and experience the wonderful things about life again. Take care, and if you get the chills, order a hot blanket, they're great!

Analisa

One day, while trying to bathe, I was quite weak. The task, with the rashes and nausea, was particularly taxing. Brian stepped out for a while, and then returned to help me. He was very quiet. I could tell something was wrong.

"So, how are the others (patients) doing? Did you see any of them?" I asked.

"No, I just saw some of the families."

"How's Harold?"

He paused, not wanting to tell me, but I pressed him.

"He died this morning."

My heart sank. The news was more than I could handle. Suddenly, I felt vulnerable and needed to get back in bed. I started crying. "I can't believe it, he's gone, just like that! Leaving a wife and three kids in Ohio. Oh, that poor family!"

Although I never met Harold, I did see his wife often, and felt a special bond with them because he was also Mormon. Now he was gone. I worried what was in store for me. He had begun his transplant one week prior to mine, and was doing well from what I had heard. Then all of the sudden he developed a bad liver infection, which often meant almost certain death. From one hour to the next, we could be put on the critical list. Angie, my nurse, said his biggest fear was catching this liver infection. If he got it, he knew he wouldn't make it.

My mind raced. Prior to isolation, Brian and I took daily walks on 10 West and always looked at the names on the doors. His wouldn't be there anymore. I was nervous and panic-stricken, as if there was no tomorrow—questioning life, death, and where I stood in the middle of it. Was I appointed to death too? I know I had been given a healing blessing; Brian constantly reminded me of it. But it wasn't a sure thing; doubts still crept in.

While Brian helped me finish my bath, my parents arrived. Just as I crawled into bed wanting to shut the world out, the phone rang.

Dad answered it in his usual, unique way: "O'Rullian residence." Suddenly, he got a surprised look on his face. "Oh, well, I'm her father. Would you like to speak to her?" He handed me the phone.

"Hello?"

"Hello Analisa, this is Howard Hunter."

"Oh President, it's a pleasure to hear from you." Hearing his soft, kind voice filled me with profound humility and gratitude.

"I just wanted to call and see how you're doing."

"I'm doing okay, President. It's just a very slow and hard process. I'm really sick and continually nauseous. I just learned that my neighbor, Brother Harold, passed away today."

He felt bad.

"Tomorrow morning when the Counsel of the Twelve meets in the Temple for our morning session, I will add your name to our special prayer list, and we will pray for you, Analisa."

In tears, I thanked him.

Our conversation was brief, but the thought of him calling me at this critical moment left me surprised and humbled. A miracle had taken place.

Although I couldn't stop thinking about Harold for the rest of the day, and wondering what was in store for me, I did feel that the Lord, through President Hunter's call, was reminding me that I wasn't alone.

By the middle of the third week on 10 West, I knew of three people who had not made it. I and my closest comrades, Rick, David, Anthony, Ragen, and Peter, were still struggling to hold our own. Like a soldier slowly marching on the battlefield, I tried hard to remain focused, and tried to not look back at my fallen comrades. Another of my notes to Rick went as follows:

Rick,

How are you faring? Somehow I got a good night's sleep—the best since my transplant. Have you gone into isolation yet? I'm going on eleven days. I very much miss seeing people's faces. Once in a while, Brian gives me a peek after I beg him.

Isolation is really tough. What I hate most is the "heaving." It really takes a toll on me. I've only been throwing up 1-3 times a day now, and I can't stand it! Brian says it's not bad compared to before. It's the only thing that gets me down. I have no control over it. Other than that, my days are basically okay to good. Taking naps during the day gives me energy for visitors at night and I try to pace the floor often.

Well, everyday I ask Brian how you're doing, since you seem to be handling this pretty well. Let's just keep taking it one day at a time. Give yourself plenty of rest and keep a positive attitude! I hope your day is a happy one.

Your pal,
Analisa

On July 27, Brian noted that I began hallucinating while on the drug Methadone. It was a strange experience. Whenever I closed my eyes I would see all sorts of images and colors and would hear voices talking to me. Unintentionally, I would answer these voices, only to open my eyes and see no one around. The racing images were very tiring. I wanted so much to turn off my brain and get rid of those "ghosts." But the drugs were so vital for the pain.

Every day while I was in isolation, doctors continued to examine me thoroughly and ask me questions. Eagerly, I shared my symptoms. Thinking of myself as a sort of lab rat, I thought that perhaps their findings would help the next poor soul coming through. They documented everything, but never seemed to stay long enough.

I most eagerly awaited Dr. Champlin's visits. His shyness often tempted me to grab him by his tie and tease him, wanting him to know that I remained positive about the transplant. There was no doubt that he was the expert, and I felt completely at ease in his care. But every time he came in, I yearned to hear new words or any signs of progress. My entire daily mood relied on his communication, and I often wondered if doctors really knew just how much their visits truly meant to their patients. I couldn't complain about the care I was receiving. But sometimes, I just wanted one of them to put his arm around me and caringly say, "Analisa, I know this is so hard. Just hang in there, it'll be okay!"

During each visit, we asked several questions and they always gave adequate answers. One day I informed Dr. Champlin, "This is no Sunday picnic. I feel like I'm going through a metamorphosis; like a crispy critter that's been fried."

"You're right where you need to be," he said, as he thoroughly examined my legs, feet and fingers, looking for rashes and signs of engraftment. By then, a whole new set of nails was beginning to grow in. For now, no news was good news.

Each day, I eagerly awaited the mail. How I appreciated those cards and letters, which now wallpapered my room, reminding me that I wasn't forgotten. Our friends in New Jersey were ever faithful in writing; their strength and prayers were carrying me through.

To get out of isolation I needed 1,000 white cells. Each morning the results of the previous night's blood drawings were in. Every day they fluctuated. If I was low on platelets, Mom or my brothers would donate theirs. If I was low on red blood cells, I would receive a transfusion. I received several while in isolation.

One day, approximately two and a half weeks after I received Alfred's marrow, Dr. Michaels and Dr. Fazio came in. My one and only goal was getting out of isolation, and since my counts were up that day I was in a good mood. Dr. Fazio, a native New Yorker, chatted with me about the East, then we discussed my blood counts.

"I'm so excited, my counts have gone up," I said anxiously.

"Well, those are just weekend counts, they don't mean anything. They can change at any time," he said apathetically.

Not expecting such indifference, it was as though he had stabbed me in the chest with a dagger! What did he mean, "they don't mean anything"? It was the *only* thing I was living for! His words were like a death sentence, crushing all hope.

"Boy, you really know how to kill a person!" I said as I burst into uncontrollable tears. Couldn't he see how hard I had been working to keep a positive attitude, or how much I depended on any sign of progress? Couldn't he have lied just to appease me? How could I go on if I couldn't believe in my own progress?

He handed me a tissue and tried to console me. "The weekend counts don't mean much because the technicians are off, and sometimes the results aren't entirely accurate."

But the damage was done. The floodgates had been opened, and nothing he said helped. He pointed to the picture of the Savior pasted on my refrigerator. "Think of Him. Remember your strong faith?"

But nothing worked. I couldn't stop sobbing, even to answer him. As he left, he encouraged me not to worry; to relax and get some rest. I was left alone feeling hopelessly deflated.

Not a minute had passed before the door suddenly flew open, and Nickie came rushing in, with her mask barely on.

"Analisa, are you okay?" she said urgently. "What's wrong?"

Seeing me in tears, she looked frightened. Surprised by her sudden appearance, I started telling her what had just occurred. She breathed a sigh of relief and said, "Let me wash up first." (Anyone coming in had to wash his or her hands.)

"Did you just see the doctors outside? Did they just send you in here?" I asked.

"No, I was down the hall, ready to see another patient, when suddenly I got this awful feeling that 'Analisa's in trouble,' and I came running! I don't know what it was, I just knew I had to get here fast."

"But they just left…Are you sure they didn't tell you to come and see me?" I insisted.

"No! I was way down the hall; I'm just glad you're okay!" she said, relieved.

Nickie sat on my bed and grabbed my hand. I was so relieved to not be alone. In between sobs, I said, "All I wanted was a bit of encouragement. Growing cells is all I'm living for." Nickie listened as I unloaded. "I wanted him to grab my hand or tap my shoulder and say, 'It's okay, you're going to be all right.' But he didn't! *None of them do!* If they only knew how sensitive patients are—how much we rely on every positive word that comes out of their mouths. Do you think I taught him a lesson on how to treat patients?"

"Well, probably not," she said. "The doctors *are* very good and they work very hard on each patient. Don't let that bother you."

My emotions were ultra-sensitive, childlike, and I needed much encouragement. She sat with me and gave me a lot of sound advice, until I calmed down. Nickie's quick response was a direct fulfillment of President Hunter's blessing—that those caring for me would be able to analyze and help me with all my needs.

I told her of his blessing, and how much I believed in it, and that she must have been inspired to come to my aid!

Nickie, with her big blue eyes, had become like a sister. She even reminded me of Stella. Indeed, I was surprised and humbled by how the Lord sometimes gave me immediate support when I least expected it. I will always remember that incident with Nickie.

MOM'S DAILY QUOTES

Rosemary supplied a daily quote for me and displayed it on an easel. Each day I looked forward to these bits of wisdom done in calligraphy. Even the nurses and doctors seemed to enjoy them. I'd often reflect on my new marrow and let my mind feed on these quotes:

"They shall mount up with wings as eagles; they shall run, and not be weary; and they shall walk and not faint." (Isaiah 40:31)

"A merry heart doeth (a body) good like medicine; but a broken spirit drieth the bones." (Proverbs 17:22)

"The words 'brother and sister' describe to me the ultimate sacrifice, the ultimate acceptance, the ultimate benefit."

"My body will rejoice in the compatibility of my cells with the cells of my brother's."

"Yes, my body will be a safe and welcoming harbor for this precious donation."

"For God hath not given us the spirit of fear; but of power, and of love, and of a sound mind." (2 Timothy 1:7)

"I will travel the places of my mind for refreshment and freedom from care."

"Lake Tahoe, shimmering from emerald deep blue, cleanses my weary eyes."

"It shall be health to thy navel and marrow to thy bones..." (Proverbs 3:8)

"Trust in the Lord with all thine heart; and lean not unto thine own understanding." (Proverbs 3:5)

"Being bald is a sign of courage, nobility and sexiness!"

"I thank thee that thou hast heard me...abounding therein with Thanksgiving." (John 11:41 and Col. 2:7)

"My wonderful new cells produce the living stream of strength, of renewal, of healing."

"...Pray unto him with exceeding faith, and he will console you in your afflictions." (Jacob 3:1)

"Ye are the temple of the living God." (2 Cor. 6:16)

"Counting your blessings gives you unlimited, personal power!"

"Look unto me in every thought; doubt not, fear not." (D&C 6:36)

CHAPTER 9
GETTING OUT OF ISOLATION

Three weeks after I received Alfred's marrow, Kristen and several nurses swung open my door and filed in without their masks. With big smiles they cheered, "Congratulations, your white count is eleven hundred!"

Puzzled, it took me a moment to realize what that meant.

"You can be out of isolation!" they shouted.

"Really?" Overcome with elation, I burst into tears. The long grueling weeks (nineteen days) of confinement within these four walls were over! No more pacing the bed or marching in the bathroom. No longer would I have to stare at a closed door in front of me—the value of freedom was certainly understood. For weeks I had longed to roam the halls and was "dying" to get out of isolation. It was great to see smiling faces and teeth again, instead of a pair of beady eyes examining me every hour.

Brian helped me with my robe and slippers. I was filled with excitement, yet feared to venture outside. Could I handle it? Somehow I had gotten used to my little jail room; it had become my comfort zone.

Getting out of isolation, I now had to wear a mask for protection against germs. I quickly realized the inconvenience Brian had lived with during the last three weeks—and he had never complained about it. How he slept with one was hard to fathom. I could barely breathe with my mask on, and he insisted that I wear it snug and tight.

As Brian pushed my pole, now a six-wheeler cradling four machines, we slowly made our way down 10 West. I was anxious to read the names on the doors and see who was still with us. Most were still there, but some of the names had changed.

An eerie feeling struck me as we walked the floor. It was a tangible feeling, as though the destroying angel had gone door to door, entering many, and had even stood at our door, yet we were passed by. With each step that I took, I felt my faith and the faith of loved ones carrying me forward. I felt somehow totally protected and untouchable.

Walking to the nurse's station was all I could handle. The energy required and the emotional adjustment were overwhelming. So Brian put a chair at the entrance of my room, and I was content to sit and watch people walk by.

This spooky, eerie feeling remained as I sat, looking down the hall. I could almost envision this "shadow of death." I mourned for my lost comrades. We were all in different stages. Some never even made it out of isolation. I wondered about the fate of the new patients, and said a silent prayer. Many were just starting, and I was glad to be past those first stages. It was every man for himself, and not an ounce of energy was expendable. Unfortunately, it was necessary to concentrate and channel all of my energies on myself. There was nothing we could do for each other but pray.

I sat staring and reflecting—-grateful to be out of isolation. Another goal met. Now I could focus on the next one—going home!

The days following included more walks down 10 West. The task was physically and emotionally challenging, for often we'd see the other patients and their families. One day their spirits were up, the next down. We could surmise their loved one's progress by the look in their eyes. Our destiny was unpredictable, seemingly relying on a wing and a prayer—and a broken wing at best!

Feelings of terrible guilt came over me when comrades weren't doing well. Other days I became slightly envious, if suddenly I was doing poorly and they were doing better. It was awkward dealing with life and death on such an abrupt basis.

Two days after leaving isolation, I ventured to visit dear Rick. Upon seeing him I was reminded of the horrible treatment to which we were all being subjected. I was struck by how drastically he had changed! Having gained fifty pounds from water retention, he had completely blown up like a balloon. His wife said you could feel the water right under his skin.

As he lay there, he told me how he woke up in a puddle of urine and water from head to toe, and how they were extracting liters through the dialysis machines.

I encouraged him not to lose faith, and that I too had gained up to fifteen pounds in one day. All we could do was try and joke about it. As I walked back to my room, my heart was filled with sorrow. With the loss of his hair and all the bloating, he had become totally unrecognizable! His nice tanned skin was now beet-red. I said a silent prayer for him—for all of us. Surely, this was no way to live, or die.

Back in my room, I looked in the mirror. I too had been transformed. I knew for certain when one day, a cleaning worker came in and, seeing a recent photo of Brian and me on the windowsill, asked, "Is this you?"

"Yes," I replied.

"Oh, you *were* pretty," he said.

Understanding the circumstances, I didn't pay too much attention to hurt feelings. This was part of the "process." Sometimes, looking at other patients, one could not even tell if they were male or female. I, too, fell into this category.

Although I lost all my hair, I was left with enough to retain some sense of dignity. I did not lose my eyebrows, eyelashes, or the hair on my arms. And, although I suffered from rashes and bloating, I was hopeful to someday get my normal face back. For now, I couldn't worry about my looks; I'd have to deal with that later. The worry for now was getting out, and recovering.

Sometimes, while in bed, I'd quietly contemplate my fate and the fate of others. In so doing, I was impressed to believe that there are hundreds of angels assigned to administer over hospitals because of the many prayers from patients and loved ones. Often, I glanced down the hall yearning to see them. I never *really* saw one, but I did through the eyes of the nurses.

Another unforgettable experience came soon after I got out of isolation. Although I was glad to be out, the days were still very difficult. This particular day was no exception. As I sat up to heave for the hundredth time, Brian gently rubbed my back. My nerves were rattled, and I was tired of the whole process. Brian faithfully cleaned out my bucket and listened patiently as I complained.

"I just want this all to stop. I want to get out of here. I have no control of my life. I'm like a puppet and never have any privacy. It's like Grand Central Station around here. Everyone has a different function— one to mop the floors, one to clean bathrooms, another to count machines, another to take out the trash twice a day, the food servers three times a day, the nurses every two hours to check vitals, the doctors, the dentist, and sometimes the dietitian, the social worker and the chaplain. If I spike a fever it brings in another whole entourage of workers to draw blood and take x-rays."

"I know, Ana, I'm sick of it too."

"It's just too much, Brian. What's happened to our lives? We had it so good, baby! Will I ever be the same? Oh, I hate this," I moaned.

He continued rubbing my back as we sat on the bed, both of us feeling hopeless. Just then, a cleaning lady came in and made her way to the bathroom. Brian and I looked at each other, and I rolled my eyes and shook my head in disgust. I wanted to scream, but he motioned for me to be polite.

When she finished and came out, she glanced up at Mom's daily quote, grabbed her chest, and fell against the wall. In a thick Italian accent, she said, "Oh! Oh, my God, are you Mormon?"

Startled, we replied, "Yes." (I thought she was going to get mad at us; she appeared so shocked.)

She said, "I knew you were Mormon! I knew it! I have a tremendous feeling in my heart. I never look at the patients. I just do my work and never look up because it's too hard. I always work on the fourth floor and I never come up here, I never do, but today I had to. Walking in here, I felt a strong feeling."

She paused, and we wondered what she could possibly be trying to tell us. Then she said, "God is here…God is here and He take care of you. I don't know you and I don't know what you have, but you gonna be okay," she said firmly, as she waved her hands at me. "You gonna be fine. Don't worry. In two weeks, you not gonna be here anymore."

The spirit in the room suddenly became so strong that we were teary-eyed before she could even finish. This woman, who just happened to be LDS, was unbelievable. All we could do was thank her for her faith and spirit.

"Oh no, thank you," she replied. "You don't know what this has done for me—you don't know! I never had this happen," she repeated. "I never come up here and I never look up. I'm gonna pray for you, and you see. In two weeks, you no be here," she said, shaking her hands.

She quickly finished her chores, and within minutes she was gone. Brian and I were left alone and astonished. We looked up at Mom's quote displayed above the refrigerator: "Ye are the temple of the living God," a quote from the Bible which gave no indication that we were Mormon.

Ironically, I had snickered when she came in. And she—a cleaning lady, no less—so humble and yet so sure of herself, was like an angel who entered to trumpet hope and promise. We were filled with humility and thanksgiving. Certainly it was another reminder to us that peace and miracles can come when you least expect them.

We never saw her again. (However, her prophetic words did come true—within twelve days I was released to go home.)

VISITORS

Brian tried to keep them to a minimum. Although it was tiring to have visitors, it was a great boost. One day, I received a visit from Karen and Andrea from New Jersey. I was reluctant to see them on account of my appearance.

Brian had them wait in the lounge on 10 West. I was nervous and didn't feel ready. Fearful of their reaction and of "talk" that would go back to New Jersey, nevertheless, I put on my cap and mask, and Brian pushed my machines into the lounge. One look at them and I would know my status. If they looked happy, I would be relieved. If they looked scared, I'd be worried. I couldn't control it. Not seeing anyone sometimes seemed to be the solution. But as we said hello and lightly hugged, I knew things would be okay. They greeted us with baskets of treats, and assured me that everyone in our New Jersey ward was deeply interested in my progress. We discussed our mutual fears of seeing each other.

We laughed about old times and how Andrea accidentally learned of my illness the night she and Gary went to Mieke's for dinner.

Brian insisted that I give them a peek of my bald head. We shared with them our struggles, and I assured them that Brian was taking good care of me.

Then Karen said, "Remember Analisa, when one door closes, another one opens."

I later reflected on this statement on several occasions.

LAST WEEK ON 10 WEST

Sometimes I felt like a guinea pig, yet I continued working hand-in-hand with the doctors, not hesitating to verbalize my symptoms. They were usually receptive. By doing so, I was hopeful that the information might help other patients.

Because the development of bone marrow transplantation is ongoing, we were asked to participate in a research study called "DHPG." The study was designed to evaluate the safety and efficacy of a new drug called ganciclovir for the prevention of serious cytomegalovirus (CMV) infections. The study required patients to administer the "DHPG" drug through an IV five days a week for four months, upon returning home. The patient would either get a placebo or the real drug. Upon completion of the study, it would show which patients improved with or without the drug.

As usual Brian and I were asked to sign consent forms. I skimmed through them, not wanting to know the details. But one paragraph stated that, "based on animal studies and tested in only 600 humans to date," ganciclovir could cause these side effects: decreased white blood count, decreased platelet count, skin rashes, hives, nausea, vomiting, dizziness, bleeding and bruising, irritation of the veins, possible impairment of reproductive ability/sexual function, abnormalities in liver or kidney function, low blood pressure, fainting, headache, anemia, swelling of the body, fever, damage to nerves, loss of hair, perforation or bleeding of the intestine, diarrhea, abdominal pain, damage to the heart muscle, blood in the urine, seizures, psychological changes including confusion, irritability, nightmares, hallucinations, or psychosis, deterioration of mental status, and loss of hearing. In addition, it stated that the study of glanciclovir posed cancer-causing affects, such as tumors in mice, and that the significance of this finding in humans was not yet known.

At this point, we had nothing to lose. We could only hope that the drug would help. Throwing my fate to the wind, we agreed to be pioneers and signed the forms. (We later learned that I was one of eighty-five patients involved in the study, and one of the forty-five to receive the real drug. The results of the study showed that ganciclovir indeed helped in the prevention of CMV infections, and it's now given as part of the routine care for BMT patients.)

During the last week at UCLA, my blood counts increased. Before I knew it, they were preparing to send me home, if I could prove to them that I could eat and learn the DHPG process.

It was a psychological process learning to eat again. I felt childlike. I had absolutely no desire to eat, as I had become accustomed to not chewing and swallowing for weeks. My insides were raw from the radiation, so trying to tackle a tray of food was impossible. Only at certain times of the day, and while under no stress or pressure, could I handle small, easy-to-swallow foods. Although food tasted bland, I didn't entirely lose my taste buds—a side effect that was quite common.

Nurse Kristen spent half a day teaching Anthony and me how to administer the DHPG to ourselves. It was a lengthy process involving the changing of needles, injecting medication into an IV bag, and then hooking the IV to our catheters. With my hands shaky from all the medications, it took real effort and concentration.

While at UCLA, Brian kept in contact with AT&T in search of a job transfer. On one occasion, he went to Mesa, Arizona, for a job interview, and a few days later was offered the position. We were so excited! Although we preferred California, Arizona was good enough. For days, all I could think of was Arizona, and buying a big home with a pool!

Later on, however, his boss advised Brian not to take the job, due to possible downsizing there. Instead, he asked if Brian would consider a quality consultant position in Irvine, California. Not only was quality consulting his area of expertise, but also Orange County was where we dreamed of living. The job would be another miracle!

The last day at UCLA finally came on August 15, 1989. That day, Brian was offered the Irvine position. He was to report to Monterey Park (the East L.A. area) for the first three months. It created an ideal situation, allowing Brian to commute from his parents' home while I convalesced. We could be together. Hopefully, in three months I would be ready for the move to Irvine. We could hardly contain our excitement.

The last day was a happy and busy one. I was glad, yet nervous about leaving. Strangely, it seemed too sudden. My coordination and concentration were poor and I was extremely vulnerable, but my spirits were high. Anthony was going home too. David had been released a few days earlier. Peter and Rick were still there. Peter was slowly improving. He had been there the longest. I'm sure it was hard for him to see others come and go.

My doctors said I had come through well—thirty-five days, to be exact. The nurse carefully unleashed my IV pole, releasing me from my lifeline of the last five weeks. Although it was great not to push a pole around, I felt insecure to go it alone.

Volunteers loaded a wheelchair with cases of the take-home medications. I was given a long list of instructions for my catheter and DHPG. Brian and I were apprehensive about the overwhelming responsibility being placed on us. But if the doctors felt we were ready to go home, we weren't going to argue with them! Kristen warned me that I'd still have many good and bad days ahead.

As I gathered my clothes from the closet, I reflected back on my first day. So much had occurred. I had survived a war zone and made it to the other side of the mountain, with new marrow in my bones. And we were moving to California! So great were our blessings.

Since I wasn't ready to wear my regular clothes, Brian helped me with my sneakers and robe. I reached for my wig and positioned it into place. It felt like sandpaper on my head. The nurses teased me, saying they had gotten used to my skinhead.

Dr. Hart, the intern, came to tell me that my blood counts were normal. Hallelujah! He encouraged me to eat a banana each day for potassium. As I said good-bye to the nurses on the floor, Dr. Champlin arrived. I hugged him and told him I loved him—and thanked him for saving my life.

That same day I was introduced to Kathy Bartoni, the clinical nurse who would follow my DHPG study. She was very friendly and bubbly, and we clicked right from the start. (She would provide countless words of encouragement!) I couldn't help but admire her short sandy-blonde hair. She was adorable, and I wondered how many days it would take for mine to grow that length.

I made my way to Rick's room for a last visit. It was hard to say good-bye to my dearest friend; I felt I was abandoning him. We were all pulling for each other, but we *had* to let go. It was very hard. It was the last time I ever saw him.

I can't say enough about the staff. The vigilant care would continue for the next several months. I was scheduled to see Dr. Champlin once a week at the Bowyer Clinic, located next to the hospital. Also, between clinic appointments, I was to have blood drawn at another location near our home. I had strict orders to call 10 West with *any* problems, especially fevers.

As the escort wheeled me out of the hospital, the smell of car exhaust and smog hit me like a brick. For five weeks I had been in a ventilated, sanitized room. Suddenly, I was subjected to the filth and germs of the world. Brian and my family became overly protective about what I touched and did.

As Brian's dad drove us home to Granada Hills, I became nauseous. The thirty-five-minute ride was more than I could handle. I was glad to get home! The house was decorated with yellow ribbons and balloons.

Everyone was happy, and I was in a state of bliss. We sat on the patio and Mom served us soft drinks and tortilla chips. I nibbled on a chip and was mesmerized by the pretty flowers on their back slope. They had never looked so beautiful! We enjoyed the afternoon, recounting our blessings and the miracles we had received from the beginning. I appreciated *everything*, and was especially glad to finally flush my own toilet again!

My mind darted ahead to the future. Each day, each week, each month that passed from today would take me further into my healing and away from the transplant. Though the next few months would be critical, a month couldn't come soon enough.

That night it felt awkward to sleep in a bed without rails, and with Brian next to me. He kept repeating how happy he was to have me home. His care and patience had been so faithful, loving and tender. I worried about my ability to reciprocate; to regain the physical and emotional happiness we had once shared, and which he deserved. I lay there— fragile, feeble and nervous—but it was so comforting to feel his body next to mine, his big arms around me, and to know that I was home.

HOME AGAIN

I remained in a state of bliss for days, until reality began to sink in. Although content to have crossed the finish line alive and to have "conquered the world," I didn't have the strength to jump up and down about it. The loss of energy was astounding. I was completely dependent upon others. I was weak, feeble, and unsteady. All my physical movements were calculated. Everything appeared to be in slow motion. I had nervous twitches and heart palpitations caused by the medications. Also, I maintained a steady low-grade fever (supposedly normal in my state) that gave me ugly chills. My whole body temperature was off balance. I felt dehydrated and in constant need of water.

My in-laws' tri-level house was gigantic compared to the hospital room I was used to. Brian or his parents often helped me from room to room—many times just helping me get off the sofa. Each day Brian monitored my medications, helped me clean my catheter twice a day, and helped with the DHPG. The DHPG took over an hour to infuse and a half-hour just to hook up. It was several days before we mastered the strict procedure. We agreed that the effort should have earned us some kind of nursing certificate.

The weekend after I got home, we daringly took a drive to Orange County to see the area we would be moving to. Although it was a risky trip, I lay in the back of his parent's car, with pillows, blankets and a jug of water. The traffic was awful. Although I didn't have to do the DHPG on weekends, I had to take eighteen pills of Bactrim instead, along with several other medications. Seeing Orange County gave us a boost. We even checked out apartments. Afterward, at dinner I ordered spaghetti and was proud to eat a sizeable portion. However, Bactrim made me terribly nauseous, and that night it all came up. It was going to be hard keeping food down on the weekends. I was very disappointed that a weekend break from the DHPG wasn't going to be any easier.

The days were full, between tracking my medications and cleaning my catheter. Cyclosporhine (anti-rejection), Leucovorin (anti-fungi), Prednisone (steroids), Bactrim and DHPG were some of the medications I took.

Time passed slowly. Within a couple of weeks after I came home, Alfred was reassigned to serve the remainder of his mission in Corpus Christi, Texas, just as anticipated. He was to leave in October. After three weeks of convalescing, Alfred was eager to resume his mission.

My recovery was very slow. Extremely exhausted, I pushed myself along, trying not to overdo it. I was able to take short trips to the bank, grocery store and pharmacy. Often, just the trip in the car was more than enough. Brian spent much of his time catching up on lost sleep before reporting to work on September 1.

I had been home for three weeks when, against family's wishes, I chose to go to church. The doctors had cautioned me to avoid large crowds, and to wear a mask when in public. It felt awkward putting on a dress after being in pajamas for months. I couldn't wear anything binding like a bra—let alone nylons or heels. I slipped on whatever I could, and off we went.

Wearing a mask, and holding a cup of water in case I burst out in coughs, we sneaked into the back row. What a different world to be among the living again! I marveled how swiftly people moved around, never taking thought of their hearts pounding, or how many steps it took to walk from one side of the room to the other. Where have I been? I mourned to myself. My world was small. I wondered if I'd ever be like them again—perfect, whole and beautiful.

I wanted to cry. I felt like a fish out of water, a prisoner released from a concentration camp. For a moment, I envied everyone coming in and out, children quietly playing with each other in the pews, and a woman holding a baby. I observed the simple physical things, which for me were impossible to do. And I couldn't help but notice women's hair.

My envy, however, turned into gratitude as I thought of the love we had received and continued to receive from friends and family. I was glad to be alive and at church. I didn't have the strength to sing the hymn, so I whispered it.

The talks given at church were often excellent. I was eager and in need of spiritual nourishment. One of the speakers shared a story. He told of the time he had been released from serving a mission. Soon after he came home, his Mission President visited his ward. The young man felt proud of his visit and eager for his Mission President to speak, hoping he would tell the congregation of all the young man's successes. When the President got up to speak, he told everyone that the young man had indeed served an honorable mission. And although he had worked hard and earned a welcome-home party, it didn't excuse him or give him permission to feel proud, high and mighty. He shouldn't feel that his work was over, and that from then on life would be easy. Nor should he sit there thinking he had earned his place in heaven. Instead, the Mission President said that life would get harder, and that because of his knowledge the Lord would expect more from him.

His story left a strong impression on me. I went home fearful that his words were meant for me. Yes, I was home and proud that I had won the race. But would it get harder? And if so, how much more would be expected of me?

Little did I know how many unexpected turns lay ahead.

PART III
UNEXPECTED TURNS

CHAPTER 10
ADJUSTING TO CHANGE

SEPTEMBER 1989

Because of my need for constant care, we alternated our stay between my in-laws and my parents. Fortunately, they lived only fifteen minutes away from each other.

Progress was slow; my energy level was improving at a snail's pace. It was hard to tell if I was getting better. I'd have good and bad days, with many phone calls to 10 West for support. A usual night owl, I now couldn't stay up past 8:00 p.m. I required at least twelve hours of sleep per day, plus naps in-between. The trouble was, I couldn't put my mind to rest. I'd often just lay in bed thinking about everything. Even my dreams seemed to be an aerobic workout.

RASH

Within two weeks after coming home, I began developing a rash on my torso. Dr. Champlin increased my Prednisone, which was in the process of being decreased. Concerned that the rash could either be GVH or an allergic reaction to the eighteen Bactrim pills I was taking on the weekends, he immediately terminated the Bactrim.

"I hate to do this, and lose the protection it gives you, but we've got to get this rash under control," Dr. Champlin said.

As the days passed, the rash spread over my entire body, including my face, ears, and legs. My skin turned beet-red. It didn't itch, but it burned and felt tight—like severe sunburn. It hurt to move or roll over in bed. My only comfort was to sit still. Certainly the rash couldn't get any worse, but it did. Within days it spread to my lips, head and eyelids. I could barely open my mouth to eat. The skin around my mouth and eyes became raw. This went on for several days, until it turned into a dirty charcoal-like color around my face and neck. I was losing my pigmentation and looked like a Dalmatian.

The Prednisone didn't seem to help. I wasn't in any immediate pain, so I didn't complain much. I was told to rub lotion all over my body. But that was just one more heavy chore to handle. My lips gave me the most trouble, since they were chapped and bleeding. (Months later, my mom admitted that when she saw my skin so raw and chapped, she often went into the other room to cry.)

The rash continued to worsen, and Dr. Champlin continued to increase my Prednisone, which gave me a bigger moon face. Between the rash and being bald, I looked like a burn victim and felt like a leper. I avoided any company. It's a wonder I didn't fall apart, seeing what was happening to me. But what was I to do? I had been through so much already. Symptoms would go away as fast as they came. I just had to roll with it. My skin was one more compromise in order to survive.

The following week I went to "clinic." It was common to wait two hours before seeing the doctor. We learned to arrive an hour late to time it just right. Often, we'd run into fellow comrades. We learned that David's transplant didn't take, and they were considering a second transplant. Supposedly, the regimen was less severe; however, the thought of a second one was unimaginable!

At clinic, I was examined thoroughly, and several vials of blood were drawn. The practitioner, Linda, would spend a long time with me, asking questions and documenting my progress. I often had a list of questions, and the staff was good at responding to my needs. They were interested in me, and like family, saw me through thick and thin.

When Dr. Champlin came in, his look of concern was visible. "How are you, Analisa?"

"Fine, I just feel like I'm being eaten alive," I replied.

(Physically I was a mess. My energy level was low; my concentration was poor; my movements were calculated; my eating was at bare minimum; and I had lost a few pounds. In addition, my body temperature was out of whack—I was always stone cold or suddenly extremely hot. Although it was ninety-five degrees outside, I had to wear sweatshirts and jackets to stay warm. My body felt unpredictable and vulnerable, causing great insecurity about my slightest capabilities. Nonetheless, I still answered, "Fine," because I based my wellness on my emotional state. If I could handle it, I was fine. It took a great deal of effort to control the only thing I *could* control, and that was my attitude. They seemed pleased.)

"I'd like to take a biopsy of this to find out what this is," he said, as he examined the red and dark blotches.

Within minutes he was surgically snipping a piece of skin from my torso. As he did so, I asked how the others were doing. I even asked after his family. I learned he had a wife and two daughters. I asked how he ever spent time with them; he was always at the hospital. Sometimes he'd call me at home during off-hours to check on me. I expressed my appreciation for his care.

"How much worse can this rash get?" I asked, half jokingly. I knew I was asking too many questions.

His impatient reply revealed his concern. "I don't know. It can get worse and turn into blood blisters, or spread internally and cause other problems."

I shut up and lay quietly as he finished bandaging me. It was then that I realized that doctors don't know everything, and they have to deal with emotions as well.

"I'm going to increase your Prednisone to 120 mg a day. And I want you to call me in two days, to tell me how you're doing."

"Will that stop it?"

"Let's hope so." He expressed his further concern. "The increase of one drug to help one part of the body can cause serious problems to other parts of the body. This increase of Prednisone might affect your liver and kidneys. Decreasing the Prednisone will have to be done gradually, posing further risks. Still, we've got to get this under control. If you have any problems at all, I want you to page me, okay?" he insisted.

"Okay," I said soberly. Again I expressed my appreciation. I wanted to cry and hug him, like a daughter to a father. My whole life was in his hands. Whatever he said, I did. I was confident in his knowledge. Sometimes I prayed for him, that nothing would happen to him while I was still sick.

Two days later, he called me to get an update on my rash.

"I think it has finally halted the progression. It's not burning as much."

"Good."

"But my vision is blurry. I have trouble seeing things."

"We'll have to start decreasing your Prednisone," he said.

The rash was finally under control. Although other complications arose, I could only focus on the immediate problems at hand. My skin continued to take on a dirty "blotchy" look, becoming excessively dry and scaly. Like a snake shedding its skin, my entire body peeled—for the third time. Every ailment was always in excess of the norm.

Because the transplant caused the inability to sweat or perspire, for months I had no body odor or body moisture, thus further drying my already excessively dry skin. It was a scary sight seeing my face and head turn a scaly white, like cradle cap. I worried that I'd never have normal skin again.

One day, my concerned father-in-law said, "Analisa, why don't you rub Vaseline on yourself?"

"I can't keep up with it, Dad. No amount of lotion is enough. I am so weak; I can barely take care of my catheter and DHPG."

Often I stood in front of the mirror, staring at my dry, rash-ridden face, wondering where my face had gone. I looked like a monster—unrecognizable even to myself.

In total, it took well over a year for the dark marks to finally dissipate. It was never determined whether it was GVH or an allergic reaction to the Bactrim. Still, I went out in public, huffing and puffing as I went. When you're stripped of personal dignity, you find yourself doing things you never thought you would do under normal circumstances. I did it for survival. In public, I hid my hands and wore a scarf to hide the dark blotches. Yet people still stared.

One day while in church, the woman conducting asked my mom to introduce me. I had known this woman for years. Apparently, she didn't recognize me. Afterward, she sorrowfully apologized.

"It's no big deal. I've been through a lot worse," I replied. Others commented on how much I had changed and offered words of encouragement. Some even shed tears. I could feel their love and empathy. All that mattered was that I was alive.

At the end of one church meeting, a woman shared a poem she had written. It summarized my feelings exactly. I added it to my pep list and often read it for comfort.

"Someone In My Corner"
By Barbara Tanner. tannerpoetry.com. Used by permission.

I'm not all I ought to be,
And I see so much that's wrong.

Still the Lord has a place for me,
And in Him the weak can be strong.

`Cause He knows me,
And He knows what I can do.
And He loves me.
It's hard to believe,
But, I know that it's true.

Sometimes, when I start to slide,
Deep inside a voice cries, "Hold on!
Don't let go. Let the spirit guide."
Faith is mine, when all else is gone.

`Cause He knows me,
And He knows what I've been through.
And He loves me.
It's hard to believe,
But, I know that it's true.

There's someone in my corner,
When the whole world walks away.
Someone in my corner,
Let the heartaches come what may.

Someone who believes in me,
And everything that I can be.
There's someone in my corner,
And He's always there for me.

Mountains tall,
I will climb them all.
If I fall, I'll fall on my knees.
Then I'll rise,
Like an eagle flies.
On the wings,
Of God's faith in me.

`Cause He knows me,
And He knows what I can do.
Yes, He loves me.

It's great to believe,
And I know that it's true.

There is someone in my corner,
When the whole world walks away.
Someone in my corner,
Let the heartaches come what may.
Someone who believes in me,
And everything that I can be.
My Savior's in my corner,
And He's always there for me.

Reality continued to slap me in the face. Each day I realized how robbed I was of the slightest abilities.

In awe, I'd watch my mother-in-law make the bed or work in the kitchen. She'd fling the sheets into the air and whip around the bed like a jackrabbit. The daunting task was physically impossible for me, and it made me sad. One never really appreciates the slightest chores until they lose the ability to do them. I felt guilty and worried that she might think of me as a lazy daughter-in-law.

"One of these days you're going to see me make my own bed, and whip around like you, Mom."

"Oh, Analisa, you will. You will," she'd say.

But I had doubts about the return of my full strength. My only desire was to have the energy to physically care for Brian and myself—nothing more.

One day we took a trip to the mall. It was good to get out. As my father in-law tried on some pants, I sat on the floor. When he came out, I couldn't get up—my knees were like spaghetti.

"I've fallen, and I can't get up," I announced.

Dad had to pick me up and put me in a standing position. We chuckled over the stupid commercial, but it was awful to be so weak. The next day I tried a couple of knee bends to strengthen my knees. However, the attempt resulted in pulled muscles, causing me misery for days. Recovery was a continual adjustment of trial and error; progressing two steps forward one day, one giant step back the next, all the while inching along and trying not to overdo it.

Always having had a fear of getting old, I felt like an eighty-year-old! Consequently, I noticed elderly people everywhere. I was envious because many fared much better than me. How did *their* bodies make it to a ripe old age? It's not fair, I thought. Why was I suffering these things, especially in the prime of my life? And what if I didn't recover fully? The prospects were frightening.

I struggled to push away my frustrations. On the one hand, I was grateful for surviving. On the other, I felt bitter and mad, since I still wasn't out of the woods by a long shot. My mind was always racing, not allowing me to relax—not allowing me to get proper sleep. I suffered from nervous little twitches, either in my hand or my whole body, mostly due to the medications. They were very tiresome and annoying.

In September, we learned that dear Rick passed away. I mourned his loss the most. He had had a terrific attitude. We had helped each other much, and were going to go to dinner someday and celebrate our triumph. My heart was full of sadness for him and his family. The news that others were not surviving brought on much guilt and stress. Why them and not me? And would I continue to recover?

Rick was in a better place. I knew it. His death wasn't in vain. Indeed, my fallen comrades had all contributed to the hope and success of future transplant patients.

Nevertheless, each day I plugged along. The mood swings were difficult to control. I'd go through periods of deep sadness, then fleeting moments of joy. I yearned for lasting peace and comfort. I tried going on more errands with family, or taking vitamins to build my endorphins. But obstacles always popped up. On two occasions, Dad had to perform the Heimlich maneuver on me when I nearly choked on the vitamins, so I stopped taking them.

EATING

Everyone was continually after me to eat more. The radiation and chemotherapy had caused temporary damage to my esophagus, so I had no appetite. It was a psychological struggle. Therefore, the environment for eating had to be quiet and non-stressful. Also, my stomach and esophagus had shrunk; hence the vulnerability to choking. I dreaded anyone asking me what I wanted for meals.

"I don't know what I want. Just serve me anything and I'll do my best," I'd tell family.

I put them through much aggravation when at times I eagerly requested an item, only to sit at the table and not be able to eat.

"Why can't you, Analisa?" Brian or his family would ask.

"I just can't. I'm going to throw up if I do." The pressure was frightening and stressful, for I knew I must eat. I was eating out of pure fear, rather than necessity. Certainly I could relate to those who suffer from anorexia or bulimia.

As the weeks passed, my eating improved. A kid's meal from McDonald's was more than enough. Brian would tease me for "overeating," and I believed him. I had no concept of what was too much or too little. I got nicknamed "just a little bit," because every time somebody offered me something, that was always my reply. And, like a child, I frequently got accused of playing with my food instead of eating.

My father-in-law, a naturally slow eater, was always the last one at the table. We chuckled, because I would often look over at his plate for reassurance to know that I wasn't too far behind in finishing. We'd talk for hours after everyone else left. He'd give me much-needed advice, and I would share my concerns.

"Dad, there's so much suffering in the world. I came home with this attitude of "if I can just make it home, then everything is going to be perfect." But I come home and realize the world hasn't stopped for me. Contention still exists, murders still occur, and family and friends are still unhappy for whatever the reason. It's very scary. People *really* need to change. We don't have time for all this."

"I know, honey. This has been a real hard experience for you, for all of us. We're all learning from this trial."

"I think I've got post-traumatic stress. Sometimes I feel deep loneliness."

"You just have to take it slow and work through it. The worst part is over. For heaven's sakes, do you realize what your body has been through? You can't expect to bounce right back into everything you were doing. You've got to give yourself time."

I soaked up his words like a sponge. I needed to hear them over and over again. He was kind, gentle and unselfish. He and Mom were like a model couple, having spent decades immersed in the service of others.

He was a retired Technicolor employee, and she was a homemaker and a volunteer at a local hospital. I could see many of Dad's attributes in Brian.

Living with them during this time of crisis was a godsend. I very much enjoyed their company. They stayed busy, and had their own routine. In the morning, they would run errands and do household projects. At about 2:00 or 3:00 p.m. they would take a nap, and starting at four p.m., Dad would watch the news until dinner was ready. Their routine fit my needs ideally.

Just like watching Mom make the beds, I'd sit on the patio and watch Dad weed the backyard slopes. I marveled at this sixty-five-year-old man maneuvering around the yard so quickly without looking tired. The tables seemed turned. I felt like an old retired person, whose life had taken a turn for the worse, with weakness as my biggest struggle. And although I was basically doing well, I constantly had to push away feelings of sorrow and bitterness.

Alternating back and forth from one set of parents to the other required many adjustments. I love my own parents. They were extremely helpful and encouraging. Yet it was difficult. Under normal circumstances, it would be hard for any adult to live with their parents again, especially while being sick.

My dad was retired, yet struggling financially. Coupled with my illness, this didn't ease the tension in their home. When I was with them, they spent most of their time caring for me and taking me to my appointments. I wanted to help them, but I was forced to close my eyes to their problems, trying to deal with my own.

I wanted to share more happy moments together, but the tension in the house was sometimes more than I could handle. During the first critical months, it was easier to stay at my in-laws, where things were a little more predictable.

TWO STEPS FORWARD, ONE STEP BACK

Just as one problem was taken care of, another one evolved. One day I twisted my ankle while carefully coming down the stairs. My bones were so brittle, someone could practically say "poof" to my face and I would tumble to the ground. I had to be extremely careful not to overdo things. The problem was finding the balance, because just about any activity was too much. I had to listen carefully to my body and work with it, even if my mind and heart wanted to do more.

In September, Brian returned to New Jersey to put the house up for sale. "I'm going to take care of the whole thing. You just concentrate on getting better," he insisted.

I tried not to think of the stress of our cross-country move. Instead, I concentrated on our future home in Orange County. It was going to be heaven!

CHAPTER 11
NIGHT IN AGONY

As the rash came under control, Dr. Champlin decreased my Prednisone levels. Then, one evening in the second week of September, while at my parents' home, I suddenly developed excruciating knee pains. The intense pain brought immediate tears. My mom quickly wrapped my knees in hot towels, but nothing helped. I called 10 West. The nurse suggested Dilaudid, but even my miracle drug didn't quell the pain—it just made me queasy. A few hours later the pain subsided.

The next night at around the same time, the pains started again. My worries increased and I wanted Brian near me. He was still in New Jersey, and I felt uneasy without him. I called 10 West again, but no one had any answers. I continued to have strong hot and cold flashes and pain in my bones and joints. However, the pain in my knees was the worst! No medication helped. Then mysteriously, a few hours later the pains would cease as quickly as they had started.

The next day, September 13, I returned to my in-law's house for the week. With Brian still in New Jersey, I was very nervous about how the evening would go. It turned into "a night in agony." The pain started at about 1:30 a.m. Hesitant to wake up my in-laws, I hobbled downstairs and grabbed the cordless phone, in case I needed to call 10 West. The intense pain traveled down my shins to my ankles and feet. I couldn't tell if it was bone pain or muscular pain. My legs felt like they'd been hacked off at the kneecaps. I paced the floor for relief. I debated calling my parents but fearing that it would scare them, I chose not to. I resolved to sweat the night out alone.

By 3:00 a.m. I could no longer tolerate the pain. I slithered around the bed for relief, all the while praying for the gripping pain to cease. My thoughts became irrational, as I stubbornly refused to wake up my in-laws. I needed to get to UCLA or have an ambulance come. But being so protective of my sleep, I figured the hassle would deprive me further of much needed rest. So I delayed the moment as long as possible.

Minutes passed like hours. I lay in bed, exhausted and delirious. At one point, I envisioned my in-laws finding me dead in the morning, never knowing the cause. Numerous thoughts raced through my mind. Why is this happening? What the hell did this transplant do to me? Am I going to loose my legs? Pain was all too familiar; I've been down this road too many times, I thought. But this was the worst! What price do I have to pay to be healed? I'd rather die right now than live like this. Nevertheless, as the night wore on, I was determined not to disrupt my family—a sort of martyr. Angrily, I gave in to the pain, absorbing every throb melting its way down to my ankles and feet.

Rosemary and Bill were early risers, so I stared at the clock hoping to doze off. The minutes seemed endless. Finally, at 4:30 a.m., I called 10 West. Fran, the night nurse, answered. Panting, I told her what was happening.

"Analisa, if you are in pain, just swallow your pride and wake up your in-laws—they won't care! Your needs are more important. Just do it."

"Okay." I replied obediently.

She stayed on the phone with me for a while. It was comforting. Before we hung up, she made me promise to wake them. But afterward I couldn't bring myself to do it. Although I was close to my in-laws, I had imposed on them enough, and like a child, I feared they would be angry with me for disturbing them.

At 4:45 a.m., I decided to wait fifteen more minutes. In tears, I agonized those final minutes. I could hardly make it to their room.

"Mom, Dad, I'm in a lot of pain. It's my knees again. I've got to go to UCLA right now! Can you please take me? If not, I can call my parents."

Rosemary darted out of bed, as Dad groaned, "Oh no, can't this wait till morning? What time is it?" His words were dreadful.

"No, Dad. I'm so sorry. The pain is killing me," I said tearfully. "I've been sweating this out all night long!"

"Oh honey, you should have just woken us," Rosemary insisted.

"I thought it would go away. But it's worse. I called 10 West and they said to go to the emergency room."

They quickly got ready. The pain was so bad that Dad had to carry me down the stairs and lay me on the floor. We were all frightened and nervous. I wanted Brian so badly. It had been a sleepless night and I feared the exhaustion alone would do me in. They loaded me into the car with pillows and blankets.

The sun was just beginning to rise as Dad got on the freeway. The traffic on the 405 was awful. "Why didn't you get us up earlier, so we could beat the traffic?" Dad remarked.

A rush of anxiety ran through me, and I felt short of breath. Traffic had never crossed my mind! The ride, which normally took thirty-five minutes, took two hours! On the way, the pain began to subside and I fell asleep.

When we got to UCLA the pain was virtually gone. I felt ridiculously stupid! We waited and waited, until finally Dr. Hart came to examine me. Then Dr. Champlin arrived. Strangely, he examined my legs as though knowing he wouldn't find anything wrong. I told him about my horrifying night and was surprised at his lack of concern. Nobody had any explanations. The pain had vanished.

Later, my parents arrived and descended upon me, as concerned as ever. In childlike fashion, I sought their love and comfort. During these critical moments, I felt more comfortable that they be responsible for me, in case something happened in Brian's absence.

"We're going to keep you here a couple more hours and then send you home," Dr. Champlin said.

"You're not going to admit me? What if the pain comes back? I can't have another night like this, Doctor. Please, I need to be here. This is worse than the transplant!" I declared.

"You should be okay," he said, as he wrote up another prescription for Dilaudid.

The ordeal was puzzling. Why such intense pain for several hours during certain times of the night, and now nothing at all? They sent me home, and I went with my parents. I didn't have any more pain the rest of the day, and I was walking around as if nothing had ever happened!

Toward evening, the pain started up again. I was petrified. However, it wasn't as intense or as long lasting. Mom slept with me for support. The next day, Dad set up an intercom system so I could signal for help, as needed.

A few weeks later at clinic, I met another BMT patient and asked him about knee pains. He immediately gave me a look that told me he fully understood the excruciating pain I was talking about. "Yes, but I got mine every morning instead of every night," he said.

"Did the doctors ever give you an explanation?"

"No, they never could. But I spoke to another patient who had her BMT in Seattle. The conclusion was that it was caused by a rapid decrease of steroids in too short a time for the body to adjust."

Bingo, a logical answer! I'd been on 120 mg of Prednisone and Dr. Champlin had decreased my levels rapidly, to ensure no damage to my organs. Finally, the pain could be attributed to something.

I'll never forget the trauma and suffering of that endless night. For months my family gave me a hard time for not waking them up. The pains finally went away. However, for months my bones and joints ached, especially my fingers. I certainly gained an appreciation for those who suffer from any form of arthritis.

BEING BALD

Many times at night I would lie in bed and soothingly rub my head. I felt love for my tattered little body, as though it was separate from my soul. This is me, I thought, rubbing the uneven nubs that were beginning to sprout. It was soft, like baby hair.

Being bald made me feel naked and vulnerable, and made my whole body feel cold. Just like an amputee feels a phantom limb, I felt phantom hair. When putting on a coat, I would instinctively reach up to pull out my hair from underneath, forgetting I had none! It took getting used to. I learned empathy for bald men.

Since my body was stripped of its oils, I did not sweat. It was an awkward, dried-up feeling. Yet when I first came home from the hospital, I would wake up in the middle of the night drenched from night sweats. The doctor said it was the medications.

By the end of September, I began to get the sniffles, so Dr. Champlin put me on an antibiotic. "We've got to nip this in the bud, in case it develops into something worse," he said.

I wondered how I would ever get through the winter without catching something. Even a cold could be fatal. I was always freezing; my body temperature was off balance. The chills continued in varying degrees. I tried to ignore them, figuring they were part of the recovery.

HANGING ON

I relied very much on my in-laws. Rosemary and Bill were solid people—in character and in testimony. I love that about them. They were planning a trip to Philadelphia for two weeks in early October, to see Robin and Craig. I felt uneasy about them leaving. But I tried to assure them, and myself, that I would be fine. It was clear that they needed a vacation.

On the surface, I was pulling through well. But deep down, I felt great despair and sadness looming. The blissful feeling of leaving the hospital had faded, and I had trouble sleeping. Life really hadn't changed. The world hadn't stopped for me. Problems still existed and I didn't see my life getting any easier. Instead, it seemed to be getting harder. Depression was coming on, and I tried to fight it at every turn.

I couldn't watch the news or listen to other people's problems. At times I was even afraid of my own shadow. Although the family was so happy to have me home, I felt great loneliness. Visitors would come and express their love. I couldn't explain my heavy heart. My body felt sick and my soul ached.

I had mixed emotions and was confused. One minute I wanted to jump for joy for surviving, and the next minute I wanted to cry out and release all the pain. There was still a need to hold back, for I was certainly not out of the woods. I remained vulnerable to any kind of setback.

On October 4, Victor called with some bad news. Their best friend, Sandy, with whom we had spent the Fourth of July, had been in a serious car accident. She was in a coma and not expected to survive. If she did, she would remain in a vegetative state for the rest of her life.

The news was horrifying! This beautiful twenty-seven-year-old woman was leaving behind her husband, John, and their three children. How could this happen? In a matter of moments, their lives were forever changed. We felt so sorry for them.

For months I thought about Sandy and how, the night we left Victor's house, we would have given a million dollars to be them! From then on, I vowed *never* to wish to be in another person's shoes, no matter how bad our circumstances were. The transplant was horrendous, *but I had survived* and my prognosis was hopeful. I struggled to concentrate on these blessings, and not on my sorrows, nor anyone else's.

Sandy lived in a nursing home for over a year before finally passing away.

MIEKE'S VISIT

Mieke was coming the first week of October. I very much looked forward to her visit, even though I wasn't quite ready. She was arriving the same week that Brian's parents were leaving for Philadelphia. Mieke was going to take care of me for two days, until Brian returned from New Jersey.

Many events were happening, and I felt uneasy. Just seeing Mieke would be hard enough. How would I entertain her, and would she understand my severe limitations? I pushed away my fears, hoping all would go well.

The week prior, she called from Northern California. Fighting a bad cold, she delayed her trip a few more days. Brian got upset when he heard about her cold.

"Analisa, you can't get sick. If she is not over her cold, she can't come. You can't overdo it," he insisted.

He repeatedly expressed his concerns, until I started to feel sick. Any kind of pressure was too much.

"I'll be okay. We're just going to sit around and talk, and maybe catch a movie." Somehow, I knew it wouldn't be that easy.

On October 7, Brian left for New Jersey. I worried for his safety, and he for mine. Nevertheless, he had to go. On Monday, October 9, Mieke arrived. When the doorbell rang, I nervously took off my cap and put on my wig. In an exerted slow pace, I walked to the entrance hall mirror and adjusted my wig one last time. How would she react to my awful rash? I had warned her, yet I still felt nervous. As I opened the door, she was pulling stuff from her car. One look at each other and we both started crying. We hugged, even though I wasn't allowed to hug anyone. She had been my closest friend, besides Robin. When we left New Jersey, I didn't know if I would ever see her again.

We sat in the living room and talked for hours. I showed her my rash and gave her a peek at my bald head. I shared with her the difficulty and guilt I was having adjusting to real life again, and how hard it was to cope with family and their problems.

She was like a breath of fresh air—a much needed boost. We reminisced about New Jersey and our real estate days.

"Brian will be back on Wednesday, and his parents are leaving at 6:00 a.m. tomorrow. I just need you to take me to clinic tomorrow. I've got to go in for a blood transfusion—I'm a pint low," I chuckled.

"Yeah, that's fine," she said.

That evening, I still felt nervous about being alone without Brian or my in-laws. I did not feel well. It was crucial to get plenty of rest, and already I was feeling overwhelmed. I looked forward to the transfusion. Perhaps it would boost my energy.

The following morning, Brian's parents left at 5:00 a.m. As they loaded the car to leave, I opened the sliding glass door and turned on the balcony light to wave good-bye. Then, I closed the door and slowly made my way to the bathroom, barefoot and half-dressed. The house was cold, and I was freezing. Chills were on the rise, and I was anxious to get back in bed. When I got in bed, I noticed the balcony light still on. But too weak and cold to get up, I decided to wait until later to turn it off.

Suddenly, I heard loud banging at the door, and Dad calling out to let him in. Startled, I jumped out of bed, frantically put on my pants and robe, and ran downstairs, barefoot and bald, as quickly as I could—a physical task which, in my present condition, normally would have taken *several* minutes.

Dad came rushing in. "You left the balcony light on. You forgot to turn it off."

"I'm sorry, Dad. I was going to turn it off." I felt awful!

Finally, after they left, I couldn't sleep at all. My body, a bundle of nerves, couldn't relax. Any minor incident could cause anxiety. Since my best time for sleeping was in the morning, I felt deprived all the more. Finally I dozed off, just as Mieke was getting up to the crisp, cold morning.

It was strange being in the big house with only her, and knowing that my in-laws would be gone for the next two weeks. I was already missing them. It was going to be a busy day. We had to be at UCLA by 10:00 a.m. In addition, I had to take my DHPG medication. However, when I awoke, I felt sick and had terrible chills, a clear sign of a fever. I denied it, thinking that once I got some blood in me I'd be fine.

By the time we got to UCLA, I knew for certain that I was sick. The nurse took my temperature. "You have a high fever, and we can't give you a blood transfusion until it comes down. I'll have to call your doctor. It looks like you're going to be here a while."

As I lay on the gurney, she wrapped me in warm blankets and called the lab to return the unit of blood I was to receive.

A few hours went by and nothing changed. Mieke waited quietly. The chills got stronger and I felt worse. I lay there denying my feelings and determined to will my fever away.

Finally, the nurse came in again. "There's no change, which means an infection is on the rise. Dr. Champlin said that you will have to be admitted."

"I was afraid of this," I replied. "I'm so sorry, Mieke. We were going to have such a nice week together."

"It's okay," she said.

Mieke left to call my parents, and Brian in New Jersey. Brian's biggest fear was that he would leave and I would get sick. Later, Mieke returned and said, "I got a hold of Brian. He was just leaving for Robin's house. He was talking to the neighbors when I called. I hated to break the news to him. He said he had just spent a terrific three days visiting with friends and telling them how well you're doing. He'll be home first thing in the morning."

I lay there in a daze, feeling terribly guilty. When would my body ever kick into gear and feel normal again? It would be another adjustment—all the needles, nurses, and doctors. What could be wrong this time?

CHAPTER 12
RE-ENTERING 10 WEST

Later that afternoon, I was back on 10 West—a real unexpected turn. It had been a long day for Mieke, especially being the only one responsible for me. Months later, she admitted that she had returned to New Jersey pretty shaken up. She had no idea the transplant could be so difficult.

When my dad arrived, the look of concern in his eyes made me worry even more. He and Mieke took a long walk while I got some rest. Later, I asked Mieke how it went.

"Good. We talked a lot. I understand where he's coming from."

In my growing-up years, Dad was always happy and cheerful, full of pep and energy. I relied on him heavily for encouragement and strength. Now, it was obvious he was under a lot of stress. Like a ship taking on water, I could see that he was sinking. But *my* "ship" was also taking on water—way too much water. I felt guilty that I couldn't help. How could I even think about his problems when trying to survive was all I could do?

I lay in bed, concerned for my family and myself. I was anxious for Brian to come home safely.

Finally, Brian arrived and Mieke left, cutting her visit short. I was sorry to see her go. But it was a relief to have Brian back. He helped me take walks again, and we stood at our usual window spot by the elevators.

The fevers persisted.

One day as we stared out the window, I said, "For one and a half months I was free from this 'cell.' Now I'm back again."

"You'll be okay, Ana. Don't worry. The doctors are experts; they know what they're doing," he maintained.

I yearned for the days when I had taken short trips to the bank or the mall. My impatience to be among the living grew stronger. The longer I stayed at UCLA, the slower my recovery. The nurses were nice, but it was different. They didn't spend as much time with me anymore. The doctors were concerned too. They knew all too well that the longer a patient stayed, the chances of survival decreased. They, too, wanted me home.

After being on 10 West for six days and going through a battery of tests, it was determined that I had some kind of fungi infection in the blood. They treated me with antibiotics.

Finally, the fevers subsided, and by Sunday they decided to send me home. The new intern discharging me could hardly explain my diagnosis and the course of action, nor could he answer my questions. My patience grew thin. (At times, I felt more knowledgeable than some of these interns, and that was scary!)

As Brian wheeled me down the corridor and through the parking lot, we both felt great relief to be back among the living!

"Oh Brian, I don't ever want to come back here again. It's just too hard."

"Don't worry. You're not going to, if I can help it. You're going to be fine. We're just going to take it slow and easy."

This unexpected turn pushed my recovery back further, causing many anxieties. The thought of administering the DHPG by myself again was distressing. I also worried about losing weight, since the antibiotics caused so much nausea and my eating was still at a bare minimum. With Brian working, and with my in-laws gone for another week, I was nervous about who would take care of me.

"We'll have to stay at your parent's house," Brian said.

"No. It will be better if I just stay up in Granada Hills."

"You worry too much, Ana," he said, as we drove over the Sepulveda pass into the San Fernando Valley.

We had a quiet Sunday, just the two of us in the old house. It truly felt strange without his parents. Their absence left a big void in me, and the house seemed much too big. I missed the sound of Rosemary banging pots and pans in the kitchen, or watching Dad work in the yard. I worried that I might never see them again. The fall weather brought colder nights and mornings. My body felt fragile, and I thought I would freeze.

We went to bed early and slept in their master bedroom. It alone seemed too immense. It took too many steps to get to the bathroom. I realized how weak I was when, for a moment, I missed 10 West. But, at least I didn't have to push my IV pole around.

I worried about the adjustments of being home. My arms were sore from the needle pricks, and there were no nurses to check on me frequently. I was nervous over the slightest deviation of my routine, and being unable to care for myself added to my insecurities.

With a heavy heart, I struggled to push away bad thoughts. I wanted Brian to hold me. He was my anchor, my lifeline. I moved my arm toward him and gently touched his back, not having the strength to rub it.

"I'd be lost without you Brian," I whispered.

He quickly turned, and as usual, reached for my bald head. "Oh, my little peach fuzz, your head is so soft, I want to lick it," he said, automatically checking my cheeks for fevers.

He had a way of making heavy things light. I was the deep thinker, and he was light-hearted and passive. More than ever, I loved that about him. He was a great listener, too. He could read me like a book and could always tell when something was wrong. He knew how to soothe my worries.

My mind was racing again and my body felt like it was in overdrive. I didn't feel well and yearned for sleeping medication. All I wanted and needed was valuable sleep. I vowed to ask Dr. Champlin for some Ativan at my next appointment. Perhaps by morning I would feel better.

CHAPTER 13
TAKING IT ON THE CHIN

The following morning, October 14, my mom and Jim came over and stayed with me. It started out as a nice, quiet day, even though I felt depression weighing heavily on me. Perhaps it was a form of denial, but I wouldn't allow myself to openly grieve. I was still struggling to hang on, and I needed to conserve every ounce of energy. Therefore, I blamed my anguish and mood swings on the medications.

Jim and Mom took me for a drive around the neighborhood. A few minutes in the car was all I could take. When we got home, Mom asked, "What do you want for lunch?"

Her question brought on immediate stress. Being continually nauseous, I was at a complete loss regarding food.

"I don't know, just anything."

"Analisa, you have to eat," she insisted.

"I know, Mom, I'm working on it. I just can't decide. Whatever you make, I'll try to eat it."

My body despised food. Eating was a chore, an unpleasant experience. It made me jealous watching others eat, envious of how their bodies could function so perfectly.

I went upstairs hoping to get some rest. It was critical to be in a quiet environment. The problem was, I would lay there agitated, my mind racing like a pack of wolves. There was no way to turn off what felt like electrical currents running through my veins and causing my eyes to twitch. Many of the strong drugs—Methadone, Dilaudid, Ativan, Halcion, and Benadryl, to name a few—were still in me. It would probably take months for these drugs to finally dissipate.

That day the hours dragged by, and I longed for Brian to get home. I didn't feel well and my biggest fear was returning to the hospital. Over and over, I reminded myself to go with the flow, listen to my body, follow its lead and don't fight it. This mental process required intense concentration.

A PIVOTAL EVENT

The incident that followed, in retrospect, was not a big deal in and of itself. However, due to my vulnerable childlike state, it was all-consuming and threatened to undermine my recovery.

At about 4:30 p.m. Dad arrived. I heard tension brewing, and my heart raced faster. Dad, in his short-tempered mood, had been like this for quite sometime. In my heightened state of anxiety, any kind of stress was exaggerated far beyond the norm. Knowing the situation would probably turn volatile, I was in no position to deal with their problems, especially at the house of my in-laws, which I considered sacred territory.

In survival mode, I listened and my blood began to boil. Slowly, I made my way to the stairs and stopped halfway.

"What's wrong?" I said, as the adrenalin kicked in.

"Oh, I just can't please everyone. Nobody can decide what to eat. Your mom wants chicken and Jim wants pizza. What do you want?"

His voice made me want to explode as he continued complaining for several minutes. And, although it was a combination of many things, past and present—finally, I could take no more. As I stood in the middle of the stairs, my voice, which for months had been merely a soft whisper, roared back.

"I can't stand this! All I want is peace and quiet. I'm doing everything I can to survive, and all you do is argue. Can't you see I'm FIGHTING FOR MY LIFE? Is this what I'm fighting for? If so, then I don't want to live anymore. Can't you see what you're doing to yourselves?"

They were stunned, and so was I. All the grief and pain that had been bottled up for months came gushing out. I began crying hysterically and gasping for air in between.

"I'm hurting really bad, trying to make it through each hour. Please, you're making me sick."

Dad immediately ran up the stairs to calm me down, but it was too late. The floodgates were open and there was no stopping.

"Please honey, calm down. I'm so sorry! I promise I will never do it again. I should have thought of you. Please stop crying," he pleaded in deep remorse.

"It's everything, not just you. I haven't cried this hard in a long time," I panted.

"It's okay, it's okay...go ahead, let it all out," he said.

The more I thought about how angry I was, the harder I cried.

"Take it easy now…control yourself," he said. "Brian's going to be here in a half-hour, and if he sees you like this he's going to wonder what in the world happened."

Finally, I stopped crying. The physical exertion was more than my body could handle. I felt sick. I looked over at Mom and Jim and they looked horrified. They knew it wasn't their fault.

"Don't tell Brian what happened because he'll be very upset," Dad insisted.

That made me even angrier, but like a confused and vulnerable child I obeyed. "Alright, alright," I said. I quickly concealed my grief so that Brian wouldn't notice.

As the minutes passed, Dad went out to buy dinner, and I went to my room to lie down. My heart was pounding faster than ever and I feared for my life. My world was collapsing, and for the first time I could feel myself slipping—wanting to throw in the towel. I knew it was wrong, but I was desperate. Suddenly, I yearned for my room on 10 West, where nurses checked on me constantly. A place where I had my little space and felt safe and sound.

Brian finally arrived. He walked into the house bursting with love and smiles. He kissed me on both cheeks, as usual, checking for fevers.

"How are you feeling, sweetie?" he said, giving me a big hug.

"Oh…okay," I responded. Inside, I was dying.

"Well, you don't have a fever!" He checked again and turned to everyone. "Isn't it great to have Analisa home again?"

My family nodded, and I cringed. All of us were trying to cover up what had just happened, and my anger was kindled. Brian didn't notice. He put his briefcase down and took off his coat.

Meanwhile, Dad returned and Mom set the table. Before eating we always bless the food. Certainly, none of us was in the mood to pray, and I dreaded whom Brian would ask.

We sat around the table and nobody said a word. The tension was so thick. Still, Brian didn't notice. His face was beaming with joy. Innocently, he looked at each of us, and with all the love in his heart, he said, "I'm so glad you are all here. Isn't it wonderful to have family?"

I wanted to scream! The words stung like needles. With my jaw clenched, I nodded. Everyone nodded.

"I want to say the prayer," he said.

I felt the tears coming fast, as we all bowed our heads.

"Dear Heavenly Father, we are so thankful we can be here with our family, and the love and support we have received from them..."

With that, I started sobbing, and Dad started crying too. Brian quickly finished.

Thinking that his prayer overly touched us, Brian remarked, "Gee, I'm sorry. I'm just so happy you're all here, and that I don't have to drive to UCLA anymore!"

I never felt so horrible in my life, forced to hide my anger. I hardly ate a morsel.

Soon after dinner, Dad insisted that it was time to go, even though Brian pleaded for them to stay.

As we said our good-byes, the look of deep sorrow was evident in their eyes. They looked fearful, worried how this incident would affect me, yet nobody said a word. I couldn't bear to look at them. I just wanted everyone to leave. Brian never caught on.

After they left, we sat and watched TV. My head was spinning and I couldn't concentrate. I found it difficult to breath. The minutes seemed like hours. All I wanted was to feel calm.

"Brian, will you just hold me and talk to me," I whispered. I couldn't bring myself to tell him what had happened, nor did I have the energy to.

He held me close, as he comfortably watched TV. I tried to give hints, but he didn't notice my grief. Instead, he got so wrapped up in the movie that I decided not to worry him. Yet I saw myself at the edge of a cliff, and tonight I had been pushed off. It could have been any situation or person who could have caused it. Unfortunately, it happened to be my dear dad.

We went to bed early, my thoughts still spinning with emotion. My strength was like that of a mosquito. How would I last another night? The plans were that I was to spend the week with my parents. Every hour with them was terribly important, but I was scared. Why was I feeling like I never wanted to see them again? I agonized over my anger and sorrow.

"Brian, I'm nervous," I said.

"About what? You're not going to get sick again?"

"Can you take the day off and be with me?"

"No, I can't. If I could I would, but I have an important meeting in Irvine. I'm taking you to your parents first thing in the morning. That means we'll have to gather all your IV medications and pole into the car around 5:00 a.m."

"I can't do it, Brian. I can't do it," I insisted.

"I'll help you. We'll just bundle you up in blankets and I'll load everything. You just have to get up early."

Naturally, I couldn't sleep a wink. The whole night my body twitched from excessive fatigue, and I continued to have trouble breathing. Nobody knew my personal agony. The room was cold, and so was I, yet my blood felt like it would boil over. I held my head high on the pillow to get some fresh air and prayed for calmness, that I might wake up feeling rejuvenated, but it didn't happen.

The alarm went off, just as it seemed I was starting to doze off. I awoke even more stressed. Brian got ready and then he helped me. I hated being so dependent. I was in an awful dilemma, physically and emotionally.

"I think I need to call the doctor. I'm having trouble breathing," I said.

"Oh, Ana, please don't get sick on me again. You're getting me very worried. You don't have a fever. Besides, you have a clinic appointment today. You definitely need to ask the doctor for some Ativan."

"Okay," I replied.

The morning was too cold to change my clothes. I hardly had the strength to put on my shoes, so Brian did it for me. Tenderly he loaded me into the car, along with my IV pole and medications.

He looked fresh, tall, and handsome in his suit and tie, while I, still in pajamas, felt like a dark, strange creature from another planet. I was weak and freezing. I didn't bother to put on my wig. I felt worlds apart from him, and wondered how he could still love me. It was hard to believe we belonged to each other, or what he had ever seen in me. It made me think of the novel *Jane Eyre*, by Charlotte Bronte, where the husband locks his crazy, demented wife in the attic to hide her from society.

Traffic on the 118 freeway was heavy. I just tried to stay calm. I wanted Brian to drive me directly to UCLA, but there was no way to impose on him now. By the time we got to my parent's house, I was really struggling.

ANALISA MARQUEZ O'RULLIAN

"You'll be okay, Analisa," he said reassuringly. He knew I had become so dependent on him. He was running late and left in a hurry. It killed me to see him go, and he knew it.

I lay down on my parents' bed for a while, but I still couldn't catch my breath. Mom and Dad kept checking on me.

Finally I announced, "I need to see the doctor now. I'm hyperventilating and am dehydrated. I need some Ativan. The sooner I get it, the sooner I can rest."

Very concerned, they quickly helped me into the car.

"Shall I take you to the emergency room or to clinic?" Dad asked. The buildings were right next to each other.

"The emergency room." I needed instant relief.

In a rush, Dad backed his car into a cement column at UCLA. I felt awful, causing my family so many problems.

In the ER my vitals were checked, and then we waited. They finally decided to send me next door, since I was already due for an appointment.

"You don't have a fever and Dr. Champlin will be able to evaluate you just as quickly. I've just called him and they'll be waiting for you," the doctor said.

We lost precious time in the ER and made it to clinic right about the time of my scheduled appointment. What a relief to see Dr. Champlin again! He would take care of me and make things better (so I thought). The nurses quickly came to my aid. They put me in a wheel chair, checked my vitals, and wrapped me in a blanket.

"I feel like I've got electricity running all through my veins," I said to the nurse.

"You're having an anxiety attack. You just feel like jumping out of your skin, don't you?" she asked.

"Oh yes, it feels awful! All I want is sleep. I can't make my body relax. I'm scared."

Finally Dr. Champlin came in. "Analisa! What's wrong?"

"I don't know, I don't know. I feel awful. I need to sleep and relax. I need some Ativan."

He looked puzzled. "Well, we got the results of the last blood tests we did before you left the hospital on Sunday. It looks like your infection didn't go away. We're going to have to put you on some stronger antibiotics again. But we won't have to admit you. We're going to send you home with some oral pills and see how you do first."

"No, I can't go home! I want to stay here. I just need some rest," I insisted. "I'm so thirsty and tired. I just want a good night's sleep."

Troubled, he glanced at the other nurses. "Well, you can get better rest at home than you can in a hospital. Remember how you couldn't wait to get out? We'd much rather have you home on oral antibiotics."

I became irrational and demanded some Ativan. "Can't you give me something?"

"We'll wait and see. Just lay right here for a while and try to be still and relax. We'll see how you do."

He opposed admitting me and instructed the nurse to hook me up to an IV line. "The saline should help you a bit."

Like a drug addict in need of a fix, I again insisted on some sleeping medication.

"We can't give you sleeping pills in the middle of the day, Analisa. Otherwise, you'll sleep all day and be awake all night," Dr. Champlin replied. He wanted me awake to keep an eye on me.

My world was disintegrating and I couldn't understand why they weren't accommodating me. Finally, in all seriousness, I looked at him and said, "Dr. Champlin, if I go home I'm not going to make it. I need to stay here just a couple of days and get some sleep."

The worry on his face was evident. He paused. "Fine, alright. But I can't put you on 10 West—it isn't critical."

"I don't care. I just need to sleep."

"While you're here, we'll give you IV antibiotics for the infection."

I had become non-functional. I was relieved that I wouldn't have to make any decisions, worry about administering my DHPG, or who was going to feed me what.

By late afternoon I was on 4 East, the cancer wing. Dr. Ho was the attending physician. I'll never forget the look on his face when they wheeled me in—it seemed to say, "Oh no, not you too!" Many patients returned with complications. They knew all too well that with each re-admittance, the harder it was for patients to recover. Patients became so dependent on the hospital that they wouldn't want to leave. Part of the recovery included weaning them off this dependency that had been created.

On 4 East I shared a room with two other patients. Fear was present. I falsely believed that if I just got some sleep, the fear would go away. The nurses refused to give me Ativan until the evening. I was confused. They had given me something for every medical problem before. Why not now for my aching soul?

Brian arrived and stayed as long as he could. There was no room for him to spend the night. He, too, was puzzled at my sudden inability to cope, and spoke to the doctors.

In the doctors' eyes, I had a blood infection—likely caused by my catheter. Nevertheless, they were puzzled as to why I was in such emotional distress. In my eyes, for the first time I was dealing with the reality of not only being sick, but the seemingly harsh reality of how my family had inadvertently pushed me over the edge. This incident jeopardized my recovery and I was angry that I had been sworn to secrecy. All this added to my misery.

The doctors' main concern was getting rid of the blood infection, which could easily turn fatal. My main concern was getting rid of the rising fear and despair. There were no miracles on 4 East, and the next few weeks proved to be the hardest yet.

CHAPTER 14
4 EAST

My desire to be back in the hospital was short-lived; I quickly realized the terrible mistake I had made. Because of the bacterial infection, what I thought would be only two days on 4 East turned out to be two weeks, and I blamed myself for being there.

4 East was the pits compared to 10 West. It was busier and noisier due to ongoing construction renovations. Rooms and bathrooms had to be shared with other patients, and there were no showers. Patients had to take sponge baths, or venture out to the one shower stall on the unit floor. I even spotted a cockroach in the bathroom. All this added to my distress. During my two weeks there, I was moved to three different rooms. I also had to adjust to a new set of nurses and doctors.

On 10 West, I always turned the psychologist away. Now I welcomed her. However, her attempts were futile. Nothing she said could comfort me. She asked several questions, trying to figure out what was wrong.

"Are you afraid you're going to get leukemia again?"

"No, that's not it," I said.

I couldn't express myself. I was drowning in self-pity, anger and guilt. I began telling her about the difficult aspects of the transplant.

"Well, I've never had a BMT, so I can't say I know exactly how you feel. I can only imagine," she said.

She didn't know what I was talking about. Not very many did. That's what was so scary about the transplant. I never felt so alone, nor did I have the energy to share my anguish. Where could I begin?

"Maybe you can draw your feelings on paper," she replied. "I could provide you with the materials."

But before she could finish, she realized I was in no condition to hold a pencil, let alone draw. Nothing she said helped and she knew it. With so much emotion penned up, it would take weeks to divulge my grief of all that I had suffered—and weeks I didn't have left.

My grief was so deep on 4 East that when the doctors came in, I could barely talk. It was terribly painful. Like a bubble, my positive attitude had burst.

The ladies from the UCLA Ward continued to visit me: Susan, Leona, and Marney. Even a few young couples from the Westwood Ward came to pledge their support, but nothing seemed to help.

Guilt plagued me as I looked at the faces of family and doctors who were trying so hard to help. The radiation had affected every part of my body; it seemed only natural that there would now be neurological repercussions.

Within a couple of days I was moved to another room. They continued to run several tests to pinpoint the origin of my blood infection. They called in the infectious disease specialist, Dr. Drew Winston. Dr. Ho came in with consent forms to run HIV tests, just in case I had been infected through one of the blood transfusions. All this furthered my anguish. Thankfully, the results came back negative.

My roommate, Mrs. Ortiz, did nothing but cry and moan. Her IV machine would beep frequently and I'd have to call the nurses for her. Her ugly moans, coupled with my anxieties, made each minute insufferable.

I had despised moaners. Why couldn't they control themselves? I had prided myself for months on not groaning and moaning. But now I felt uncontrollable urges. Then, it happened. One day I involuntarily moaned, my body needing to sooth itself. It was not a good sign.

There was no way to relax with a host of people constantly parading through the room. When my roommate began sneezing, I blurted out, "That's it! I'm going to catch pneumonia and die." The problems were mounting, as though everything was turning against me.

During the day I tried to walk the halls at least once. The nurses were nice. They tried to minimize my stress by allowing me to flush my own toilet, without having to measure everything.

Still in sorrow over my family's blowout, I was really in pain. All I knew was that I couldn't tell anyone. Mom and Dad came to visit, but Dad's presence made me nervous. I'm sure he was worried. I dreaded dying in such a state, leaving matters unresolved. Mom quietly stayed for long hours, while Dad left for the day. It worked out well. In the evening, Brian arrived and they would go home.

Dr. Ho asked my parents if they knew what was wrong with me. Dad told him I did not have a history of instability. The doctors were concerned.

Three days after I was admitted, the psychologist returned. This time, I divulged the incident to her, and how I had been sworn to secrecy.

"It's okay, Analisa. Your family has been under a lot of stress. You really need to tell Brian when he comes in tonight." Her words were soothing and I agreed to heed her advice. What a relief! Now I could try to deal with the main issue—getting well.

That evening I related everything to Brian.

"Now I know what's been eating at you!" he said, relieved. "Dr. Ho and I just couldn't figure it out!"

"I thought I was going to die without you ever knowing the truth of what really sent me over the edge!"

He consoled me. Later, when my parents arrived, he talked with Dad and assured him not to fret about the incident. Nothing was ever said about it again.

Meanwhile, I was still hurting. Doubts about surviving were taking over. I couldn't stop grieving as I looked all about me. There were sick people everywhere, and I was one of them.

Mrs. Ortiz moved out and I got another roommate, Shauna. She was another BMT patient in her late thirties, who also had CML. She received her sister's marrow and was one month further out than me. She, too, was struggling emotionally—having been readmitted for the third time. It was difficult to say anything; we were both in such need of comfort. We showed each other pictures of what we used to look like, but it was too hard to talk about the past. We couldn't talk about the future. Who the heck knew where we'd be in three months, or if we could lead productive lives again? So we talked about our present conditions. She was in for stomach GVH and some liver problems; and we were both struggling to eat. She was on steroids, which gave her a big moon face, and she complained about a bump on the back of her neck.

Although curious about each other's problems, we didn't want to hear each other's war stories, for fear they would become self-fulfilling prophecies.

"I want to turn my body in for a new one. Do you know where they're giving them away?" I said, half seriously.

"No, but if I did, I'd turn mine in too," she quietly replied.

We kept our conversations short and simple, agreeing that what we had survived thus far was unspeakable. Oftentimes we just glanced at each other, in hope and in fear. She had lost her pigmentation and was charcoal-colored. She also had a huge mouth sore on her lip. Yet I still felt envious because she was one month further out, and seemed to be faring slightly better. She had more nubs on her head, and besides, she was going home the next day. It was a terrible thing to compare myself, but we all did it, and it easily affected our own progress.

Her husband was very sweet and often talked to me. Married for over ten years, they too did not have children. He had stood by her side faithfully through this entire process.

LOSING FOCUS

The construction, along with the unfamiliarity of the floor, added to my anguish. When the doctors asked, "How are you?" I couldn't answer, "fine" anymore. I felt numb, like when a loved one has died and you want the world to stop while you catch up. Life was slipping away from me, and I didn't want to surrender.

One day, Dr. Ho and the fellow came in and sat at the foot of my bed. The fellow had a clipboard and took notes.

"We're worried about you, Analisa. The hardest part of the transplant is over. You don't have leukemia anymore. You have a serious infection, which we are treating. What do you want us to do for you? How can we help you? We have done all kinds of other tests and there is nothing else we can find wrong, except for this blood infection," Dr. Ho said.

I could hardly utter the words. "I don't know, Doctor. I just can't do this anymore."

He looked worried. "We're going to give you an anti-depressant, Elavil. It will take about a week for you to feel it."

But a week was too long—I'll be dead by then, I thought. Nevertheless, I appreciated their genuine concern.

The nurses brought in magazines, but I couldn't read. Lack of concentration prevented me from watching TV. In addition, the San Francisco earthquake hit that week, toppling freeways and crushing people. It was terrifying to see all the damage. To make matters worse,

Brian had a two-day business meeting in Oakland the following day. There was no way to change it. I worried for his safety, especially given the recent tragedy.

My cup of faith, which once 'runneth over' was now bone-dry! How quickly I had fallen victim to throwing in the towel! I thought back to my days on 10 West, when my vision was sure and my faith unshakable. Now, I was looking into an empty satchel, with no ammunition to fight anymore.

My spirit didn't feel separate from my body anymore, like it did on 10 West. It felt chained. The adversary was screaming at me that there was no chance to survive now, and I was a fool to believe I ever could. Yet deep down, a small whisper was still saying, "Hang on." At times I'd talk out loud to myself for consolation, and to un-clutter my racing mind.

"Trust in the Lord with all thine heart; and lean not unto thine own understanding" (Proverbs 3:5), I'd whisper to myself. I prayed as never before, earnestly pouring my heart out to God.

On 4 East, a wave of fevers and chills continued to attack my frail body and suck up precious energy. All the while, my new marrow fervently labored to make my body its refuge. I couldn't keep track of the medications anymore, and I barely had the strength to use the bathroom. Luckily, I never used a bedpan.

After a short walk or a trip to the bathroom, I'd slump over in my bed, unbelievably weak and unable to adjust my position. So great was my exhaustion that I preferred to sleep uncomfortably. An "I-don't-care-anymore" attitude set in.

"Lord, I'm hanging by threads, there's nothing left. Please help me!" I'd whisper.

The weight of my head and body pushing me against the bed felt like a ton of bricks. It seemed that only a spatula could scrape me off. This is what it's like to die, I thought. I had made too many compromises to my illness—to the point that as long as I was breathing, I felt I was okay. But I wasn't okay anymore. Each night I went to bed convinced I would not wake up in the morning due to exhaustion. And each morning I'd awake, surprised that I was still alive—and, in many ways, disappointed.

My soul yearned to be freed from these mortal chains. Yet I wrestled. Somewhere, I'd gone down a dead end and couldn't find my way back. I began telling Brian that my time for healing had run out.

Tenderly, he would console me and encourage me not to be afraid. He, too, was worn out. "Just hang on. The doctors are doing everything they can."

"I'm giving it my all, Brian. I don't have any more to give."

"Oh Ana, don't talk like this. You're worrying me."

"Only a miracle will get me out of this!" I replied. "I'm sorry, Brian. I'm really, really sorry."

How was I going to climb out of this mess? If I wasn't going to survive, then I wanted to speed up my demise and get it over with!

I began to devise an elaborate plan. I could unplug my IV machine to prevent it from beeping. Next, I could unhook my IV line from the medications. This would cause my blood to back up and drain out of my catheter. I could then drain it into my emesis bucket, which I could place under my bed. It was a demented plan, which I knew I would never carry out! Nevertheless, I was tempted, as each passing day on 4 East grew harder.

GUILT, ANGER AND FEAR

I called it the big "G": Guilt. I felt guilty that many of my comrades were not surviving, and I was angry that I had been brought this far to suffer far beyond my wildest expectations. Then there was fear, tempting me to curse God, or say He didn't exist. Still, I reminded myself to just hold on. My analogy was like walking a tight rope with an enormous weight on my shoulders and soon I'd be squished. I even drew a picture of it. I also worried that the Lord would be angry with me and throw me out onto the "scrap heap"—like the *Trials* story.

Brian came to see me after work each day and relieved my mom. His parents were still in Philadelphia, and not expected to return for several more days. Shauna left, so I had a few nights to myself. Brian, exhausted from work, would stay for hours. Once, he slept in a chair in his suit all night.

Finally, one evening I decided to tell Brian that I didn't want to live anymore. It was heart wrenching. He was worn out by my instability and so was I. I hated being like this!

With my roommate gone, the other bed was empty, so Brian lay down on it. I started to unload my feelings for the hundredth time. I wept as I began telling him how much I loved him and how sorry I was to have come to my decision. I begged his forgiveness. He was always such a good listener. But this time, it was different. When I finished my drawn-out speech, he didn't respond. I turned to look over at him, wondering about his reaction, and he was sound asleep!

At that moment, I chuckled and realized that I was completely alone in this matter, and probably out of line. I stared at the ceiling. "I guess it's just you and me, Lord, to wrestle this out." I could only surmise that I had no right to decide my fate, but that I should suck it up; and that certainly Brian wasn't meant to hear those words.

As the days wore on, I watched a little more TV. I wanted so much to remove the pain—to transform myself into a fixture, or anything. Even the cockroach scurrying across the bathroom floor seemed more fortunate. Brian asked what he could do to help.

"I don't know. Maybe more letters from friends. Funny stuff."

He got on the horn and made some calls. Within a couple of days, more letters arrived with words of encouragement. God bless those good people in New Jersey!

FEVERS

The relentless fevers continued to plague me. Dr. Ho said the blood infection called "fortuitum infection," had most likely been caused by my catheter. Because I was in need of IV medications, they chose not to remove my catheter. They again tackled the infection with strong antibiotics. The medications and Tylenol given for those never-ending fevers caused so much nausea I could barely eat.

After a week, I realized the only way to cope was to tune out. The daily events played out like a suspenseful action drama, etching every scene ever so vividly into my memory. On several occasions I found myself pacing the hall faster than my body could handle. I continually reminded myself to slow down and hold steady. I forgot what it was like to smile or feel happy. I was at rock-bottom, and my moaning increased.

I waited for Mom each day to help me bathe. She would help me push my IV pole into the large shower stall on 4 East. It was a long drawn-out process, since I was slow and needed a great deal of assistance. Sometimes the nurses helped.

One day, I was just finishing when a knock came to the door. "Analisa? Analisa? Are you in there?"

I opened the door and, to my surprise, it was Nickie from 10 West! I painfully cracked a smile.

"Oh, Nickie!" I cried out.

She gave me a half-hug. "I just came down to say hello, and to see how you're doing."

"Oh Nickie, it's really hard! I'm really suffering—look at me!" My rash was still noticeably ugly.

"I know. But you just hang in there, okay?"

"Oh, you've made my day! You're an angel!"

She chuckled. "Look at your nubs; they're starting to come in! I've got to go now," she said, "but you've got to promise me to hang in there!"

"Okay, I will."

Although her visit was brief, it meant the world to me. It was truly my first smile in over a week, causing my cheeks to ache! She'll never know how much it meant, to know that I hadn't been forgotten.

A NEED FOR SELF-ACCEPTANCE

The days on 4 East continued to be difficult, in my quest to gain emotional control. My visions of flowers or lying on the beach were spent. So, I read my pep list over and over again.

Although I could barely hold a pen, I scribbled positive notes to myself to be of good cheer, that there was still a future left for me, and that someday I *would* be well enough to care for myself. Still, the anxiety wouldn't leave. I needed to talk to my dad, in case something happened. I needed him more than ever. I needed his pep talks. Yet, I was in a catch 22 dilemma with him. The pain and guilt were too great.

One afternoon, I stood at the hall window observing the busy world of people below, walking, talking and smiling. To be among the living seemed miles away. I thought back to Karen Smith's saying, "When one door closes another one opens." But, I couldn't look back, no matter how painful it was—not even to 10 West. I must press forward, searching for that open door, a window, a peephole—anything leading to new life and progress.

Although I felt like a speck in the universe, a peon amidst millions of others with needs, I *knew* the Lord knew me and knew my name. Maybe He had just forgotten me for a while. I thought I had God all figured out, but suddenly I knew so very little. In fact, I didn't know anything!

I whispered, "This one's on you, dear God. I'll just try and stay out of your way. Just help me get through this."

I noticed people's clothing. They looked beautiful in their dresses, suits and ties—so full of life and promise. Here I stood in a robe and cap, feeling deprived. Surely I would never be like them again. I was too removed from that life.

Nurse Penny walked by and stopped to see what I was staring at. "Hello," she said.

"Hello," I solemnly replied as I kept staring out the window.

"It's hard, isn't it?"

"I'm just trying to get through each day," I replied.

"Sometimes you have to try and get through each hour, don't you?"

"Yes."

I looked up at her. She couldn't have said it better, and I appreciated her thoughtfulness.

I needed someone to talk to. So I scanned the floor again for allies. The only other patients seemed to be Ron and Joe.

Ron, a nice-looking man in his late twenties, had just been diagnosed with ALL (Acute Lymphocytic Leukemia). His room was across from mine. Sometimes we just stared at each other until one of us would wave.

One day, we sat by the elevators and talked. He was in for his second round of chemo, and a transplant was eminent if he went into remission. He told me that his wife had given birth to their first baby a month ago. Since they lived several hours away, she was unable to come see him. His mother came often. Like two zombies from different planets, we shared the same pain. We both sought encouragement, rather than giving it.

Then there was Joe, who wore a dark blue beanie cap and constantly paced the floor. He had been fighting cancer for years. He was going through chemo again and also waiting for a donor.

As we talked, it was clear they still had a long way to go. I refrained from sharing with them the unpredictability of the BMT process. And, although I wrestled with my own mortality, and even envied those who had died and were out of this misery, I had every reason to count my blessings. My transplant was over with. I just needed to accept my present state, and myself.

Every day the doctors made their rounds. They were my closest allies. Some days they would pull close, other days they would pull back. When they began pulling away, it was devastating. On one occasion

I ran into Kathy Bartoni, who had spent countless hours counseling me and regulating my DHPG levels. She was very caring and really understood BMT patients. Yet this time I felt her pulling away too. How could I blame them? At some point they had to draw the line with their patients.

On 4 East, my life continually flashed before me. I could only think of the story of the man who falls off a cliff and manages to grasp a branch as he's falling. He holds on with all his might and begins praying earnestly. "God, help me, please. Don't let me fall to my death!"

After a while, the clouds part and the voice from heaven asks, "Do you have faith that I can save you?"

The man cries out, "Yes Lord! Yes! Don't let me die!"

The voice replies, "Then let go."

As I thought of this story, I wondered how far I'd have to fall before the Lord would save me, or if He would at all. Perhaps I hadn't truly let go in the BMT process. I was hanging on to my last threads, and it was time to truly let go of my will. Like a candle barely flickering, the storm was blowing me out.

Spiritually, I felt unprepared to die. I told Brian, "It wasn't supposed to happen like this or end this way. It's all wrong! I'm supposed to be at peace. I don't know anything. Why was I getting mixed signals all along?" I asked.

Brian listened with great concern, also feeling puzzled.

"I don't know, Ana. We just have to have faith. You can't give up yet. Think of President Hunter's blessing. We've been through so much. I don't know exactly how you feel. I just know we've come too far."

One day my brother Jim came to see me and gave me some sound advice.

"Jim, I want to turn back time and be normal again. I want to work. I want to eat and sleep, take showers, and go for walks. I want to have goals. I'm going crazy here!"

"I know what you're going through, Ana. You want to turn back time, and wish this all hadn't happened. But, you can't. You can't live in the past." He looked at me squarely and said, "ANA, YOU'VE GOT TO HAVE PATIENCE. YOU CAN'T HAVE IT ALL AT ONCE. PATIENCE IS THE WAY TO RECOVERY!" He even wrote it on a sheet of paper and hung it on the wall.

This was my turning point. His words left a lasting impression that strengthened me. For months we had patiently endured the transplant. Now, we were struggling to endure patience.

After several days of high fevers and strong antibiotics, the fevers finally broke—what a relief! I was sick of the medications, blood tests, transfusions, x-rays and needle pricks. The fevers were monitored closely. Although I had a constant low-grade fever, I could go home after three days, if I didn't spike a "real" fever above 101°F.

Now a veteran patient, I "had it out" with a nurse when she insisted that I was spiking a fever two days before I was to go home. The nurse had taken my temperature and called the intern, who then ordered another ten-days round of antibiotics and blood tests.

In a fury, I argued with her that it was due to Mom's back and leg rubs, which warmed my circulation. Finally, the intern came in. I begged for another chance to prove that I didn't have a fever. They conceded, waited an hour, and took my temperature again. It was within normal range, so they cancelled the antibiotics.

It seemed so easy for them to speedily make decisions affecting my life. I was tired of being a puppet. Toward the end of the two weeks, I changed rooms for the third time. It was calmer, quieter there, except for the yelling and moaning of the patient across the hall.

"Who is that?" I asked Brian.

"It's Garrett (another comrade from 10 West). He's back with shingles. They say it's very painful."

"We're all like yo-yos, aren't we? I hope I don't get them," I said.

We were told that seventy-five percent of the patients got shingles as long as two years post transplant.

My happiest day on 4 East was the day Rosemary and Bill came to see me. I cried like a baby!

"Analisa, we shouldn't have gone out of town. It was a mistake to leave you. We won't do it again until we know you're better," they assured me.

"Oh, Mom and Dad, it's been awful here. I never thought I was going to see you again! I miss our daily routine and naps. Tell me all about your trip. I need to know how wonderful life is out there."

They proceeded to give me a report of their travels. I felt rejuvenated like I hadn't felt in weeks.

Finally, my fevers ceased for three days, and on Saturday, October 28, I was released to go home. Surprised that I had survived; I vowed never to voluntarily admit myself again!

CHAPTER 15
PATIENCE AND MORE PATIENTS

Although glad to be home again, the fear of returning to the hospital remained. So, I repeated Jim's advice to myself; if ever I needed patience, it was now!

My body was beaten-up. I had regressed much. My energy level was still abysmal, and I didn't dare go upstairs unless it was absolutely necessary. When I did, I crawled. The struggle to eat continued. Constantly thirsty, I had to keep a cup of water nearby.

The next day a large package arrived from New Jersey. Dad helped me open it. It was a beautiful quilt made by the young women of the ward. Each square conveyed words of encouragement and love. The soft, fluffy quilt was exactly what I needed to combat those darn chills! I wrapped myself in it and imagined the girls were giving me a big hug.

I was humbled at the loyal support that continued to pour in from friends. My high school friend, Selma, sent me a wonderful story entitled:

Welcome To Holland
by
Emily Perl Kingsley
©1987 by Emily Perl Kingsley. All Rights Reserved. Reprinted by permission of the author.

I am often asked to describe the experience of raising a child with a disability—to try to help people who have not shared that unique experience to understand it, to imagine how it would feel. It's like this...

When you're going to have a baby, it's like planning a fabulous vacation trip—to Italy. You buy a bunch of guide books and make your wonderful plans. The Coliseum. The Michelangelo David. The gondolas in Venice. You may learn some handy phrases in Italian. It's all very exciting.

After months of eager anticipation, the day finally arrives. You pack your bags and off you go. Several hours later, the plane lands. The stewardess comes in and says, "Welcome to Holland."

"Holland?!?" you say. "What do you mean Holland?? I signed up for Italy! I'm supposed to be in Italy. All my life I've dreamed of going to Italy."

But there's been a change in the flight plan. They've landed in Holland, and there you must stay.

The important thing is that they haven't taken you to a horrible, disgusting, filthy place, full of pestilence, famine and disease. It's just a different place.

So you must go out and buy new guide books. And you must learn a whole new language. And you will meet a whole new group of people you would never have met.

It's just a different place. It's slower-paced than Italy, less flashy than Italy. But after you've been there for a while and you catch your breath, you look around...and you begin to notice that Holland has windmills...and Holland has tulips. Holland even has Rembrandts.

But everyone else you know is busy coming and going from Italy... and they're all bragging about what a wonderful time they had there. And for the rest of your life, you will say, "Yes, that's where I was supposed to go. That's what I had planned."

And the pain of that will never, ever, ever, *ever* go away...because the loss of that dream is a very, very significant loss.

But...if you spend your life mourning the fact that you didn't get to Italy, you may never be free to enjoy the very special, the very lovely things...about Holland.

Indeed, "Holland" was a difficult place. Yet I still had hopes to make it back to "Italy."

Selma was coming in a few weeks to attend our ten-year high school reunion. It was obvious I wouldn't make it. I was far too weak. Besides, my hair was still in nubs and growing unevenly. I looked like a dark-brown pigeon that had met up with a power line.

At home, baby chills and low-grade fevers persisted. I resigned myself to the fact that I'd probably live with this discomfort the rest of my life. I took Ativan and Elavil to help me through. However, I preferred Ativan and discontinued Elavil after about a month.

On my second evening home, while watching TV I began to feel a boiling sensation throughout my body. My legs felt numb, as if life was literally being squeezed out of me—like my body was shutting down and dying.

As I wondered what could be wrong this time, I glanced over at Rosemary and Bill. I yearned to be in their shoes. I strained to deny my feelings, demanding normalcy, but my body wouldn't comply. I didn't dare share my concerns. I was too worn out for the attention it would command. The heat persisted to run through my veins like fire. I decided to go to bed. I took my temperature, but it showed the usual low-grade fever. Brian came in to check on me.

"You don't have a fever," he said. "Do you want to call 10 West?"

"No, I don't want to go back to UCLA. I'll be all right. Maybe I just need rest."

He prepared my bedadine solution and alcohol swabs and helped me clean my catheter.

"Well, I'm not going to make my ten-year reunion," I said sadly.

"Oh, don't worry about it. Those reunions are only filled with everyone passing out business cards and bragging about their kids. Remember mine?"

"Yeah, I guess you're right."

"Hey, next week, our Grand Am will be delivered from New Jersey and you'll be able to drive it!"

How I longed to drive again, to have something from home. We talked about our move to Orange County. The cross-country move made me nervous.

"I'm going to take care of the whole thing. You just get well," he insisted.

I felt like a child, as Brian lovingly tucked me into bed and piled the covers high. The way he treated me, I knew he'd make an excellent father. For now, I suppose I was his child. I apologized again, like I had so many times before.

"It's okay, Analisa. I don't mind. You're my wife, we're in this together, and I'll always take care of you."

"Even if I never get better?"

"You will! Either way, I'd still take care of you. Now get some rest; you've got clinic tomorrow."

He kissed me and went back downstairs. By morning the boiling feeling was gone, but I still had chills.

OCTOBER 31, 1989—CLINIC

On Tuesday, Rosemary and Bill took me to UCLA. I was nervous—the last two times I never made it home.

My appointment was scheduled for early afternoon, so I was hopeful that it would go by fast. I wonder if the doctors ever realized how taxing it was for BMT patients to make it through clinic. Well, this day was no different. Luckily, Mom brought along lunch.

In the hall, I ran into Shauna's husband (my comrade from 4 East). He was teary-eyed, and I feared the worst.

Hesitantly he said, "She's being admitted again. She's got GVH of the intestines."

I felt so bad. I didn't know what to say. GVH of the intestines was very serious—the body's way of rejecting the new marrow. It could be mild or severe. In her case, it didn't sound good.

"We'll keep her in our prayers," was all I could say.

Then another bombshell hit. I learned that Peter had passed away, leaving behind a wife and an eleven-year-old son. I had never met anyone as courageous as Peter. He gave it his best to the very end. I worried for my comrades. I worried for myself.

The minute I saw Dr. Champlin, he urgently announced, "We've got to take your catheter out today."

"What, today? Really?"

"Yes, right now! We're going to give you a port-a-catheter on your arm. The nurse will show you how to use it. We've been holding out to see how you'd do, but the infection in your blood is just not going away. And it's the only place where we can pinpoint it." He seemed nervous, but determined.

"Okay, whatever you say," I said, as blood was being drawn from my arm.

My life was in his hands, and he knew it. He called the shots. Sometimes it was evident that he was nervous about having this awesome responsibility. There was no way we BMT patients could survive the first three to six months without their *vigilant* care. I often prayed for their good health and wisdom.

"We're going to do it right here in the office, with local anesthesia. It should only take about twenty minutes," Dr. Champlin remarked.

It's strange how adrenalin kicks in when a sudden change in plan occurs or something is demanded of you. It put me in an electrified mood—an instinctive way of pushing out stress for a later time.

Within minutes I was lying on a table in a small room, waiting for the surgeon. I pondered about my catheter coming out sooner than necessary, and the risks it might pose. Many patients kept their catheters in for up to six months. I couldn't feel it unless I tugged at the tubing. However, it didn't feel natural having something protruding from my chest. For three and a half months it had been my lifeline. Now it was posing fatal threats. The infection gave me nothing but fevers and chills.

After a very long wait, a young, handsome surgeon came in. He was about my age and pleasant to talk to.

"We usually do these in the hospital, but occasionally we remove them here. It should only take a few minutes," he said.

Rosemary stayed with me. What should have taken fifteen minutes took more than an hour. He kept tugging and tugging at my chest, trying to snip and clip the catheter out, but it wouldn't budge. A nurse came in frequently to offer assistance.

"They had trouble putting it in, so it's not surprising it's not coming out," I said as I lay awake.

The minutes passed and he began to perspire in frustration. I was bleeding a lot, so he stopped frequently to apply pressure to my chest. I glanced over at Mom, who was sitting against the wall. She looked squeamish.

What was to be a simple procedure was turning into a bloody scene. At times it hurt, so he gave me more anesthesia and kept apologizing. He even left the room for a few seconds to get more tools. I turned to Mom. "I wonder if he knows what he's doing?"

Mom motioned to me and said, "Shhh." In my condition, I had a habit of saying exactly what was on my mind.

He came back within seconds and apologized again. "I've taken so many of these out and I've never had this problem. This darn thing just won't come out," he said.

To ease the tension a bit, I asked, "While you're snipping and tugging, don't remove my breast, okay?"

"No, I won't," he replied firmly.

"Well, if you take part of it, I'll still have plenty there!" I just had to find humor in all this.

The nurse returned and finally decided to assist. My nerves were wearing thin, as I kept looking over at Mom. Finally, he was able to detach and pull out the long spaghetti-like tubing.

He wiped the sweat off his brow in relief and apologized again. He sopped up the blood, cleaned the area, and patched me up quite well. By now, I was stressed, having gone through what seemed like extensive surgery. Mom looked equally worn out.

Within minutes, two nurses rushed in—each armed with large needles. They, too, had been waiting a long time, and were racing to get to me. One wanted another sample of blood, and another to hook in my port-a-catheter. Linda Genkelman and Dr. Champlin were right behind them, and began asking me questions. I was overwhelmed!

Dr. Champlin, seeing the commotion, asked that one procedure be done at a time. The phlebotomist went first, and had to do it twice to find a good vein. Then the IV nurse shoved a larger needle into my forearm and hooked up my port-a-catheter. Boy, did that hurt! She taped it down, handed me a case of heparin vials, a metal instrument to flush it out in case it clotted, and began instructing me on the intricate caring technique. Mom and I just glared at each other. Everything was happening too fast!

Dr. Champlin said he was putting me on oral antibiotics and gave me instructions. He examined me and regulated all my other medications (Cyclosphorine, steroids, etc.).

By 5:30 p.m., I was the last patient still there. As I stepped out to leave, a nursed stopped me again. "Dr. Champlin needs one more vial of blood."

My eyes welled up immediately. It was my fifth prick! Linda Genkelman, seeing my anxiety, put her arm around me. She could see that I had had enough!

Dr. Champlin came by and apologized for the long day.

I sighed. "As long as I have some Ativan to get me through the night, I think I'll be okay."

He quickly scribbled out another prescription right then and there. They said good-bye and wished me well. Their concern for me was visible.

"Don't hesitate to call if you have *any* problems, or spike any fevers," Dr. Champlin insisted.

"Okay," I said, as we made our way to the elevators.

I glanced at their Halloween decorations. The day's events played out like a horror movie on Halloween night. Only this was real life, and it really was Halloween!

On the way home, the anesthesia began to wear off. I had patches everywhere. My chest ached, my wrist ached, and my arms felt tender from the blood tests.

Mom and Dad felt so sorry for me. I felt bad for the long day. Dad had sat in the lounge for more than four hours.

"I can't believe you had to lay awake on that table while he performed surgery!" Mom remarked.

"I didn't think I'd make it, but at least I'm going home and wasn't admitted," I insisted. That's all I could think of.

"I ought to take off my wig and go trick or treating. Surely, I'd scare the hell out of every one with my dark rash, patches and bald head!"

We all chuckled. I was glad to find humor in my condition. There were many times when the events of this process caused me to shake my head in amazement. When we got home I took some Ativan. How much more would I have to endure? How much more did they expect me to endure?

The next day, the chills started up again. I tried to ignore them. Family members continually asked, "How do you feel?"

"Okay," I replied, although my heart was telling me otherwise.

By the afternoon of the second day, I spiked a high fever. I lay in bed like a zombie, staring at Mom's tastefully decorated walls. With a fever, I was sure to be hospitalized again.

Rosemary came in. "Oh, Analisa, we're so worried for you."

"I know, Mom," I whispered.

"You better call Dr. Champlin."

"I'll wait until Brian gets home, so he can take me in."

When Brian arrived around 7:00 p.m., my fever was 102°F. Reluctantly, I paged Dr. Champlin, and he promptly returned my call.

"You're going to have to be admitted," he said.

"I figured. How about tomorrow morning?"

"No, I can't have you at home like this."

"Can't I just wait? I'll come in first thing in the morning. It's just a fever, and I'm responding to Tylenol every two hours."

"No, we can't afford to have you go into shock and lose you, Analisa. You've come too far. Any one of your organs can begin to shut down. We don't want you to get CMV pneumonia."

I sighed.

"You need an IV. We've really got to get this infection under control. It looks like you'll be in for at least three weeks, with some very strong antibiotics."

"Okay," I moaned. "But no way am I going back to 4 East."

"I can't put you on 10 West because there's no room. I can't give you a private room."

"Please Dr. Champlin, I won't survive if you put me on 4 East. I mean it!" I said emphatically.

"Maybe I can put you on 10 East, but it's quite expensive."

"That's fine."

"Okay, I'll call the ER and tell them you're coming, to speed up the admitting process."

Although I was reluctant to go back, I felt calm—almost happy. This time I could focus on why I had to go in and how long I was expected to stay. Just knowing I wouldn't be on 4 East made *all* the difference!

As usual, the wait in the ER was very long. Several doctors examined me, and each questioned my need to be on 10 East.

Brian and I discussed the cost—two hundred dollars more per day out of our pockets would mean three thousand dollars, should I stay the entire month of November. If ever our savings was meant for emergencies, this was the time to use it.

Finally, by midnight I was back on the tenth floor, overlooking familiar views. Although it was going to be a long stay, we were grateful for the attentiveness of my doctors in managing my care. We felt total confidence in them. Somehow, Dr. Champlin *had* to get emotionally attached to his patients when their lives rested so heavily on his decisions. Still, he remained reserved, zeroing in on my illness and not on me personally. This fortified our trust.

NOVEMBER—10 EAST

On 10 East, I was introduced to the new attending physician for the month, Dr. Stephen Nimer. I felt at ease with him. He was kind, knowledgeable and friendly. The only doctors I felt leery about were the interns. They were like kids, and at times I felt I knew more than they did. The fellow was Dr. Gary Schiller. Brian and I would chuckle, because we'd occasionally refer to them as "Dr. Nightmare" and "Dr. Chiller," even though they were both terrific doctors!

The antibiotics ordered by Dr. Champlin were the strongest available: Amikacin and Immipenen. They caused as much nausea as the chemo and radiation. Immipenen was the worst of the two. Therefore, I was back to throw up sessions. This, along with my never-ending high fevers, made eating impossible.

"Dr. Nimer, if I don't have to worry about eating, I think I can do this. Can you give me TPN (Total Parental Nutrition)?" I begged.

"It's hard on the veins without your catheter. You're going to have to try and eat, even a little bit."

I panicked. "But, I can't hold anything down, and I'm feeling worse each day. Please," I pleaded.

Finally he agreed to give me partial IV nutrition. "But, you can't forget about eating altogether, otherwise you'll have problems later. We need to keep your insides moving."

They didn't understand how awful it was to be throwing up for weeks, even months. It was perpetual, indescribable suffering, physically and emotionally. Nevertheless, I was relieved to get some help.

I was calmer on 10 East. The treatment was more catered. However, I preferred the softer foods of 4 East than the steak and lobster I was being offered.

The fevers were a roller coaster of highs and lows. Still, my body only responded to Tylenol for an hour or two before the temperature would shoot up again. When my fever would rise, a hundred blankets couldn't keep me warm enough!

Chills plagued me twenty-four hours a day. I was freezing cold, yet burning up. They switched me back and forth between ice packs and heating packs. Only a BMT patient can fully understand the misery of having chills.

Olga, my nurse, had a good sense of humor.

"Do I have a fever?" I'd ask. (Again, low-grade fevers of 101°F and under were normal, so I constantly felt lousy.)

"Don't say that "F" word," she'd say in her German accent. She was always smiling.

On November 4, our car arrived from New Jersey. Mom brought in pictures, and I could only hope to someday drive it. For now my future seemed foggy.

On November 6, I spent my twenty-eighth birthday on 10 East. Brian brought in balloons, and the nurses brought in a cake.

The best birthday present was a call from President Hunter. He had heard that I was hospitalized again. Although his call was brief, he assured me that he would again put my name on a special prayer roll, which the Brethren would pray over in the Salt Lake Temple.

Every bit of encouragement helped. My spiritual antennas were on alert again, searching for inspiration and comfort. However, it didn't seem to come fast enough.

MORE TESTS

My condition worsened; I remained suspended in fevers around the clock. More tests were done to see if all my organs were functioning properly, and to pinpoint the infection.

Then, my white count dropped below 1,000, thus sending me back into isolation for several days. Another rash broke out on my legs and was terribly itchy. The original rash covering my body was still very noticeable. It had extended to my legs, and blackened my underarms and the backs of my knees.

One day, after being asked, I became the class project for the dermatology department. Two dozen students filed in to glance at my legs and arms, to observe the condition of the skin after a BMT. My only consolation was that maybe they would learn something.

Every three or four days my port-a-catheter on my wrist had to be changed to a new vein. The painful procedure sometimes took several pricks to get the extra large needle in correctly. This, along with at least two or three additional daily pricks for blood, drove me nuts. Tired of being a pincushion, I cringed each time the phlebotomist came in. At any time they would demand blood. I had no say in the matter.

I tried to establish a daily routine, which included eating. Breakfast was a chore, and usually by dinnertime I would throw it up. However, I was pleased with having started each day with good intentions.

Although several doctors visited me, now including the infectious disease specialist, my world revolved around that one visit by Dr. Nimer. For weeks my condition did not change. "No news is good news," he'd say.

One day, to my delight, Dr. Champlin came in. Occasionally I'd see Dr. Ho. Dr. Champlin assured me that they consulted together daily on my condition. Each still carried "update" cards in their pockets.

After getting out of isolation, I took a walk down 10 West to visit the nurses. They looked surprised to see me still there. They kept their distance, and I tried not to think that they were giving up on me. My mind wanted to play tricks on me. I did my best to "tune out", because reality was too painful.

Anthony was back, and so was Ragen. Anthony came down with chicken pox in October. Doctors said it was a miracle he survived. He even infected one of the nurses. Ragen was also having complications. He caught an eye infection and lost sight in one eye. In our shared struggle for survival, we just observed each other in wonderment.

We also met a woman named Jenny who was in for a second transplant! She thought she was cured from leukemia after her fifth year post transplant. It came back in her sixth year.

"I debated doing it again, but I'm a single mother with a young daughter and I want to be around to raise her," she said.

I admired her courage and couldn't imagine considering a second transplant. She was a tall, attractive woman, and within days she became transformed from the harsh regimen. She lost her pigmentation. My heart went out to her as I often saw her swiftly pacing the halls with her IV machine, almost nervously running to get her health back. She reminded me of myself on 4 East.

VISITORS

I received visits from friends, old and new. I looked forward to Sundays, to receive the sacrament from the UCLA Ward. We became acquainted with two couples. They were students at UCLA. I marveled at their beauty and young love, and it saddened me that at the prime of my life I was being deprived of the joys of married life. I wondered if I would ever be like them again.

Selma flew in from Utah to attend our high school reunion. I warned her not to come see me because I looked awful, but she came anyway, and treated me like normal. It was good to see her and her sister. I was glad I didn't go to my reunion. In my present condition, it would have been difficult to see everyone.

Although Brian worked every day, he continued his faithful support. I was terribly lonely, but unlike on 4 East, I was able to cope with my anxieties. To keep from worrying, on good days, I listened to music. Whitney Houston's "One Moment in Time," or Gloria Estefan's "I Don't Want to Lose You Now," really hit home. I also busied myself with a new address book, transferring addresses. It took much concentration, since my hands were shaky.

The nurses on 10 East were very good. Olga, my favorite, was always teasing me. I was able to enjoy TV more. *Cheers* and *Gilligan's Island* reruns were my favorites. Historical events were also unfolding. From my bed I watched the Iron Curtain fall.

I remember the deep sorrow I felt for the hanging of U.S. hostage, Col. Higgins, in Beirut, Lebanon. I felt empathy for all the hostages. I even had dreams of them. I worried for anyone suffering. It was during this time that President Reagan had brain surgery and half his head was shaved. They showed him waving from the window of his hospital room.

"Well I'm glad I'm not the only one bald," I told Brian.

"At least he "half" understands what it's like!" he quipped.

On our daily walks, I noticed others staring at us. I tried not to let it bother me, but sometimes it did. I wanted to cry out "I AM NORMAL, "I WASN'T ALWAYS LIKE THIS." All I wanted from people was a smile. But very few people, other than the nurses and doctors, looked at me directly. After months of sickness, it was better to ignore how others perceived me. What mattered were the feelings in my heart and how I could cope.

SURGERY—MISTAKES AND BLUNDERS

By the middle of November, despite all efforts, the high fevers persisted. Like a yo-yo, I was being dragged up and down. Finally, they decided to try and clean out the location of my catheter, concluding it was the origin of the fortuitum infection. The surgeons were hesitant, deeming it risky. However, my doctors insisted, as it was their final attempt to clear up this infection that otherwise was going to kill me.

On the morning of November 14, an escort volunteer wheeled me to surgery. I was alone. Brian was at work and my family was due to come in later.

What should have been a twenty-minute procedure turned into a repeat of my clinic appointment on Halloween! Here I lay again, with local anesthesia, hearing the snipping and cutting just inches from my face.

A large clock hung to my right, and I wondered how long it would really take. Being hooked to an IV required frequent trips to the bathroom, so I hoped it would be quick. In addition, I was low on blood, and Olga said I would receive a transfusion as soon as I returned.

As the surgeon cut away, a nurse was busy at the sink on the other side of the large room. I talked to the doctor as he worked. It was my way of calming my nerves; however, he wasn't very pleasant.

"You're bleeding a lot," he said as he kept sponging me off.

"How much longer?" I asked, about forty minutes into it. I wasn't actually sure what all he was doing.

"We're almost done," he said. "Tell me if you feel anything, and I'll give you more anesthesia."

The minutes passed. Occasionally, I'd feel a sting and he'd give me more anesthesia. Time lapsed and I began to worry! More importantly, I worried about getting back to my room to use the bathroom. The rate of my IV drip required me to use the bathroom every fifteen minutes—like clockwork.

Suddenly, I felt an excruciating pain in my chest and instinctively I cried out, "UGGGHHH!!" Warm liquid ran across my chest.

"I just cut an artery!" he declared, as he called to the other nurse. "Can you get Dr. Zucker to come and assist, please?" he said urgently. He quickly administered more anesthesia.

She left, and then returned. "He'll be here in a minute."

She immediately checked my vitals, and kept doing so. Drowsiness came over me, and she engaged me in conversation to keep me awake. Inside, I was mad because I knew what was happening—they *goofed* and I *still* needed to use the bathroom!

The surgeon came in, quickly scrubbed up, and introduced himself to me, while the other young doctor continued applying pressure to my chest. It took several minutes to get the bleeding under control.

"I'm low on blood and due for a transfusion," I managed to say.

Finally, they finished. The new surgeon patched me up. The procedure had lasted more than an hour! I was mad, even in my dazed state. All I could think of was getting to the bathroom. They made me lay still for a while, and then helped me to the wheelchair. Too weak to mention the bathroom, I decided to wait until I got to my room. They parked me out in the hall, where I waited for the escort. The surgeon checked on me again, and apologized once more.

At last, a young escort arrived. Unlike some volunteers, this young man in his teens maneuvered my wheelchair and IV machine well. I could hardly wait to get back to my room!

When we got to 10 East, a passing nurse said, "There you are! We were worried. You've been gone a long time!"

I didn't say a thing. I was so full of liquids I was ready to explode!

When I got to my room, this unusually friendly escort said, "Don't you worry, I'll plug in your machine and get you situated."

"Okay," I replied. "But I think I'll use the bathroom first."

As I stood up, terrible dizziness came over me. "No, I think I'll just sit a minute..." I moved toward the bed, and that's all I remember before passing out.

The next thing I knew, several doctors and nurses were hovering over me in a frenzy! Olga was holding something to my head and yelling, "Speak! Speak! Talk to me, Analisa."

I had fallen and hit my left eye on the bed rail and was bleeding. My bladder released all my liquids. I soaked the sheets, as well as Olga! The young escort had broken my fall, as he saw me go down, and called out to the nurses. An emergency plug was pulled and the staff descended on my room within seconds.

"They cut an artery!" I managed to mumble.

A doctor examined my eyes, and made me read whatever he could get his hands on. He kept repeating, "How many fingers am I holding up?"

My instincts were to get even and shout "two" instead of "three," but I dared not scare them. From my point of view, it was like watching a movie in slow motion. For them, it was panic and chaos. I wanted to get back at everyone for screwing up my day!

They patched my eye with a Band-Aid and Olga stayed to keep a watch on me. She added new sheets to my bed and helped me change. Finally, I received my blood transfusion.

"You gave me the biggest scare, young lady. Don't ever do that again," she exclaimed.

"It was a crazy incident. I could have died from the dumb surgeon's mistake!" I replied.

"They should have known better! They should have sent you back on a stretcher for having kept you so long!" she remarked.

Thoughts ran through my head. What would have happened had I died? What would they have told my family?

Brian later couldn't believe what had happened. Dr. Nimer was also upset and spoke to the surgery personnel.

Afterward, I noticed a blind spot in my left eye. I went through a battery of tests at the Jules Stein Institute next to UCLA. They surmised that due to my suppressed immune system, the force of my eye striking the bed rail probably caused the gelatinous part of the retina to tear away. It could have been much worse. To date I still have the blind spot.

Another incident happened later in the month when a new intern ordered the wrong medication. I didn't like her pushy approach and she wouldn't always answer my questions.

One evening, a nurse came in and handed me eardrops. I insisted that I didn't have an ear infection. I was so upset that I didn't notice the new medication she put into my IV. The following morning, another nurse came in to give me a second dose of "who knows what"!

The doctors always informed me of new medications. It didn't feel right. As I lay in doubt, I began feeling jittery electrical impulses throughout my body. I got out of bed, put on my robe, and pushed my pole to the nurse's station.

The nurse checked my chart, and then checked the levels on my IV. "Everything looks okay," she said. "The intern ordered it. It says here on your chart."

"Please call Dr. Nimer. He would have told me of any new medications." I begged.

She paused. "Okay, I'll check."

Moments later, she got off the phone and immediately unhooked my IV. The medication ordered was a complete mistake! The nurse apologized.

It was unbelievable; who knows what I was getting! The mixture of drugs I was receiving could have been fatal. I never found out what it was.

Brian threw a fit and spoke to Dr. Nimer, who chewed out the intern. That afternoon, Dr. Nimer apologized and said the intern would be in to apologize also. But she never did.

In both situations, I was alone. Had I died, I wondered what explanation they would have given Brian—after all we had been through. I suppose there could have been several reasons for lawsuits, but it was never a consideration. We weren't the type to sue, and we didn't want to make waves. Just getting through this was hard enough. These incidences assured us the importance of always asking questions and staying aware of everything.

PATIENTLY ENDURING—NOVEMBER

By the third week in November, the fevers continued their attack. "We're doing all we can, Analisa. The antibiotics just take time," Dr. Nimer reiterated.

Each day we waited for updates. Several doctors examined me, and due to the strong antibiotics, they often asked if I had yeast infections or trouble urinating. My answer was always no.

Then one day, the fellow and the resident came in and stood on either side of me. "Analisa, we've got to check to see if you have a yeast infection."

"I don't; I'd tell you if I had any problems," I insisted.

They looked at each other, "Well, we need to check anyways, to make sure."

"Fine." I pulled down my panties and said, "There, see?"

Embarrassed, they quickly examined me with their penlights and seemed satisfied. It was humiliating.

Another day, a nurse came in to give me some medication. "How are you doing today, Analisa?"

"Not good. This nausea is doing me in. It's like I'm on a bicycle racing downhill and have lost all control. I'm barely hanging on, bouncing over rocks and heading for a big crash! I can't stop or jump off," I said worriedly.

Brian paused, wondering how to respond. "Well Analisa, just remember you're on a bicycle built for two, and I'm in front, steering!"

We all broke into laughter.

"You both make a great team," she said.

He turned my image of forthcoming disaster into one of hope.

Another image plaguing me was that of walking along a narrow mountain ridge. On both sides were steep drop-offs into rivers below. I was walking along this ridge with millions of other people. No one was allowed to stop and help. Brian was with me, and somehow I had lost my footing. The crowd had to keep moving forward, and I felt life passing me by. Time was running short. Brian, too, would have to move on if I didn't get up fast enough. I was helpless, and disappointed that I had lost my way. Down below I could see the river. If I fell, I would land in the river, where people were waiting in boats to take me to the end. There I'd have to wait to meet Brian again. I could see others sitting in these boats, being carried off. I didn't want to go. I wanted to remain with all the people moving forward. I just needed more time to regain my footing.

Occasionally, Alfred called from Texas. "Alfred, if there's one thing I'd love to inherit from your marrow, it's your *patience*!" I told him. He had recovered well, with only occasional back pain when he exercised.

In late October, Cindy, my sister-in-law, gave birth to their third baby. They named him Brian. In late November, Victor and Cindy brought him into the lobby so I could see him. I wore a mask and sat several feet away. I enjoyed looking at their beautiful baby boy dressed in a little Santa suit.

<u>November 20, 1989</u>—journal entry

Today is four months since I received Alfred's marrow. The healing has been slow and taxing. However, everybody says I'm doing well, considering.

I'm *so* tired lately. I've hardly eaten a thing for three days and I've been throwing up for weeks. Amidst the miracles, we *must* keep pushing forward. I love the Lord and hope He will continue giving us the strength to endure.

The next day, Brian arrived with a gentleman from admissions to notarize papers for the sale of our New Jersey home. They caught me at a bad time. I was so out of it. It seemed ridiculous that they would bring up such a matter at that moment, or that I was expected to sign so many papers.

"I can't do this! There's no way! Can't they just take my word?" I begged Brian.

"No, we've got to air express these papers back today."

Hardly able to hold the pen, I reluctantly scribbled my name on numerous forms. It was an emotional moment to know our house in New Jersey was sold and we were now "homeless."

<u>November 22, 1989</u>—journal entry

Tomorrow is Thanksgiving. I never thought I'd be here for it. We just need to see one more miracle! The nausea is still bad. There's nothing worse than being nauseous *all* the time. Will I ever get the desire to eat again? It's scary to think so. Brian has been very kind. I can't begin to express his dedication. I guess that's what marriage vows are all about. He's continually telling me how much he loves and needs me, and I do the same. We look forward so much to getting our lives back.

GALLIUM TEST—NOVEMBER 20, 1989

I sweated the days out calmly on 10 East; however, I yearned deeply for guidance and inner peace. I needed to know my fate. One day, I verbally prayed for one more miracle; anything or anyone to let me know I was going to be okay; that I was going to be fine—whatever the outcome!

The following day, I was scheduled for a two-day Gallium Test, to pinpoint that darn blood infection. The test involved injecting fluid into the bloodstream, which would attach itself to white blood cells, consequently leading it to any infection in the body.

As usual, an escort wheeled me to the lab. It was an opportunity to leave my room for a while and brush with the world. A nurse injected the fluid, then set me out in the hall for about thirty minutes for it to circulate. The wait seemed endless as I sat in the wheelchair, dressed in a robe and head cap.

After months of illness, I was functioning at bare minimum, becoming numb to the world. I no longer put too much attention on wanting to *be* everyone that walked around me.

Still, as I sat in the hall, observing the activity of people coming and going, there I was, suspended in a holding pattern. "They" were in control of my life, I thought. Feeling old and semi-worthless, I accepted the fact that I couldn't leap out and scurry down the hall like them. It was useless and painful to compare myself anymore. Those that passed hardly looked at me. I vowed that if I ever recovered and passed by someone in a wheelchair, I would always acknowledge their presence, look them in the face, and smile or say hello, rather than looking away.

Finally, a young Filipino man introduced himself as Alex Casasola, the technician. He wheeled me into a small room that had a long white table with a machine over it. Along the wall was a large computer to maneuver the apparatus.

He was friendly and we clicked immediately. He helped me out of my chair, laid me on the table, and then sat in a chair next to me. He looked at my chart. "You seem very young to have leukemia. How old are you?"

"I just turned twenty-eight this month."

We chatted a bit. He was married and had three kids under the age of six.

"Well, tell me about yourself," he said eagerly.

It was unusual to have someone genuinely interested in me. So I slowly began telling him the story of my diagnosis; how Alfred matched, how his vials of blood were sent from Peru; and how he came home to save my life and baptize my parents. I told him about Brian, what a great husband he is. How family and friends throughout the country rallied and prayed for a match. How I couldn't have survived without the letters, cards and prayers. And, that since my diagnosis, we truly had been blessed.

By the time I finished telling him about President Hunter, a glimmer of hope began igniting my heart as I recalled the many miracles *we indeed had experienced.* He listened intently.

"You know, I really feel impressed by what you're telling me," he said. "I really have a good feeling inside my heart."

"Really?" I asked.

His eyes opened wide, and with a very assured look and a warm smile, he touched my shoulder and said, "YOU ARE GOING TO BE JUST FINE!"

"What?" I said, in amazement.

"I really feel it, just listening to you."

Overcome by his conviction, my eyes welled up with tears. "You don't know how much that means to me."

The miracle continued. "I'm going to pray for you," he said. Then he paused. "I don't normally do this, but can I pray for you right now?"

"Yes, that would be fine," I humbly replied.

He quietly closed the door and asked me to repeat after him. He said a beautiful little prayer on my behalf. I was so grateful!

"I seldom ever do such a thing at work, but I just felt the urge so strongly. I know you're a good person, and I couldn't help myself!"

"This means so much to me. You're an answer to my prayers!" I said.

He beamed. He proceeded with the Gallium test. I had to lie very still and quiet while he pulled the large apparatus over me. We chatted between segments. I told him about our church. He said he practiced preaching a little on his own with friends, but didn't belong to any particular denomination. I teasingly told him I would send the missionaries to his house. He said, "Okay."

He owned a small apartment building on Western and Beverly and had just started working at UCLA. He was thinking of moving to San

Bernardino. We had such a nice time talking. I felt like a real person! When he finished, he helped me back into my wheelchair.

For having never met each other, we were like two old friends catching up on lapsed time. I know he felt the same.

"Since we'll repeat this test tomorrow, I promise I'll be here to take care of you. Okay, Analisa?" With a big smile he said, "I'll be looking forward to seeing you."

"Okay, Alex. Me too."

"Take care now."

"Okay," I said.

As the escort wheeled me back to my room, my soul was overjoyed and I was humbled. My prayer had been answered through Alex. I couldn't wait to tell Brian!

The next day I eagerly waited to see Alex. When I got to the lab, another technician was there to assist me.

"Where's Alex?" I asked.

"Who?"

"Alex Casasola, the technician who helped me yesterday."

"Oh, he must be the new guy. I don't know, let me ask around." A few minutes later he returned. "I don't know where he is right now. They must have moved him to another area. He's no longer here."

"Oh," I said. I was so disheartened.

He proceeded with the Gallium test and not much was said. I felt cheated.

I never saw or heard from Alex again. But his face and the sweet prayer he offered on my behalf in that little room will never be forgotten. I have often wondered what happened to him.

The incident with Alex reminded me again that God, in His tender mercies, does place people in our paths to meet our needs. Like many times before, my needs had been met by these "angels".

One day, my nurse came in with a prospective transplant patient named Jasmine. She was a beautiful Persian woman in her mid-thirties, also with CML. The nurse asked Brian and me to talk to her, since she was indecisive about undergoing a transplant.

For the first time, I was giving advice to someone else. She stared at my arms and face, and with fear in her voice asked bluntly, "Am I going to get that ugly rash too?"

"Not everyone gets this rash. I'm hopeful it will go away."

I reinforced the importance of swabbing and exercising every day; taking care of unfinished business; and putting all her faith in God, or whoever she believed in. She was Muslim. By the time we finished talking she was in tears, but determined to go ahead with it. She asked, "Do you think I should do it now, or wait until after the holidays?"

"Enjoy the holidays with your family. Otherwise, it will always be a miserable reminder of the hospital."

Helping someone else made me feel better. (Jasmine went on to have her transplant. She had a few complications, but did quite well—and she never got the ugly rash.)

Meanwhile, Brian and I spent a quiet Thanksgiving. He enjoyed my turkey meal with all the trimmings. I could barely look at his food without heaving. He finally convinced me to take a few bites, but it didn't stay down.

Finally, after months of battling those endless fevers, the antibiotics were successful in killing off the infection.

I was scheduled to go home on November 30. The last days were spent eagerly counting white cells, checking for any fevers, and proving to the nurses that I could eat. It was a wonder, being on such hard medications and with the never-ending fevers that I didn't come down with a secondary infection.

Toward the last week, I was given Pentamidine, a lung inhaler, to aid in preventing a form of pneumonia. The specialist administering it had absolutely no personality. I also had one more bone marrow test, to see how well Alfred's marrow had engrafted. They would be able to tell by seeing his XY chromosomes.

November 30—final journal entry

I go home today exactly four weeks after being admitted for the fourth time. The fevers have finally subsided, and I'm so glad! Things are really coming together.

I'm so grateful this chapter of "hospitals" is over. I won't be coming back anymore! Amidst these tremendous trials, the Lord has been with us, and I feel like I've been tested to the eleventh hour.

Everyone was happy to see us leave UCLA. I had gone full circle—seeing doctors eager to help, to their look of worry that I might not make it, and now happy and relieved that I was going home! They were like family. They knew my body better than I did. Many couldn't help but get attached, including the food servers and cleaning people. Except for those two unfortunate incidents, the staff was excellent. We were glad to leave.

PART IV
THE HEALING

CHAPTER 16
DECEMBER 1989—
GETTING THE YEAR BEHIND US

T he following weeks were extremely difficult. I had to convince myself that I didn't need the hospital or doctors, and that I could make it among the living. I worried about it being December, since December always brought bad news. The possibility of catching infections was still high. Therefore, the possibility of dying in December haunted me. I tried imagining December as a vacation month and that I was in California for the holidays.

PHYSICAL STATE

The first week I suffered from a very stiff neck, probably because I wasn't accustomed to holding my head up. The smallest discomforts posed the greatest discouragement.

As usual, I was functioning at the bare minimum. My body still demanded at least twelve hours of uninterrupted sleep, with naps in between. My skin was excessively dry and scaly. I still had no body odor or ability to sweat; yet strangely, I continued with the night sweats. With a constantly dry mouth, it was imperative that I keep a glass of water near at all times.

I was on high dosages of Prednisone, Cyclosphorine, and other medications, which caused my joints and bones to ache. I felt like an old lady suffering from arthritis.

I appreciated the intense pleasures of smelling fragrances and seeing things of beauty. I even savored fleeting moments of appetite.

EMOTIONAL STATE

It was a struggle to gain a balance between body and spirit. I spent so much energy trying to stay alive that I had forgotten who I was. Childlike, completely vulnerable, and easily frightened, I was prone to anxiety attacks. Sometimes I'd have moments of joy where I wanted to jump up and down, but doing that was impossible.

My concentration level was poor, and I forgot things easily. Struggling to recapture a zest for life, I scribbled out a new pep list. It was a daily task to push myself forward, inch by inch. My vision of leading a normal, productive life seemed obscure and virtually unattainable. One day, I wrote in my journal:

> I've run a marathon in the Olympics, and everyone has been cheering me on. Now that I've reached the finish line all I can do is cry. I feel violated—no longer innocent. Looking around, I feel alone. No one *really* knows what I've been through. Happiness seems foreign, and I've lost track in which direction I am going. Gosh, I have been through hell! I've faced the fire, and now what? I look in the mirror at my poor body—bald and covered with this horrifying rash. I see a burned victim. Who am I? How do I pick my life up and go on? Surely, there must be some recompense for this suffering! I desperately search for self-acceptance and direction to get "back on track." I just want a day without pain. What is it like to be normal? To not feel complete and total exhaustion all the time? To not have to pre-meditate my every move of how I'm going to get up the stairs or across the room?

A big part of me wanted to reject my body and remain angry and bitter. I had survivor's guilt, having watched my comrades fall, yet I praised myself daily for having made it this far. Still, negative thoughts easily cluttered my mind. It sounds egotistical, but I had to remind myself that there was still enough self-love to pull myself out of the depths of sorrow.

Ativan helped a lot. It took the edge off the stress. I took it sparingly. Sometimes I felt guilty, but Kathy Bartoni insisted that I take it as needed.

I also had long talks with my dad. We were able to patch up our falling-out. One afternoon, he helped me take a walk around the back yard.

"I feel so lost, Dad. I'm giving it my all, trying to find my way back," I said.

"I know, sweetheart, I know. Me too," he said softly.

We circled the yard, arm in arm, both of us shedding tears of pain and love. I was so grateful for him. What a relief to know I had not died without making amends.

Each week at clinic, I saw Dr. Champlin and Linda, the nurse practitioner. Linda often came into the waiting room and talked to the families about the healing process. She always spent quality time (up to an hour), and never rushed me through appointments. Her counseling was invaluable.

"You're going to have good and bad days. Physically, it takes about a year or more; emotionally, about two years—three to really feel good again," she'd say.

I continued to be amazed at the excellent care I received from these wonderful people. They examined me thoroughly, wanting to study every detail. Slowly I was being weaned off steroids, and in my struggle to eat again, my weight dropped to 104 pounds. I worried. I didn't want to look emaciated. In the hospital, they didn't allow me to lose weight.

Occasionally Linda would call me at home. Even a year after my transplant, I called her whenever I had problems. She'd talk me through my eating dilemma. There was just no desire. It pained me to see my brothers scarf down their meals. I couldn't drink hot or cold drinks. For the next two years I was a very slow eater, taking up to twenty minutes to eat a small bowl of cereal, or a half a sandwich. Sweets were out of the question.

In December, Dr. Champlin announced that he was leaving UCLA to head the Bone Marrow Transplant Unit at MD Anderson Medical Center in Houston, Texas. He was to leave at the end of January 1990. Although I was sad to see him go, I was glad that he had seen me *all* the way through. I wrote him a thank-you note and wished him great success with future transplant patients. Dr. Champlin will always be special to me!

Dr. Stephen Nimer was now my physician. I really liked him. He and Dr. Ho were both very familiar with my case, and I felt at ease under their excellent care.

SETTING NEW GOALS

During this time of healing, it was crucial to regain my identity and set new goals. I needed to create new, happy memories to replace the painful ones. However, I couldn't picture myself even a month into the future. I lived hour by hour; hoping time would do its miracle, ease the burden, and help me see clearly.

I watched Rosemary send out Christmas cards and wrap presents. She helped me gather the materials so I could write a generic Christmas letter to family and friends.

She took me on small errands. I couldn't handle driving more than two or three miles before feeling panic-stricken. I preferred to stay at home, where I felt safe with my surroundings.

Slowly I improved, and was taking trips to the market with them again. I was so thrilled the first time I walked around the perimeter of a grocery store. I knew I was on the rebound!

Oftentimes while at the mall, a store, or somebody's house, I'd suddenly have the "fight or flight" impulse. I would get so nervous that I wanted to scream or run. I guess it was my body's way of relieving stress. It was a constant trial and error, searching for physical and emotional balance. Sometimes, I'd want to do something, but when I went to do it or eat it, I couldn't.

My parents often picked me up during the day, to relieve Rosemary and Bill. They would take me on drives around the Valley. Later, Brian would pick me up after his workday.

As the year came to an end, we spent a quiet Christmas. We watched *It's A Wonderful Life* and I cried all the way through. I could identify completely with George Bailey; feeling his desperation, realizing his individual worth, and then finally feeling gratitude and humility as his friends rallied on his behalf. I, too, desperately wanted "to live again"!

On New Year's Eve, as family members danced and rang in the New Year, Brian and I retired to bed early, contemplating what the new decade would bring us. We couldn't wait to get the year 1989, and the decade behind us!

CHAPTER 17
A NEW YEAR, A NEW LIFE, A NEW BEGINNING

In January, I started driving again, and within a week I got a speeding ticket near my in-law's house. Ironically, I had warned others about the officer at that intersection. As he questioned my New Jersey license, I explained to him my BMT, hoping sympathy would get me out of it, but it didn't work. (IT'S THE ONLY TIME I EVER USED MY BMT TO SEEK SOMEBODY ELSE'S PITY!) Overall, it's a good thing I got the ticket, since my reflexes were still sluggish. Thereafter, I drove more cautiously.

One beautiful afternoon, Jim, Mom and I took a wonderful drive to Lake Piru, an hour north of Los Angeles. The outings helped.

In January, Brian and I received a letter from New Jersey, containing our 1989 resolutions we had made the previous New Year's Eve at the Bartholomew's. My resolutions were short—to get my health back to normal. I was glad to be headed in that direction.

Since Brian's office was moving to Irvine in February, it was time to house-hunt. I was walking a bit more, and each weekend we took trips to South Orange County. During our expeditions we had to be extra cautious about sanitary conditions. Also, when touring two-story houses, Brian would have to push me up the stairs.

I marveled at the foliage lacing the winding roads of South Orange County. The first few trips we stayed at the Marriott. In the evening, Brian would bring back food so that I could eat in a non-stressful environment. At restaurants, one meal was plenty for both of us. Later, as I became more courageous, I scanned the children's menus. I could only nibble on enough to keep me alive.

Finally, after several trips, we found a place in Lake Forest. It was bright and cheery, with lots of windows. It was the height of the real estate market—taking three offers to come to a purchase agreement. Finally, we moved in on March 8.

I started venturing out more without my wig. Around the house I seldom wore it; I either wore a scarf, a cap, or nothing at all. Brian couldn't keep his hands off my nubs. Had it not been for the awful rash, I'd have gone without my wig sooner. Whenever someone came to the house unexpectedly, everyone scrambled for my wig. It was hilarious. The wig softened my rash and moon face, and I preferred not to frighten people.

Still, it saddened me each day to look in the mirror. I could only hope to someday have my normal face back. My hair was very fine and growing unevenly. Some patients' hair grew back a whole new color, or curly instead of straight. My hair came back the same, just fuller and wavier. By the end of January, it needed shaping. Jackie, our cousin, offered to cut it. There was always a first for everything after the transplant.

PRESIDENT HUNTER'S VISIT AND SOCIAL OUTINGS

On January 20, 1990, six months post-transplant, we attended a special regional church meeting at the Shrine Auditorium in Los Angeles. President Hunter was scheduled to speak. After the meeting we went up to greet him. He was thrilled to see us. It was a wonderful, quick reunion. We thanked him for everything!

The following week, we attended a retirement party in Long Beach for Brian's manager. Brian looked handsome in his suit and tie. I was nervous about going, since it was my first social outing. Brian was eager for me to meet his co-workers. I felt out of place to be among such happy and healthy corporate people.

As the tributes were made to the retiring manager, slides were shown of all her accomplishments, to the song "The Wind Beneath My Wings" by Bette Midler. Instinctively, I replaced her slides with images of Brian—holding me every time I threw up, shaving my head, applying lotion to my ravaged skin, wiping my feverish face, learning the IV infusions, and quietly listening to my every fear. He was the greatest in my eyes! And no corporate accomplishment could ever come close to the genuine service he rendered to me. He was the one needing recognition tonight! Even at that moment, when I still looked ugly and felt completely inadequate, he was proud to have me with him in public. The magnitude of his love and selflessness still overwhelmed me.

In February, in a hurry to get into the bank before it closed, I leaped forward and, unthinkingly, took four running steps. I was so excited that I couldn't wait to tell everyone! Since the transplant, my wobbly legs and knees had caused every movement to be calculated; otherwise, I could really get hurt.

Later that month, Robin and Craig arrived from Pennsylvania. Rosemary put out her usual bounteous spread of food and invited all the relatives. Craig and Robin invited me to the Magic Castle, in Hollywood. It was my second outing, and a terrific boost, but I could hardly eat a morsel. On the way home we conversed about the night and the "Hollywood crowd." Robin and I ran into Liza Minelli in the ladies room.

To show my appreciation, I bought Craig a souvenir shirt. I surprised him by having him magically pull it out of my suit jacket. It was a wonderful evening and great to laugh again; a sure sign that healing was taking place.

OUR NEW HOME

In March, we moved into our new home. With my health slowly improving, the timing could not have come sooner. It was a thrill to see the moving van arrive and unload our belongings. As I started sifting through boxes, the thought of Stella was the first thing that came to mind. For the first time in nine months I felt her presence. An overwhelming feeling of love came over me, as though she was whispering, "Congratulations Ana; you made it home!"

Tears filled my eyes. Her example had paved the way for me to handle my crisis. I recalled my last day in New Jersey when her favorite song "Who Loves You" played on the radio. Suddenly, I had to find that tape and listen to it one more time. I searched until I found it. By the end of the day, Brian hooked up the stereo. It was a very happy day.

The most shocking moment came when I discovered how many clothes I owned. I was embarrassed to open box after box of dresses, shoes, and belts—nothing of real lasting significance. For months, I had lived in pajamas and just a few outfits. I was ashamed, and troubled that I had placed so much value, time and money on trivial things. Certainly my time and means could have been spent on more worthy causes.

The only thing mattering now was that Brian and I were alive and together. Such was our content that if we had been asked to live in a cracker-box house, it would have sufficed. The greatest joy came when I finally slept in my own bed! I slept the best I had in months.

Lake Forest was beautiful, everything we could have hoped for. Even my favorite grocery store, Albertson's, was nearby.

The days passed slowly as I struggled to unpack. Brian did all the housework while I did the bare minimum. It was hard to be alone during the day. I unpacked a bit and took discovery drives to keep busy. My family came often to help.

Eating continued to be a problem. It was hard to swallow even the smallest foods. It also took months for the baby chills to subside. I suffered hot flashes, heart flutters and mood swings—very happy one moment, then very sad the next.

Around the end of March, Rosemary and Bill came. Mom handed me a newspaper clipping from the *Los Angeles Times*. David Saltzman, my valiant comrade on 10 West, had died earlier in the month, just short of his twenty-third birthday.

A beautiful tribute was written about this young, talented Yale graduate, who had touched the lives of so many, including us. David, in his heroic struggles at one point, wrote this stanza for the children's book *The Jester Has Lost His Jingle* that he was writing and illustrating when he was diagnosed with Hodgkin's disease:

"Whenever I feel like crying,
I smile hard instead!
I turn my sadness upside down
And stand it on its head!

When I get sad or lonesome,
Or when I get depressed,
That's when I sing my loudest
And dance my very best!" ©

©Copyright 1995 by The Jester Co., Inc. Reprinted With Permission. All Rights Reserved.
(*The Jester Has Lost His Jingle* was published by David's mother, Barbara, his father, Joe, and brother, Michael, in 1995. It became a *New York Times* bestseller. Inspired by *The Jester Has Lost His Jingle*

and David's life, the Saltzman family founded The Jester & Pharley Phund in 2000. The charitable organization (www.thejester.org) helps ill and special-needs children and literacy, providing copies of David's uplifting book for young cancer patients across the country.)

I deeply mourned David's loss and will always treasure the notes we passed to each other. I contemplated why "good people" died young— Stella, David, Rick, and so many others. They had so much to offer. I realized the Lord works through so many of us. We are all a small thread of life, each having our own tasks to accomplish, and no one person doing it all.

A part of me feels we have it all backwards—*they* are the lucky ones. Perhaps they're feeling sorry for *me*. I still remain here, having to pass through life's multitude of challenges. For a long time, Brian and I discussed life and death. At times we wished we could die, so that there would be no more struggles or decisions to make.

In contemplating our mortality, we can only find comfort in a loving God. Someday we will learn the answers to all the hard questions. Meanwhile, life must go on.

My clinic appointments were cut back to once a month, and the doctors were pleased with my progress. My face, mouth and eyelids remained raw and itchy. I couldn't stop scratching my forearms, where I had received all my needle pricks. Linda said I would have scars if I didn't stop scratching. Dr. Nimer referred me to a dermatologist, to rule out skin cancer. Upon examination, it was determined to be a mild form of GVH. Dr. Nimer insisted a little GVH was good. The rest of my "leopard marks" slowly faded. However, my lips remained purple and never regained their healthy pink color. Thank goodness for lipstick! I couldn't complain. Physically, I was doing well, in comparison to how I had been.

APRIL 1990

On April 16, I had another clinic appointment. Dr. Nimer encouraged us to visit the nurses on 10 West. They always needed to see patients who were doing well. It was equally important for us to see them.

Nurse Fran tearfully disclosed that Jenny had passed away not long after we left. "She was very special to us," she said.

"Gosh, it seems like the survival rate is only about thirty percent," Brian said. "How are patients on the floor doing?"

"Okay. Well, you know it's hard. But it's so good to see you," she said, as she wiped her tears.

Dorinda came down the hall and we hugged. We asked how Anthony, Jasmine, and Ragen were doing. Ragen had returned, but was hanging in there. Anthony was home and doing well. Jasmine had returned with CMV pneumonia, but had pulled through it.

It was nice to see the nurses, but feeling queasy, I couldn't stay. On subsequent visits, sometimes we were asked to visit patients. It was helpful to talk to them and offer encouragement.

The next day we attended an AT&T celebration at which Academy Award-winner Cliff Robertson, the voice of AT&T, was in attendance. Interestingly, it was the second day in a row that we had met an Academy Award-winner. (The first declined to be mentioned.)

It's not every day that one runs into an actor with such huge accomplishments, let alone two days in a row. Brian was so impressed with each of them that I couldn't help but insist that *he* deserved his own award, for the faithful and tender care he had given me. It sparked a big discussion on what truly is "success." Certainly, nothing could compare to the Herculean effort of going through a bone marrow transplant—or the families that faithfully supported the patient. Surely, these unnoticed and unrecognized heroes deserved their own medals of honor.

CHAPTER 18
LOOKING BACK, LOOKING FORWARD

Not long after moving into our new home, we sat on our bed and listened to the tape and read the letter I had written to Brian the day we left New Jersey. It was bittersweet as we hugged and thought how easily different the outcome could have been. We never looked at it again. This was now a new beginning, a new life!

In May I took my last doses of Cyclosphorine and steroids! Some patients had to be on anti-rejection medication for life.

Emotionally, I was still very vulnerable. I had trouble sleeping, and I had nightmares. Ativan, my "wonder drug," helped. I didn't worry about getting leukemia again; I worried about complications from all the treatments.

I felt a terrible loneliness and insecurity, and worlds apart from life's mainstream. No one understood what I had gone through. On outings, I observed others doing things I couldn't do as well, such as walking, exercising or lifting a child.

Fatigue weighed the heaviest on my chest. I was constantly short of breath. I didn't know whether I needed to exercise or rest. The saying "When you rest, you rust" worried me. So I tried to stay busy. Luckily, I could drive. I'd frequent the mall to walk a bit. But my eyes automatically focused on the senior citizens from the nearby Leisure World. Sadly, I could easily be counted among them—taking several rests on the benches, only I was still huffing and puffing.

I pasted notes on the bathroom mirror to "be of good cheer," that I *could* go on to live a happy normal life, and that someday I would be able to write about it. One read: "I've earned it, I'm going to do it, and I *can make* it happen!"

At church we were warmly welcomed into our new ward. Within two months, Brian was asked to be a counselor to the Bishop. By August, I was called to teach Sunday School. It was good to serve again. My new visiting teachers, Monique and Ann, came regularly, and I appreciated our new friendship. Ann had three children and Monique had just had her first baby. Oftentimes, I pondered how different our lives had been during the previous year.

REGAINING ZEST

As I healed, life didn't seem so magnified anymore. People weren't as beautiful or as perfect as I had thought. And every time I shared my experience with someone, it helped ease my own sorrows.

Physically, I knew I was getting better when one night I awoke at 3:00 a.m. totally famished. My body was finally craving food! I went downstairs and had a big bowl of cereal. For months, my appetite was unpredictable, but now my body was responding.

Rosemary said she distinctly noticed I was getting better when one day my voice changed back to normal. For months, I had whispered to conserve energy.

By May of 1990, my personal analogy was that of a deer grazing in green pasture, having narrowly escaped the woods. Earnestly I prayed for peace, strength, and time to heal before life's next calamity.

For months, even years after my transplant, I contemplated the strength it took to survive, what it meant now that it was "over." It was several months before I could look at the pictures Brian took at UCLA, or the boxes of letters from friends. One day while thumbing through some papers, I came across two letters written by Brian during my hospitalization. They were written in German; from what I gathered, they were two prayers beseeching the Lord for my survival.

During the healing, I wrote in my journal:

At what point do we stop fighting? Is it materialistic to want to survive? True spirituality makes me want to give up. Yet, I have fought hard to be where I am today. If I am going to be here for a while, then I want to enjoy life.

I want to do totally fun things; where there is no room for anything else. It's "now or never." If I have endured the most excruciating pain, then I will allow myself to experience the most exquisite pleasures. Savoring the littlest joys, like taking a walk on the beach, driving with the radio on, or eating a cheeseburger and knowing it will be digested!

Now that I have survived, I sometimes feel an incredible exhilaration. It's important to enjoy life to the fullest. I will explore every opportunity big or small, as long as it's within our means.

I felt a need to write, to soothe my aching heart and release my fears. Life's dreams took on more meaning. I was more committed to seeing them come true—writing a book, having a family, learning to play the piano, and turning my A.A. degree into a bachelor's.

Although I enjoyed writing, at times it was difficult to open the wounds, which were still healing. One day while feeling particularly down, and doubting whether to continue writing, I lay down on the bed and opened up the Bible for direction. Haphazardly, I turned to the first highlighted verse and read:

"Trust in the Lord with all thine heart; and lean not unto thine own understanding. In all thy ways acknowledge him, and he shall direct thy paths."

I then continued reading the non-highlighted portion:

"Be not wise in thine own eyes: fear the Lord, and depart from evil. It shall be health to thy navel, and marrow to thy bones." (Proverbs 3:5-8)

I was so excited that I immediately called Brian. It was as if the scripture had been written especially for me! I knew I must continue writing.

In May, Mieke came for a short visit. I showed off my new hair, along with a few grays that Dr. Champlin said I had earned!

In September, we treated Brian's parents with a trip to Hawaii. It was a goal we had made. As long as I walked slowly and paced myself, I was able to get around. In Kauai, I briefly swam in the ocean, and Brian and I took a tour around the island in a prop-plane.

In October, we returned to New Jersey. It was an emotional moment to address our friends of the North Branch Ward, and thank them for their support. They threw a wonderful party for us. Some said that their children were still praying for us. We also drove to our old house on Bree Court, took pictures, and reflected on our last day there.

One day, I rode the train into New York with Mieke. While she worked, I walked around Times Square. We ate lunch at Rockefeller Center, and although the day was rejuvenating, I had to take a nap in her lunchroom.

In Pennsylvania, Robin and I stayed up and reminisced about everything; laughing and talking like old times. I was so grateful for Robin. Between her and Mary (Brian's brother's wife), I had the best sisters-in-laws!

At Newark Airport, while waiting for our flight back to Los Angeles, we recapped how great it had been to see everyone. Suddenly, an overwhelming feeling of sadness came over me. This would happen often—unexpected flashbacks of pain and suffering.

"Brian, I don't like where I'm at; I can't believe where I've been; and I can't imagine where I'm going," I blurted out.

"I guess it's all a part of healing," he replied. "You've come a long way, baby. Sometimes at work, I'll be very busy and suddenly I'll think of UCLA, and how hard it was to go there every day and see you so sick; each day wondering and praying when you'd come home. I can't believe you made it. We are so blessed. We have so much to be thankful for!"

"Our needs were great, and He met them, all of them," I admitted.

Sometimes, looking back at the enormity of the BMT process, I want to crumble in fear, and simultaneously I want to fall to my knees in heartfelt gratitude for the way things turned out.

Time slowly did its miracle. Day by day my energy improved. Oftentimes I overdid it and paid the price by having to lie in bed for a few days. Slowly, my eating improved. It took a long time to enjoy cold or hot drinks, or to be able to guzzle a glass of water. My taste for sweets lay dormant for over a year. I also had to chew well and take my time; otherwise, I'd start choking.

In August, Brian and I went to the DMV to register our cars. I was delighted to turn in my New Jersey plates for ones that better described us—4EVRUNI ("Forever You and I").

ALFRED RETURNS

On October 30, 1990, Alfred returned from his Spanish-speaking mission in Corpus Christi, Texas. As his plane rolled in, our family eagerly held up the same posters we used when he arrived the first time. We were happy for his safe return. To our surprise, Alfred had gained about twenty-five pounds since the last time we had seen him. Everyone teased him. I was grateful to greet the brother who had saved my life.

"How's my marrow, Ana?" he said.

"Great! Thanks to you, Alfred! I will always be indebted to you, hermano," I replied.

A few days later he was officially released as a missionary. After his release, I turned to him and said, "Well, Alfred, you're released, but your missionary marrow in my bones will never be! A part of you will *always* be a missionary."

It was an exciting time for our family. Just two weeks later, Jim left for his mission to Guatemala. We accompanied him to Utah to see him embark on this worthy cause.

In the spring of 1991, I got my California Real Estate License. As my energy increased, I took a piano class in the fall at the local college. I was healing well, but still had trouble sleeping. I couldn't handle any type of stress. For the first few years, I would easily get sick from anything and would be down for up to two weeks at a time.

SUPPORT GROUP

In 1991, Dr. Ho transferred from UCLA to St. Joseph's Hospital in Orange, California, as Director of the Bone Marrow Transplant Unit. I began seeing him, since he was closer to our home. Dr. Ho was also world-renowned, as part of the team of doctors who went to Chernobyl. He was also fluent in Spanish, having studied and taught in South America. Dr. Ho and Dr. Nimer had followed me through the fortuitum blood infection. Since Dr. Ho was the hematologist, I would tell others that no one knew the workings of my body better than he did!

Dr. Ho organized a support group for BMT patients at St. Joseph's Cancer Center. It was the first time Brian and I had the opportunity to meet with other patients who had survived a BMT. The first meeting was comprised of the chaplain, three post-transplant patients, and one prospective patient. It was an interesting evening to finally share "war stories" with others; a much-needed element of healing that should have come sooner.

The support group met monthly and grew to over thirty-five members. There I met several other BMT survivors, prospective patients and their families. It was great to "give back," and to associate with others who knew what it was like to have a BMT. Several of the women began meeting for lunch regularly. We called ourselves the "BMT-Out-to-Lunch-Bunch."

At one of Dr. Ho's support groups, I met a man named Karl Karlsen. He also had CML and was planning to have his non-related bone marrow transplant at the City of Hope in Duarte, California. He was very fearful of doing it. However, Karl had an incredibly dry sense of humor. At the support group, he told everyone that he was going to the "City of No Hope," and that each day he was checking the obituaries to see if his name was listed.

Although everyone came down hard on him, saying he would never make it through with that attitude, I felt otherwise. Since he lived near us in Orange County, we became good friends with him and his wife, Connie. I told him that if he kept up his "warped sense of humor" he would probably get through it.

Karl survived his BMT. However, he suffered from chronic GVH of the skin and intestines. His complications landed him in the hospital several times. For years, we talked on a regular basis. Karl was my true "BMT buddy." And although his quality of life never returned to normal, and many years later his leukemia returned, he never let that stop him from enjoying life, his daughter, Marisa, or Connie, whom he adored.

Connie worked for an airline, so they often traveled whenever he could gather his strength. He passed away in 2004. In some ways Karl made my transplant look like a cakewalk. He will always be remembered for his great stamina and courage, his long suffering, and his incredible wittiness when poking fun at life and himself.

On the day of Karl's funeral, we were asked to drive his Jeep Cherokee from our new hometown back to Orange County. As Brian drove his car on the freeway, I followed behind. Suddenly, a morning dove appeared out of nowhere—and swooped down and began tailing Karl's car and darting around, like it wanted to get in. It did this for several seconds before finally flying away. Even Brian noticed it. It was amazing. I couldn't help but think it was Karl's way of "winking" at us—his way of saying thanks! He is truly missed by many.

In 1991, UCLA also started its own support group, but I couldn't attend as often. However, it was there that I learned about a BMT newsletter published by Susan Stewart, another BMT survivor. Through her newsletter, now called *BMT InfoNet* (Blood & Marrow Transplant Information Network—bmtinfonet.org), I was able to connect with other survivors and share information. Later, she and Jan Sugar went on to publish a book entitled *Bone Marrow and Blood Stem Cell Transplants: A Guide for Patients*. It is an excellent resource for anyone contemplating a transplant.

In August, I received a call from Dr. Nimer, inviting me to attend one of their monthly Grand Rounds, where doctors from all departments meet to discuss medical advances in their fields of medicine. The theme that month was Bone Marrow Transplantation. Dr. Nimer was preparing his one-hour dissertation around my BMT.

"As I review your case, I want them to be able to meet you. Can you come?" he asked.

"Do I have to say anything?"

"Well, you don't have to prepare a speech. But they'll probably ask questions; just answer honestly.

On that day over two hundred doctors and specialists filled the UCLA auditorium. Dr. Nimer introduced my case and then asked me to stand and allow for questions. I was somewhat nervous, but mostly grateful. At first, nobody asked anything. They just stared at me.

I finally said, "Hey the worst is over! Ask me anything you want."

Everyone laughed. It broke the ice and several began asking questions. I thanked the UCLA staff for the care we had received. It was hard not to feel emotional.

Dr. Nimer then proceeded to give a forty-five-minute dissertation on my case, including a comparison study using laboratory rats. It was fascinating to witness my transplant from a medical standpoint. He discussed slide after slide of statistical reports and graphs, charting each phase and setback—how they mechanically gained control of my body, wiped out my immune system, infused Alfred's marrow, mechanically sustained life, and then overcame infections with medication after medication. Much of the dialogue was hardly understandable. However, viewing my illness on screen was amazing! It was clear I had survived a holocaust! Yet here I was, whole again. I could only thank my doctors, Brian, and my Father in Heaven for such a miracle!

Afterward, Dr. Nimer received loud ovation and praise from his colleagues. We hugged him and the nurses. It was a very special day.

In 1992, we began preparing adoption papers through the church's LDS Social Services. We were told it would take up to two years to receive a baby. We were in no hurry. I was hopeful the vision of my illness could still end with the adoption of a baby. I asked Dr. Nimer straight out, "What are my chances of long-term survival? Is it worth our effort?"

"Well, put it this way, Analisa; if you were a horse, I'd bet a lot of money on you. I'll fill out any papers you need," he replied.

I was glad. It was easy to come to clinic now every three months. My blood tests were coming up perfect and it was a boost for all of us.

Although it was sometimes difficult, I continued to work on my book. Putting my thoughts on paper brought me great relief. Writing became my number-one priority.

CHICKEN POX

In April of 1992, we took another trip to Pennsylvania. I was to stay two weeks, and Brian one. While there, I felt chills coming on. I shrugged it off, thinking it was due to the cold weather.

Toward the middle of the week, we took a side trip to Washington, D.C., with Robin, Craig and the girls. We stayed at our favorite place, the Marriott, Bethesda. Craig had business there, so this time he made arrangements for us to stay in the Presidential Suite. Enjoying the lavish accommodations, complete with two bedrooms, a living room and dining area, Robin and I pretended to be ambassadors from foreign countries.

On our first day we visited some museums. I continued feeling feverish. That evening, Good Friday, we gorged ourselves at a Chinese restaurant. The chills increased, and I was certain an infection was on the rise. Back at the Marriott, I asked Robin to check my torso. Suspiciously, she said, "It looks like a chicken pox to me."

Unfortunately, I had been exposed three weeks before, from my nephew, Jesse! I had one mark on my stomach, and about four on my back. Relieved that I knew what the problem was, I was more upset about cutting my vacation short. "I guess I'll have to leave with Brian on Easter Sunday," I replied.

To play it safe, the next morning I called Dr. Ho, but he was in Israel. His assistant frantically insisted I get on medication immediately! Disturbed by his concern, I decided to call Dr. Nimer at UCLA. They paged him. It being Passover and he being Jewish, I wondered if we would get a hold of him. Within minutes he returned our call. When I mentioned chicken pox, he became very concerned.

"Analisa, you need to get on some Acyclovir as soon as possible. You might have to be admitted for a few days."

"What, you mean hospitalized? I'm coming home tomorrow with Brian. Can't it wait? Can't you call a pharmacy for me to pick up a prescription?"

"No, tomorrow's not soon enough. Besides, I'm not authorized to prescribe medication out of state. You're going to need an IV for about five days," he said.

"Five days in the hospital for chicken pox? Why?" I said, as tears began to well up. Brian and Robin listened, bewildered.

"Chicken pox could be potentially dangerous, even fatal. It could go to your lungs and cause pneumonia, or cause brain damage. Even though you are three years post-transplant, we can't take any chances that your immune system will be able to handle it. The sooner you get on Acyclovir, the better," he said firmly.

I couldn't believe it! What started out as a relaxing vacation was turning into a life or death experience! He instructed me to call a colleague of his at Georgetown University, but the colleague was out of town. Instead, I was referred to a "dumb" intern!

"Great," he said sarcastically. "You're a BMT patient from California with the chicken pox? And everyone's out of town. If complications arise, I don't know anything about your case," he said emphatically. "I'm going to have to call the Infectious Disease Specialist. You need to get in here immediately. I'll have to call you back." He complained about it being Passover, and that he was just getting ready to leave.

Upset by his rudeness and everyone's urgency, we got scared!

"What do we do, Brian? I don't want to stay here. What if complications arise? I'd rather be at UCLA."

Brian agreed. He thought about it then said, "What if we went home today, right now?"

Craig had the secretary at the hotel call the airlines for the next available flight out of D.C. I paged Dr. Nimer.

In the meantime the intern called back. I told him my plans. He cautioned, "You'd better not get on that plane! You might infect others. Just come here. We'll take care of you and have you on an IV within an hour. I'll call Emergency and tell them to be ready. I'll *have* to meet you there," he said perturbed. It was obvious that he was bothered. I apologized again, but he continued to make sarcastic remarks about it being a holiday. I couldn't believe it!

"That's it. I don't want to stay here," I said. I called Dr. Nimer again and told him we could be on a plane and at UCLA by 8:00 p.m. He expressed concern, but agreed it would be better to come home, even though it would be risky.

"What symptoms do I need to watch for?" I asked.

"Well, if you have trouble thinking or breathing, you'd better just check yourself into the nearest hospital."

Naturally, the minute he said that, I had trouble breathing and thinking.

"The decision is up to you, Analisa. They can help you there. You'll just have to be there a week."

Everything was happening so fast. We decided to drop everything and go home. Brian gave me a blessing. Famished for breakfast, we quickly ate at the hotel, to gather our senses.

With only thirty-five minutes to catch our flight, Craig speedily led the way as we followed in our rental car to Arlington National Airport. All the way there, we contemplated checking me into the nearest hospital. With no luggage, we arrived at the airport five minutes before departure. We threw the keys to Robin, and in frantic tears said good-bye.

While Brian ran in to buy one-way tickets (costing us a bundle), I ran to the pay phone to call Rosemary and Bill to meet us at LAX. I was so nervous and conscientious about my breathing that I could hardly dial! We ran to the gate and barely made it. Within minutes, we were pulling away from the terminal.

It all happened so fast! Luckily, the plane was empty, so we were able to sprawl out. The fever and chills increased, and by the hour my face and neck broke out in itchy, red bumps. I tried to stay calm, holding a blanket to my face. It was the longest flight, with a layover in Atlanta.

Finally, we arrived at LAX, and by 11:00 p.m. I was back at UCLA, on the eighth floor receiving Acyclovir. Though certainly a frightening and incredible day, all things went in our favor.

By the next day I had a bad case of bronchitis. My face, scalp, torso and back were covered in pox; it was awful. Dr. Nimer said, "It could have been much worse. Had you waited another day, you would have broken out with hundreds more! You did the right thing calling us."

My five-day stay was comfortable compared to all the previous times. The time went by faster than the flight it took to come home! I was just glad to be in California. Our luggage arrived a week later.

The day after I was released, the L.A. riots broke out with the announcement of the Rodney King verdicts. Getting the chicken pox was an emotional setback, and seeing the city burn senselessly didn't help.

After that experience, we marveled how just one little pat on the face of my nephew, Jesse, could transfer so many germs. My eyes were sensitive to light for several weeks thereafter, and it took time to regain my strength. We decided to halt the adoption process and give ourselves more time to heal.

LONG-TERM PROBLEMS

1992 was the year of making rounds with all other doctors: the gastroenterologist, dermatologist, gynecologist, dentist, and optometrist. It's a wonder I didn't go to a psychiatrist!

Now three and a half years post-transplant, my health was improving and the discomforts were minor—dry eyes and sometimes muscle cramping. My skin cleared up well, with only occasional GVH around my mouth and eyes. However, I still tired very easily and continued to have colitis problems. I could do just about anything as long as I got *plenty* of rest. Whenever I got sick, it usually lasted for about two to three weeks. Bouts of the flu and fevers decreased to one or two a year. However my stomach and hiatel hernia continued to give me frequent trouble.

As 1992 came to an end, it felt like a "resting period" from all our difficult challenges; a time to reestablish priorities and begin working on new ones.

In the summer of 1993, I went in for my four-year bone marrow test with Dr. Ho. The results came back—disease free! Dr. Ho called and left the following message: "You still have your brother's male chromosomes. Not to worry. It's all good."

I was so happy that I recorded his message on tape. That night we celebrated at a restaurant. Brian made a toast: "To your marrow and those missionary cells, still dressed in suits, white shirts and ties, doing their job!"

LEARNINGS—1993

Miracles really do happen! Life is a gift, and I have been given a second chance. We cannot take family, friends and God for granted. And, we cannot afford to dwell on the tragedies of the past. We must hold steadfast with a brightness of hope towards the future, trusting in God and having a good sense of humor.

Life is a continuous cycle of changes and adjustments to circumstances. It's a matter of focusing and refocusing while living life to its fullest, always with a heart full of gratitude.

I've learned tremendous respect for the body that houses my spirit. Its complexity and resiliency are no doubt evidence of divine creation.

For months, even years after my transplant, life felt temporary—as if it could all end the next week. I told family I'd be lucky to make it to age forty. Not that forty is old; it just seemed unattainable. Well, I passed forty, and now fifty is starting to look possible.

Not long ago I drove by a high school. The quote on the marquee caught my attention: "Success is not your income; it's what you overcome."

I am grateful I had six months to prepare for the transplant, time to decide how to handle the crisis. We applied ourselves diligently and prepared ourselves spiritually. Nevertheless, the struggle was hard. Events brought spiritual highs that were almost tangible. Others brought tremendous lows. We went in strong, determined to beat the odds. We marched forth like little soldiers. But after months of battle, we were beaten up and nearly blown to pieces, until our faith was hanging by a thread, and the adversary was preying on my soul! I was scared, very scared.

I'm grateful for our church, which has taught me about the Savior's teachings and helped me understand the plan of life—where we come from, why we are here, and where we go after we die.

Recently, I came across a quote that a friend handed me on Father's

Day, 1989: "The presence of fear is a sure sign that you are trusting in your *own* strength." How true that is. It gave understanding to my fears on 4 East.

I now understand the dream I had just prior to my diagnosis—it wasn't my time to go! But I *was* to pass through a life and death situation. Now, whenever I drive at night, the sea of headlights of the oncoming cars always reminds me of that dream. The light is so bright and beautiful that I wish I could climb in and be surrounded by its beauty.

Faith, when exercised fully, will be tested to its ultimate limit. At church, I recently heard a quote: "When we exercise true faith we only look forward; we don't look back at the past."

Another truth learned: one must continually work on spirituality. Our reservoir of faith will help pull us through any crisis. In the middle of a crisis we can't go back and make up what is not there. If you don't have faith, surviving and healing will be harder. We *can* choose to have spiritual experiences if we listen with a pure heart. It just takes work. They're not easy to find when life is turned inside out, but even if the answer is no, one can still receive peace.

In the hospital I couldn't deny the spiritual promptings. Truth and wisdom were being learned line upon line, precept upon precept. I feel lucky. In another time and place, it might not have worked out the way it did.

The only thing that brought peace and comfort was to share my faith with others. Nothing brought relief than when I testified that God lives and is powerful, and does heal. I went through the transplant because I had to. He suffered and died for us because He *chose* to, because He was willing to pay the price. This knowledge gave me courage.

A woman at church recently said, "God won't allow you to walk twenty-five miles when he knows He can get thirty, forty or even fifty miles out of you." His grace and mercy are sufficient to take over and walk the extra miles for us, and with us. No matter how much faith we exercise, part of the growth is learning to let go, even when the outcome may not be what we want.

There is also a saying: "Pray as though everything depended on the Lord and then work as though everything depended on you."

Now that life has become increasingly normal and I plug along, I realize a great responsibility for my actions and deeds. Sometimes I want to forget the whole bone marrow transplant and just move on with life.

But I know I must never forget the events that have changed my life. In those weakest moments have come my greatest strengths. So, when life's storms kick up again, it's those strengths that will pull me through.

Every time I feel I can't do something, I ask myself if it's harder than what I've been through. It has increased my patience with myself, and others. However, sometimes I'm less tolerant of people who complain about insignificant problems.

Also, although sharing my story may not convert others to turning their faith to a loving Heavenly Father, perhaps it may convince them to just experiment on a portion of their own faith, whatever that may be.

I empathize with anyone suffering from cancer. When someone mentions a BMT, I think, "big—major big." Mount Everest is before them. Yet, the transplant process is ever changing and improving. And, I am confident that the process is not quite as grueling as it was back in 1989. They now have drugs to increase white cell growth, minimize GVH, and reduce infections and nausea.

As I enjoy life again, the feelings are two-fold: on one hand it's not important if things are left undone—just sit back and enjoy it. Don't rush. On the other hand, life is short and there's no time to waste. More than ever is the urgency to make oneself useful and not sit idle. We must find that balance.

We all have much to offer and each day needs to be filled with service. Back on 4 East, when I thought the suffering couldn't get any worse, it did. Now, when I can't believe life can't get any better or sweeter, I strive for it that much harder.

I'm grateful for modern technology that offers so much hope. It's not just one person that brings about a miracle, but the efforts of many. In the end, it's the Lord's choice to intervene and complete the miracle.

I'm grateful for Brian, for suffering right along with me. A book could be written about him alone. Through it all, his love and patience never flinched. If they did, he never showed it. His genuine kindness and selflessness still keeps me in awe after twenty-four years of marriage.

I'm grateful for music. My wish is to always have a song in my heart, a good sense of humor, and a desire to serve.

Among several songs that had an impact on me, there is one that sums it all up. I think it's fitting to end with a portion of the words:

"In Perfect Faith"

11TH HOUR MIRACLES!

Lyrics by Joy Saunders Lundberg, Music by Janice Kapp Perry, ©
1985, Used by permission.

Did Moses know just where and how to set all Israel free?
When he received the sacred call that came from Deity.
With perfect faith in Israel's God he opened up a sea,
And led them to a promised land fulfilling prophecy.

Could Esther see what faith would do when asked to risk her life?
To save her people from their death and stand for truth and right.
With courage born of fast and prayer, she trusted in God's arm,
Went forth in royal robes of faith and not one soul was harmed.

In perfect faith I too believe in things I cannot see,
I only need to trust in Him and follow where He leads.
With faith secure in Jesus Christ, God's own Begotten Son,
I too go forth to do His will, and miracles will come.

With faith secure in Jesus Christ...God's own Begotten Son,
I too go forth to do His will, and miracles will come!

Life goes on...

CHAPTER 19
A FAMILY AT LAST: 1994-2006

On January 5, 1994, just before boarding a plane to Hawaii, we licked the envelope, gave each other a kiss for luck, and dropped our final adoption papers in the mail. It was a final honeymoon, sensing parenthood on the horizon.

Just ten weeks later on a beautiful Friday afternoon, I was driving through Irvine, listening to the radio, and thinking about the prospects of a baby coming into our lives. The words of a new song, "I'll Be There" sung by the Escape Club, caught my attention. The words are about somebody who has died and is singing to a loved one. It made me think of Stella. If there were truly a baby in heaven waiting to come to us, perhaps she would be one of the last people to hold this child. Tears filled my eyes as I listened. It had been years since I thought of Stella with so much emotion. Part of the song went like this:

"I'll Be There"
Written by Trevor Steel, Chris Christoforou, John Holliday and Milan Zekavica © BUG MUSIC INC. (BMI) O/B/O BUG MUSIC LTD. (PRS) All Rights Reserved. Used by Permission.

Over mountains, over trees, over oceans, over seas,
Across the desert I'll be there.
In a whisper on the wind, on the smile of a new friend,
Just think of me, and I'll be there.

Don't be afraid, oh my love, I'll be watching you from above.
And I'd give all the world tonight to be with you.
Because I'm on your side and I still care,
I may have died but I've gone nowhere.
Just think of me and I'll be there.

Little did I know that just a few hours later we would receive the most important phone call of our lives. That night around 6:00 p.m., while I was on the phone with my dear friend, Monique, the operator made an emergency break in the call. Our social worker was trying to reach us.

"Oh, my gosh, I think this is it!" I yelled frantically. I called out to Brian. Our social worker promptly called back.

"I'm so sorry to interrupt you and disturb you tonight," he said. After what felt like an eternity of intentional small talk, he said, "Well, congratulations. You have a baby boy who was born yesterday, St. Patrick's Day! He's waiting for you to pick him up. Would it be too much trouble to come tonight?"

"Of course not!" we exclaimed as we jumped up and down in excitement. It was the happiest day of our lives! When we got off the phone, we darted around the room like crazy chickens not knowing what to do first. After eleven years of marriage, our lives were about to change forever.

With only a borrowed car seat to our name, we rushed out to pick up our bundle of joy that was two hours away. It was exhilarating. On the way there, we discussed names.

"How about Blake?" I said.

"How about Brian? I want him to know that I love him so much that I gave him my name," Brian replied.

"That sounds good."

Our conversation then turned to what we refer to as "the little boy in the window" incident. It happened back in 1984, the night before we learned from the doctor that we would never be able to have our own biological children. I've never mentioned this before, partly because at the time it was hard to accept. But now it is fitting to share what happened on that cold December night in Idaho Falls.

Brian had just closed the AT&T Phone Store and was vacuuming after a busy day. I was puttering in the store, while in the back of my mind contemplating the medical test results we would receive the following day. I glanced up and noticed a dark-haired little boy about ten years old slip a folded piece of paper through the glass doors and then walk away. Now, Brian's store was located on the side of a small strip mall, which was rarely busy at night. Since it was already dark, the thought came to me as I started walking toward the door--what could this boy possibly need to tell me on this cold night with virtually nobody around? And, why would he be out at this time anyway? I picked up the paper, and to my dismay it was a flyer on adoption! Instantly I cried out, "No!" I showed the flyer to Brian, then crumpled it up and threw it in the trash. We dismissed it as any kind of warning or foretelling of the future-- determined at all costs to have our own biological children if the results did not go in our favor.

Well, it didn't turn out that way for many reasons, and it was evident by that little boy in the window that God had other plans for us. Now, as we drove to pick up our little angel Brian Patrick, we were so thrilled and grateful for the opportunity to adopt!

Upon arriving, we sat with the social worker and went over all the paperwork. After about an hour, she said, "Well, are you ready for him? He's beautiful!"

"Yes!" We could hardly contain ourselves.

She left the room for a few minutes.

"Gosh, it's so late! What time is it?" I asked.

Brian looked at his watch, "It's 11:00 p.m., exactly."

In awe, I stared at him. A tingling feeling came over me.

"Haven't our greatest miracles always come at the eleventh hour?"

He nodded. "And, it's our eleventh year of marriage, too!"

Just then, the social worker opened the door. Our joy was overflowing as she placed Brian Patrick in our arms. It was a sure sign that this precious little boy with rosy cheeks, a flower-shaped mouth, and full head of brown hair was meant to be ours. We were amazed at how much he resembled his daddy!

At midnight, like two kids with a new toy, we snuggled him into the car seat and headed for the nearest twenty-four-hour drugstore to load up on baby supplies. At last, that ever-elusive baby aisle would be a part of our lives. When we arrived home, to our surprise Monique had decorated the house with balloons, gifts, and several of her own baby items.

Later, as I reflected on the events of the day and the excitement of picking up our new son, I remembered the amazing song I had heard earlier that day. I couldn't help but feel reassured that Stella had been with us that evening and shared in our joy.

For days thereafter, I was in total bliss. I felt like Maria in *The Sound of Music,* when she's in the gazebo with her fiancé who has just proposed. Feeling unworthy of such great happiness, she sings, "...somewhere in my youth or childhood, I must have done something good." That's how I felt holding little Brian. Truly, the Lord's love had descended on our home. We were the beneficiaries of this new angel sent from heaven. Nine months later, Brian was "sealed" to us in the San Diego Temple, meaning he would be ours for eternity.

Later that year, we attended UCLA's 20th Bone Marrow Transplant Reunion. It was great to see the staff again and to have little Brian with us. Many had left UCLA, but Kathy Bartoni was still there. She presented little Brian with beautiful gifts.

I was asked to say a few words. I thanked UCLA Medical Center for everything they had done for me. The main thing I remember saying at the pulpit was, "Yes, those 'Rad' animals *do* save lives!"

BLAKE'S ARRIVAL

Two and a half years later, our busy little Brian was in need of a sibling. My health was good, so we completed the paperwork again. Nine months later, on Valentine's Day of 1997, we received the call. A baby boy was due in a couple of weeks and the out-of-state birthmother wanted to meet us.

When Brian Patrick arrived, he was like a gift. All we had to do was pick him up. This time there was more risk, and anything could go wrong.

Since Brian could only take a limited time off work, we made arrangements to stay for eleven days. We took the necessary clothing and equipment for the baby.

When we got there we had a wonderful meeting with the birth mother. Little Brian presented her with flowers and chocolates. It was strange to sit across from a beautiful young woman who was about to deliver "our" baby. So many emotions ran through my mind—from great love, to guilt, sorrow and appreciation, all at the same time. Our lives would be forever connected and yet disconnected. It's hard to put into words the feelings we felt toward this sweet young lady with long brown hair and big brown eyes. More than anything, we felt love.

That night I could hardly sleep. My thoughts of her brought tremendous guilt, and I wondered if we were doing the right thing. I said several prayers. However, the next day I awoke feeling differently. This was her life and her decision. *She* had chosen *us* and asked us to come here. God-willing, it would turn out well for all of us.

For several days we waited for her to deliver. Finally, ten days later, baby Blake was born; and on the eleventh day, the day we were to return home, he was placed in our arms. It was another eleventh hour miracle! We named him Blake Hunter--after President Hunter. We cherish President Hunter and his blessing to me, and the fact that our son would carry his name forever.

Many events were happening at the time of Blake's arrival. AT&T was downsizing again and Brian's job was going away. He was scurrying to find a new one. There was a strong possibility of returning to New Jersey. It took several months for him to convince me that New Jersey was the only way he could stay with AT&T. He tried several avenues.

For me, the thought of moving back was out of the question. Just as my life seemed furthest away from those transplant days, I was ironically being forced to confront the skeletons of the past and return to New Jersey, where my CML had been diagnosed nine years earlier. Besides, we now had two small children and I wanted to be near family. I adamantly refused to accept any subtle impressions that were pointing to the East.

We weren't seeing eye to eye at all on this. It was a difficult time in our relationship. "It's like having to go back for the kill," I'd say.

"I know it's hard, but what else can I do? It's my job and I need to provide for my family."

I accompanied Brian to New Jersey for his interview, to get a feel for things. He was offered the position. However, we needed time to decide if it was the right thing.

Back in California, we were driving one day and discussing the moving issue again. "I don't know what to do, Analisa. How come the answer doesn't come? Remember when you were in the hospital and answers would come so quickly? How come that doesn't happen anymore?"

"Yes, I remember. We just have to look for the answers," I said calmly. "Look!" I said suddenly, pointing to the New Jersey license plates on the car in front of ours! "Sometimes the answer is spelled out right in front of us and we just *have* to accept it. Even if I don't want to."

Brian had supported me in all I went through; now it was my turn to support him. I could only have faith that it was all happening for a reason.

In his agonizing decision to accept the job, Brian's personal answer finally came as he sat in the bishop's office one Sunday. His eyes zeroed in on a book lying on the table, *Go Forward with Faith,* the biography of

Church President Gordon B. Hinckley, by Sheri L. Dew. He felt strongly that New Jersey was where we needed to be.

In October of 1997, while my parents watched the boys, we took our house-hunting trip. Prices in New Jersey were just starting to rise, so we were hopeful of finding a nice home in a good area. On our second day, we came upon a new development in Bridgewater. The location was perfect and we were ecstatic. Not only would we be in a new house, we would end up back in our same ward at church. It was a great relief to know that we would be back among friends.

It took a few days to complete all the paperwork. The house would not be completed until early spring, so now we needed temporary housing. Time was of the essence, since we had only two days left before returning to California. Our intent was to find a furnished place to make the move easier.

As we toured various townships, we became very discouraged. Nobody wanted to consider a four-month lease. As the day wore on we scanned newspapers, rental magazines, and even grocery store bulletin boards, but had no luck.

Finally, at 4:00 p.m., we ended up on a bench outside a supermarket in Hillsborough, just a few blocks from our old Bree Court condo. Feeling helpless, frustrated and worn out from the week, we just stared at each other.

"We have one more day to find a place and secure it before we leave," I said.

"Yeah, we've looked everywhere. There isn't anything available. Maybe we need to say a prayer," Brian said humbly.

"Yeah, we need a miracle right now. There's no time left!" I replied.

Brian whispered a prayer and I did, too. Then we sat pondering what to do next.

We decided to take one more drive through Somerville, and see if we could find some condos, which I remembered were really cute years ago. "Maybe we'll find a rental around there," I said.

So off we went. As we drove through Somerville, suddenly we came across the development I'd been talking about. Lo and behold, there was a big "For Rent" sign right in front. We yelled out at the same time!

"I can't believe it," Brian exclaimed.

"Let's call on it."

I turned my head, looking for a phone booth and noticed a real estate office directly across the street. "I can call from there!" I replied.

We were so surprised at how quickly our luck might be changing. Hopefully, the owner would want to rent to us.

As I made the call and explained our situation to the owner, the realtor in the office began speaking to Brian. Before I knew it, Brian was trying to get my attention. Disappointed, I hung up and told Brian that the owner was not interested in us.

Brian eagerly explained that the realtor knew of a furnished place just a few blocks away being offered for sale. It had been on the market for some time, and she believed the owner might be interested in renting it to us until it sold.

Within minutes we were sitting in the realtor's car, on our way to see the unit. We were amazed by how the events of the day and our emotions had suddenly turned.

The tiny two-bedroom unit was old and rickety, but completely furnished and clean. The price was several hundred dollars less than the unfurnished apartments we had seen, and the location was perfect. We agreed to take it!

The following morning we met with the owners, who were more than happy to rent it to us until it sold.

By Sunday morning, we had accomplished everything we had set out to do! And, we returned to California excited about our future in New Jersey. We were humbled at how the Lord had indeed answered our prayers. Every desire of our hearts had been met.

Seven months after Blake's arrival, with the moving truck packed and already gone, Blakie was sealed to us in the Los Angeles Temple.

Amazingly, Blake resembled *my* baby pictures! We called him our "little love," since we received the first call about him on Valentine's Day. And Brian was our "little angel," since he was born on St. Patrick's Day. As we gathered outside the Temple for an emotional day with family and friends, Brian held Blake while little Brian ran in circles on the grass. Our family was complete and growing. We know they were divinely handpicked to come to our home and be part of our family.

My brothers, Alfred and Jim, were now married. I couldn't help but feel tremendous joy and gratitude. We had come full circle from those long, hard days at UCLA.

As I stood gazing at the beautiful Temple before me, I remembered how often I had glanced out my hospital window, staring at this magnificent edifice. How I had longed, hoped and prayed that someday I would survive, write about my experiences, and the ending would be entering this Temple with a baby. Now, my dream was truly being fulfilled—but this time with our *second* baby!

Amazingly, it's as if we had returned to California, accomplished all that we had dreamed of doing; and without a day to spare, it was time to return to New Jersey and begin our lives where we had left off.

The next day we left California.

NEW JERSEY 1997—CALIFORNIA 2006

Except for missing family out West, life in New Jersey with our two darling boys was great. We loved our new home and we were able to rekindle old friendships. Mieke and Paul were also doing great. We shared happy times together again reminiscing about our past. They had moved to northern New Jersey, and were in the process of building a beautiful home in the country.

We also shared our experiences with friends in our old ward and made closure. In a small way, we were able to serve and give back a portion of all that had been done for us so many years earlier.

While in New Jersey I joined the Leukemia and Lymphoma Society, Northern New Jersey Chapter, and became a First Connection Volunteer. I participated as a committee member and a guest speaker for a special, Keys to Survivorship Conference. It was a great opportunity to serve and work with professionals on improving the needs of cancer patients.

We were in New Jersey for three years before AT&T began downsizing again. Brian qualified for early retirement, and was able to leave just after inching passed his twentieth anniversary.

With a strong desire to get back to California, we were set to return to Orange County and start all over again. However, Brian accepted a prospective job in Seattle with AT&T Wireless.

On a busy Halloween night we received the call with an unofficial job offer. There would be some "slight" changes—the job would be located in Southern California (North Hollywood, to be exact) and the hiring manager was wondering if that would be a problem for us.

We were ecstatic, to say the least! The "Valley" is where Brian and

I both grew up. In fact, his new job would be located across the street from the old movie theaters we used to frequent when we dated. Of all the possible locations in Southern California, we were going home to our neck of the woods. It was certainly yet another unbelievable miracle!

As the weather turned colder, we waited for the official job offer. Finally it came, just a week before the movers arrived.

Our neighbors gave us a great send-off party. We were happy to leave New Jersey and to head west.

VICTOR'S PASSING

Sadly, just a year later, in January of 2002, after spending a memorable Christmas with our family, my brother Victor was suddenly taken ill with a gallstone lodged in his pancreas. All his organs began to fail and within four days he died, leaving behind his wife, Cindy, and their four children.

It was a devastating time for us. I certainly felt cheated of my time with Victor; his office was only five minutes from our house. And although our desire to see each other was strong, with our busy schedules, I only got to see him a few times since our return from New Jersey. It was very difficult to understand how quickly he had passed away. He was only forty-two years old.

As for my parents, they have been through so much. Yet, they have stood strong—handling their challenges with much grace and courage. My dad has been fighting prostate cancer for several years now, and underwent double bypass heart surgery after suffering a heart attack in 2004. He's doing well and his sense of humor keeps everyone from worrying about him.

In 2003, as home values continued to soar, we finally got on a lottery list to buy a home. As fate would have it, another eleventh hour miracle occurred. We were the final name picked in phase three of the development. Thereafter, prices increased way beyond what we could afford. For over two years we had searched for the right home. As they called our name, we were ecstatic to learn it was the floor plan we wanted, and the lot was situated just like our New Jersey home—second house from the corner at the end of a block, with no one directly behind us.

This unusual blessing for us seemed as if the Lord was saying, "See, I put you guys here! This is where I want you, and don't you *ever* forget that I have a hand in your life—in all things, big and small!"

Two years after we returned to Los Angeles, the perpetual company downsizing continued. Brian finally retired from AT&T for good. He now directs an operation in a motion picture film lab that develops film from the major studios.

As for Brian and Blake, they are growing up fast. They have made our lives complete. We truly couldn't ask for greater blessings than our two precious boys. And while parenting is wonderful and fulfilling, it is continually challenging. They keep us busy, entertained, and ever looking to the future.

Alfred and Laura have a beautiful daughter and a newborn son. They are doing great, and I will be forever indebted to Alfred for giving me his marrow.

Finalizing my manuscript for the publisher has caused me to reconnect with many great people who provided support and encouragement to me during my illness. One of them is Alex Casasola, the technician who took an interest in me by offering a prayer on my behalf. In searching him out, it turns out he lives just a mile away from us! He was excited to hear from me, and the day I called him, he and his wife, Ennie, came over. We shared a wonderful reunion as I recounted the story of our brief meeting, and how that day *he* was my answer to a very desperate prayer!

He related to us that he only worked at UCLA for two weeks before taking another job offer, and that perhaps his only purpose for working there was to meet me. We plan to continue a long-lasting friendship.

The only other comrade I keep in contact with is Ragen Hodges, and his wife, Peggy. We exchange Christmas cards every year. There is something very special about knowing them, and that Ragen is still around—hanging in there like me.

I also keep in contact with Barbara Saltzman, David's mother. We are so proud of the success she has had with the book *The Jester Has Lost His Jingle*.

Just recently, in need of losing a few pounds, I joined Lindora's Lean For Life program (a medically supervised weight-loss plan). Through Lindora, I lost twenty pounds in eight weeks. But more importantly, it was an amazing breakthrough in my health. I no longer live off antacids, and I believe my colitis problems have all but disappeared. I feel healthier and my immune system feels stronger than ever before. It's been the best investment in my health and education.

I wish I could have learned about the program years ago. It would have saved me years of suffering with my eating and colitis problems. Recently, when I spoke to Mieke, and told her about Lindora, she about fell over. Surprisingly, Cynthia Stamper Graff, President of Lindora, was her roommate in college, and also her real estate business partner in Newport Beach, California, back in the late '70s! It seems that the world is a very small place.

Also, there are plenty of organizations and foundations that cater toward children, such as the Make A Wish Foundation and the Children's Miracle Network. However, few cater to adults. For years I have had a dream—that if my book became very successful, I would begin a foundation called "11th Hour Miracles," to help BMT survivors realize a special goal or wish.

Each patient would also receive something similar to an Olympic gold medal or an Academy Award for his or her incredible achievement. It would give patients perhaps a little "11th hour miracle" to look forward to as they heal.

Finally, in closing, I often think of the photocopied picture of Christ hanging in my hospital room which read: I Never Said It Would Be Easy, I Only Said It Would Be Worth It!" How true that is! A beautiful portrait of it now hangs in our bedroom.

For this, and all our miracles, we thank God each and every day. Life goes on, and as long as we continue believing, so do miracles—even those at the 11th hour!

Alfred and Analisa on the day Alfred returned from Peru.

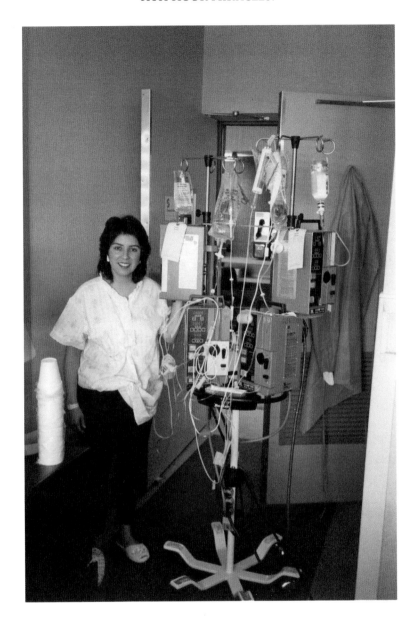

Analisa attached to a six-wheeler IV pole with four machines.

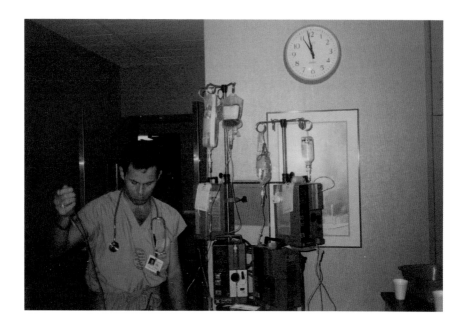

Nurse Mitchell infusing Alfred's lifesaving marrow into Analisa's
IV line. Note the time.

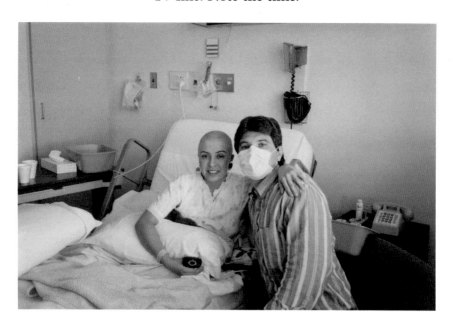

Analisa and Brian in isolation.

A weary Analisa with Brian, December 1989, five months post transplant.

Six months post transplant, January 1990. Analisa and Dr. Champlin, just prior to him leaving UCLA. He had seen her all the way through the transplant.

Analisa and Brian with President Howard W. Hunter, after receiving a blessing.

November 1997, Blake is sealed to us in the Los Angeles Temple.
It's a happy day as our family is finally complete.

CHAPTER 20
QUICK REFERENCE LIST FOR PROSPECTIVE PATIENTS

PRIOR TO TRANSPLANT

- Get educated about your illness. Learn all your options for treatment.
- Decide where you want to get treatment.
- Talk to other survivors with the same diagnosis.
- Take care of all unfinished business; write letters and make amends with loved ones.
- Write a big pep list for those down days.
- Gather favorite music, poems, and stories that will uplift you.
- Exercise if you are able.
- Surround yourself with positive people, books and things.
- Prepare yourself spiritually. Nourish your faith or what you believe in.
- Make a goal of something you want to do after you survive (a trip to Hawaii, start a family, college, etc.)
- Request the support of others by instructing them to send cards and letters and to pray for you.
- Get a box of much-needed baby wipes for the bathroom. They will come in handy.
- Maintain a sense of humor.
- Choose to get the best of your illness, rather than let it get the best of you. Count your blessings.

DURING TRANSPLANT

- Imagine you've just been employed by the hospital to get your health back. Work with your doctors and nurses.
- Take your mind to beautiful places of your past.

-   Get a daily routine going.
-   Focus and refocus on small goals—getting through chemo, radiation, isolation, going home, etc.
-   Keep a journal.
-   Refer to your pep list often.
-   Ask lots of questions. Become informed about the medications and what side effects to expect.
-   Keep busy with daily walks down the hall or marching in your room.
-   Let the experts do the worrying. Just go with the flow.
-   Don't look back; keep pressing forward to reach your goal.
-   Don't forget your sense of humor.
-   Remember, you are not alone. Have faith that God is with you. Miracles *can* come and you *can* have peace, even joy.

POST TRANSPLANT

-   Don't expect too much. Pace yourself. Listen to your body and pamper yourself.
-   Remember, it's always two steps forward and one step back. (Sometimes a giant step back.)
-   It's okay to cry and let out the pain. Love yourself.
-   Try not to feel guilty about "everything."
-   Take frequent naps.
-   You'll have many insecurities and periods of forgetfulness, and you will feel emotionally and physically vulnerable. This is normal. Have faith that things will get better.
-   Ask family and friends to keep the letters, love, and prayers coming.
-   Have patience and let time heal. Remember, you can't have it all at once.
-   Remember to keep your sense of humor.
-   Keep life simple and focus on your goals.
-   Attend support groups. Talk to other survivors.
-   Look back with gratitude, not bitterness.
-   Thank God for all your blessings and miracles. Enjoy life!